31274653

D1367261

Navajo Weapon

By S. McClain

Books Beyond Borders, Inc.
Boulder, Colorado

The following publishers have generously given permission to use extended quotations from the following copyrighted work:

The Pacific War by John Costello, Copyright © 1981 by John Costello. Reprinted with the permission of Rawson Associates, an imprint of Simon & Schuster.

The Pacific War by John Costello, published in 1981 by Rawson, Wade Publishers. Copyright © 1981 by Atlantic Communications, Inc. Reprinted with permission of John Hawkins & Associates, Inc. (World rights)

Dust jacket illustration by Teddy Draper, Sr.,
Code Talker, 5th Division Marines
Book Design by Rik Rydlun

First Edition
ISBN 1-883862-07-8

Library of Congress Catalog Number: 94-72306

Printed in the United States of America

Dedication

To my daughter, Melinda, whose love and patience supported my effort and made this book possible. And to children everywhere who have the need or desire to learn about the experiences and wisdom of their Elders.

Contents

Maps and Photos

Photos

Maps

Acknowledgments

This book could not have been written without loving contributions from the following people. To each and every one of them, my heartfelt thanks.

My mother, friend and confidante, Lee Redfield who raised me with the attitude that I could achieve anything I worked for and believed in. My sisters Dona and Beth and my brother Fred who took care of my household during research trips to Washington, D. C. and the Navajo reservation. They made it possible for this story to move beyond my desk. And a special note of thanks to my father, F. D. McClain, United States Navy (Retired) who contributed inspiration, experiences, and photographs for this story.

To Rik and Judy Rydlun, two "visionaries" who felt the power of the Navajo code talker story and believed in me 100 percent. Without their desire to have the message of this book made available to the public, this would still be a work in progress. To Jan Kristiansson, a special note of gratitude for your wonderful advice while editing the manuscript.

An extra special thank you to the following people who gave of their time, experience, wisdom, stories and devotion to the Navajo code talkers. Their resources granted me the privilege of becoming the humble messenger of an intriguing and important historical event: Carl Gorman; Mary Gorman; Zonnie Gorman; Harold Foster; Henry & Alice Hisey, Jr.; Teddy Draper, Sr.; Eugene Roanhorse Crawford (Rest gently, brave warrior); Wilsie Bitsie; Kee Etsicitty; Paul Blatchford; Bill Toledo; John Kinsel, Sr.; Thomas & Nina Begay; Samuel Billison; Lee Cannon; William Banning; Richard Boyland - National Archives, Suitland

Branch; Rebecca Lentz-Collier - National Archives, Suitland Branch; Kerry Strong, Archives Director of the Marine Corps University, Quantico, Virginia; Dave Gaddy, Cryptology Historian - National Security Agency, Fort George, Meade, Maryland; Tom Randant; Sergeant Major Dolph Reeves, USMC (Retired); Ed Hogue; R.G. Rosenquist, Director of the Raider Museum, Richmond, Virginia; Lieutenant General J. P. Berkeley, USMC (Retired); Lieutenant Colonel Palmer "Pete" Brown, USMC (Retired); Kenji Kawano.

I wish, also, to extend my deepest respect to the Navajo Nation and all the code talkers whose dedication, devotion and love of this country represent the ideals this country was founded on.

A personal note of gratitude and admiration to everyone who participated during World War II. Your sacrifices ensured that I would have the freedom to pursue my dreams and march to the beat of my own drum.

Introduction

February 23, 1945
Incoming message to the command ship USS *Eldorado*:

D-ah a-kha: Ashdla a-woh cha Ashi-hi Bih-keh-he,
Bi-tsan-dehn: Ah-jad A-woh n-kih n-kih tseebii Dzeh Nakia,
taa Has-clish-nih. Besh-legai-a-la-ih Cha Jeha Dibeh moasi
tse-gah gah tkin ah-nah ah-losz klesh Ah-jah Nakia gah tse-
nill yeh-hes dibeh dzeh be Shi-da Klesh chuo ah-jad be-la-
sana ah-tad do ye-dzeh-al-tsisi-gi Tsin-tliti a-kha no-da-ih a-
chin d-ah Dibeh dzeh bi-so-dih ne-zhoni wol-la-chee ah-di
neeznaa taa ashdla be-la-sana na-as-tso-si.

Translated message:

To: 5th Division Commanding General
From: LT 228 E Company, 3rd Platoon
1st Lieutenant H. G. Schrier's E Company raised U.S. flag
and secured Mount Suribachi at 10:35 AM.

One of the most celebrated moments in Marine Corps history was passed down through the ranks and out to the *Eldorado*
in Navajo code. This is the story of how and why this code became one of the Marine Corps's most valuable secret weapons.
The lives this code saved and the way it stymied an intelligent
and formidable foe are revealed in depth for the first time.

What began as a "pilot project" with twenty-nine Navajo volunteers in April 1942 grew to a force of more than 400 by the
end of the war. The Navajo code was used in almost every South

Pacific campaign the marines participated in from Guadalcanal to Okinawa. The Navajos who served in this integral part of the South Pacific war were in thought, word and deed the "Navajo Weapon."

The story you are about to read reveals a hidden chapter of the South Pacific campaigns during World War II and the Marine Corps's best kept secret: The Navajo code talkers.

I had no knowledge of the Navajo people or the code talkers prior to this project, nor am I a veteran of any branch of the Armed Forces. My small traces of Native American heritage stem from paternal and maternal ancestors of the Choctaw and Cherokee Nations. How I became the messenger for this unique story cannot be explained in a logical manner because I am still not sure how or why it came to me. Suffice to say that my intense curiosity to know how the Navajos and the Marine Corps merged in a time of crisis fueled my journey.

The story of the "Navajo Weapon" is based on oral interviews, first person accounts, correspondence and Marine Corps documents. The documents pertaining to the code talkers were found in various branches of the National Archives and Records Administration, Washington, D.C., and the Marine Corps Historical Center, Washington Navy Yard, Washington D.C. These records provided an insight to Marine Corps commanders, policies and attitudes toward the Navajo code talker program and validated what the code talkers experienced during crucial periods of training and combat situations.

The "Navajo Weapon" is told in chronological order beginning with a brief view of Navajo life in the years between the two world wars. This sequence also includes a historical review of the reasons behind Japan's invasion of the South Pacific territories and the subsequent attack on the United States at Pearl Harbor.

The ensuing chapters deal with the Marine Corps's search for the ways and means to create a system of secure, coded communications based on a Native American language. The search led them to the Navajos and the eventual induction of twenty-nine men for a "pilot project." The trail follows the "First 29" through boot camp, creating the first combat dictionary based on a modified version of their language, and then to their first combat assignment on Guadalcanal.

The limited but successful use of the Navajo code on Guadalcanal encouraged the Marine Corps to expedite the induction of Navajos. The students that followed the original group helped modify and increase the vocabulary to over 619 terms before the war ended.

As the war in the South Pacific progressed, so did the need and use of this unique, secure form of coded communications, which the Japanese could not decipher. The culmination of the code talkers' skills, along with dedicated marines of the 3rd, 4th, and 5th Divisions, reached a climax on an unforgettable island: Iwo Jima. The role the code talkers played during this intense battle often made the difference between life and death for the marine and navy personnel engaged in wrestling this strategic island from the enemy.

When the war ended, many of the code talkers volunteered for post-occupation duty even though their code was no longer needed. When it came time for them to finally return home, they were told, in no uncertain terms, that what they had done during the war must remain a secret until further notice. The secrecy lasted for twenty-four years.

The story concludes with chapters that concentrate on the postwar years, the progressive changes the code talkers generated within the Navajo Nation, and the first public recognition for the crucial role they played during the war.

The two compelling reasons for telling this story were (1) to correct any past misconceptions concerning the code talkers, their code, or their program; and (2) to identify and properly credit the people responsible for the implementation and creation of the Navajo code talker program.

I hope that you will enjoy the journey through World War II and Marine Corps history with a unique, dedicated and honorable group of warriors.

iv   Navajo Weapon

*We, the Navajo people, were very
fortunate to contribute our
language as a code for our
country's victory.
For this I strongly recommend we
teach our children the language
our ancestors were blessed with at
the beginning of time.
It is very sacred and represents
the power of life.*

—Kee Etsicitty
Code Talker,
3rd Division

Living Canyon*. Photo by Beth McClain.*

The Diné Bikéyah (People of the Land), 1926

A silent figure emerged from the hogan, and a quiver rippled through his body as he met the cold, predawn air. He raised his arms to stretch the night's sleep from his body, and the air pinched his lungs with the first breaths he took. He walked due east a few quiet paces from the doorway, and began a prayer the Diné had practiced since the beginning of time:

> *In beauty may I walk.*
> *All day long may I walk.*
> *Through the returning seasons may I walk.*
> *Beautifully will I possess again.*
> *Beautifully birds…*
> *Beautifully joyful birds…*
> *On the trail marked with pollen may I walk.*
> *With grasshoppers about my feet may I walk.*
> *With beauty may I walk.*
> *With beauty before me may I walk.*
> *With beauty behind me may I walk.*
> *With beauty above me may I walk.*
> *With beauty all around me may I walk.*
> *In old age wandering on a trail of beauty, lively, may I walk.*
> *In old age wandering on a trail of beauty, living again, may I walk.*
> *If it finished in beauty.*
> *It is finished in beauty.*[1]

To bless the prayer, he took a pinch of sacred corn pollen from his pouch and touched his tongue, then the top of his head, and then made an offering of the corn pollen to the east. The soft voices of his children and grandchildren performing the same ritual reached his ears. He was pleased they practiced the ways of the Diné. The ritual served a purpose in their lives: a day that had a good beginning would have a good ending. As he finished, he felt a great calm pass through him; he was ready to face the coming day.

As the rest of the household came to life, he looked forward to spending the day with his family and relatives who were due to arrive by mid-morning. These gatherings gave them all a chance to listen to the latest gossip, tribal affairs and news. The smell of lamb stew and fry bread filled the air. The happy chatter of voices accompanying the daily chores wrapped him in memories of his childhood.

Finishing his bowl of stew, he set out to find firewood and rocks for the traditional sweat house that would be used in the afternoon. He decided that today was the day to initiate his six- and seven-year-old grandsons to the cleansing of the sweat house ritual. He spent the next few hours in solitary contentment gathering wood and rocks.

Sounds of "Yá'át'ééh!" echoing around the compound alerted him to the arrival of his relatives. Strolling back toward the hogan, he was pleased to see that everyone had arrived safely. Later, as they all sat around the campfire, talk centered on marriages, recent births, tribal affairs, gossip and wool prices.

The congeniality of their conversations turned somber when the topic of the First World War and its aftermath was brought up. The tales of that war brought back by Navajos who had served in Europe made for curious speculation. This was not the first time family members had discussed events that had taken place in France, England and Germany. They could only imagine what these places were like. From the descriptions of what had happened there, they did not seem like very good places to live. Thousands of men had been left crippled or dead by clouds that stole breath from the body and guns that could fire faster than one could count.

Defending a way of life against invaders was not foreign to the Navajos. They had fought the Spanish, Mexicans, Americans, as well as other tribes in the defense of their homeland and would do so again if they were threatened. Everyone agreed that finding more sensible solutions to conflicts was better than resorting to full-scale war. A decision made in anger or impatience was not always so easy to live with later.

Thinking a problem through before making a decision that would affect the rest of one's days was the proper approach. The world surrounding the Diné was changing rapidly and making its presence felt more and more with each passing year. Change was inevitable, but change without careful thought to the consequences could weaken, not strengthen, the People.

It was time to adjourn to the sweat house. He called his two grandsons and explained that they were to begin the journey toward manhood. He instructed them to walk about 50 yards away and then race each other into the sweat house. The boys did as they were instructed and ran excitedly into the entrance. After they entered, he closed the flap behind them. The intensity of the heat enveloping them made the boys feel as if they were suffocating. He made them stay for about two minutes, then told them to go outside and rub dirt on their bodies to absorb the sweat and cool off.

This routine was repeated for nearly four hours, with one minute being added each time they stayed. Their howling protestations were gone by the third go-round as they acclimated to the heat. The communal spirit of the songs and stories within the sweat house eased any discomfort they experienced, and the physical energy they obtained from the ritual made the experience worthwhile.

At the end of the day, the family moved inside the hogan as the night air began to cool with the setting sun. As the family was settling down he realized that the young ones would ask him for a story. This was his favorite time, and he looked forward to their attention. He recalled the many times he had begged his father for a story and how much he had enjoyed learning the history of the Diné.

When their chirping pleas began, he appeared not to hear them; he just closed his eyes. This was the signal for them to become quiet as the night so that he could begin. He took a deep breath and released it slowly, taking himself back to the moment when he had first heard the story he was about to tell them. He recalled the pain and fear etched on his father's face as he told of the terrible suffering the Diné had endured during the Long Walk. He would tell the story the same way he had been told so that these children would feel and remember it forever.

The Diné had lived within the Four Sacred Mountains since the beginning of time. The Holy People had given us this place to live and instructed us in the ways to nurture and protect it forever. Many years later the Spanish invaded not only our land but that of the Utes, Pueblos and Apaches.

During the Spanish invasions, other tribes often sought protection within our lands, and together we eventually defeated them. When the Spanish were no longer a threat, we expected the other tribes to return to their own lands. This did not happen. Perhaps the Utes and Pueblos wanted what belonged to us; perhaps they wanted to conquer us just as the Spanish had. The reasons were many, and peace between the tribes was not easily found.

During the next years, livestock raids and the stealing and selling of children began to occur among the Utes, Pueblos and New Mexicans. The white government intervened many times, and treaties were signed and then broken by all parties. But only the Diné were punished and made to pay for these acts. Justice was not measured out equally after raids and counter-raids because the whites did not see our actions as self-defense but as aggression.

The Army became so angry over the latest attacks that it called a meeting with our tribal Headmen. Colonel Carson informed them that a new policy was going to be enforced as punishment for the latest fighting. It would be a policy that would change our world forever.

Carson informed the Headmen that the entire tribe was going to be removed from the Four Sacred Mountains forever, and they were to inform everyone of this decision. Carson stated that we were to surrender unconditionally at Fort Defiance in one month. Anyone who refused would be considered hostile and then hunted, captured or killed.

When word spread of Carson's order, many refused to believe that such a thing could happen. They cried and asked what they had done to bring about such punishment. Tribal tradition had instructed them never to leave this place. How could they leave and still be the Diné? The Headmen had no answers for them except to repeat that if they refused to go, they would be hunted, captured or killed. Many felt that they could not go, but they could not stay either, so they fled to places of refuge near Navajo Mountain, the Grand Canyon and Canyon de Chelly.

The ones who fled to Canyon de Chelly angered Carson so much that he sent his troops on a rampage through the Four Sacred Mountains. They pulled thousands of fruit trees up by the roots, burned every crop, killed livestock, and destroyed every dwelling they could find. Carson blocked the only way in or out of Canyon de Chelly and starved those in hiding into surrender the following spring.

Witnessing the senseless destruction of the only world they knew forced the Diné to surrender. Carson's troops gathered them at Fort Defiance and began to move them, on foot, 350 miles southwest toward Bosque Redondo, near Fort Sumner. The journey would be nonstop, and since there were few wagons or horses, the People carried what few possessions they had on their backs.

The enforced march was full of terror; each painful step taking them farther and farther from the Four Sacred Mountains. The soldiers' orders were to move them to Bosque Redondo as quickly as possible. If someone complained of being sick, the soldiers killed him. If someone stopped because he was tired, hungry or thirsty, the soldiers killed him. If a woman stopped to have a baby, the soldiers killed her and anyone who tried to help. The Diné quickly realized that there would be no mercy during this march; they did whatever was necessary to survive.

When they arrived at their place of exile, they discovered there was no shelter and there was very poor ground in which to grow food. They dug holes in the hard ground for shelter during the winter and made shabby lean-tos out of sticks to fight the fierce summer heat. They made clothes out of flour, salt and sugar sacks, but these clothes did little to provide warmth or protection. They were forced to build the soldiers' barracks and corrals in exchange for food that made them sick. The water from the nearby creek was full of alkali and made both the animals and people ill.

There was no sacred ground to perform healing ceremonies, and the Medicine men had no herbs with which to heal. Despair and disease were in the People's hearts and minds, and many believed this was their punishment for leaving the Four Sacred Mountains.

In the fourth year of their exile, a small bit of hope arrived in the form of a peace commission. The Headmen met with the commission; the fate of the Diné would be decided once and for all.

Two of the most respected Headmen, Manuelito and Ganado Mucho, pleaded with the commission for the right to return home. They told of the poor land, food, water and living conditions the Diné had been forced to endure. They feared that they were fast becoming nothing and desired to go home. Manuelito and Ganado Mucho made it clear that the Diné did not desire to go to the right or the left, but straight back to the Four Sacred Mountains. They would honor any and all provisions the commission imposed if they were just allowed to go home.

The Treaty of 1868 was signed, and the Diné began preparing for the journey home. They would return the same way they had been forced to leave, but this time they would not be under the threat of the soldiers' guns.

The return of the Diné to the Four Sacred Mountains was celebrated for many weeks. Songs and ceremonies of healing and thanksgiving were carried on with joyful hearts and thoughtful minds. The relief of returning was not lost in the reality of what they had suffered and endured. They had been forced to leave the Four Sacred Mountains and cross two rivers, and they had survived. The harsh conditions of Bosque Redondo and the white men's cruelties had not stripped them of who they were – the Diné! They would rebuild their hogans, replenish their livestock, plant new crops, and be one with the land forever. What they had expe-

rienced and survived made them stronger and more determined than ever to ensure that they would never again be
forced to leave the Four Sacred Mountains. They were, now
and forever, the Diné.

Grandfather closed his eyes, breathing deeply to bring himself back to the present. He then looked on the faces of the children and was pleased to see how attentive they had been. "Were
you on the Long Walk?" a child asked. "No. That happened before I was born. My father survived that terrible time, and he
told me the story the same way that I have just told you," he
replied.

His rising to stretch marked the end of story time, and the
children began to make their way to the sleeping pallets along
the wall. Out of the corner of his eye he noticed that one child
remained behind. There was always one who needed one more
question answered.

He flinched when the boy asked, "Why do the white teachers want to take away my language and traditions? Why is it so
important for me to know the ways of the white people? Why
must I learn to be like them, dress as they do, and believe what
they believe?"

Grandfather closed his eyes and asked for the wisdom to answer these painful questions. This boy had run away many times
from the boarding school that was located more than 40 miles
from his home. He had been severely punished for refusing to
apologize and for speaking Navajo, and he had rebelled at this
harsh treatment.

Grandfather did not approve of the methods the Christian
teachers imposed on the young ones. He did not understand why
they insisted on English only. Did they not see the value in the
ways of the Diné? He understood that the outside world was
encroaching and changes had to be made, but forcing the young
ones to abandon the traditional ways disturbed him.

"The world around the Diné is moving closer, and we must
find new ways to adapt to these changes," he replied. "We are
dealing with the white men in the marketplace, and we must learn
some of their ways if we are to be treated with respect and fair-

ness. Learning their ways will help not only yourself but also the rest of the tribe in the coming years. What you are facing is the same challenge your great grandparents faced during the Long Walk. The lesson learned from that time was that sometimes you must make adjustments in your outer way of life to protect the inner one. The ways of the Diné are there to give you strength and guidance even if you must hold them in secret. Hard lessons often turn out to be the best teachers, and learning always brings wisdom."

He was not sure that anything he said had penetrated the pain and confusion the boy was feeling until he saw the resolve deep in the child's eyes when he replied, "All right, Grandfather, I understand. I will learn the white 'talk' and read their books, but I will <u>never</u> give up the ways of the Diné!"

As the boy turned for his bed, the grandfather knew that this child would hold and practice the ways of the Diné and that he would do his part to ensure that. The hope and future of the Diné, and perhaps of the world in general, depended on the young ones learning from both worlds. As the grandfather made his way to his sleeping place, he lay down with the feeling that it had indeed been a good day to be alive.

Notes

1. Stephen C. Jett, *Navajo Wildlands "as long as the rivers shall run,"* Sierra Club and Ballantine Books, New York, 1969, p. 151.

Living Canyon. Photo by Beth McClain.

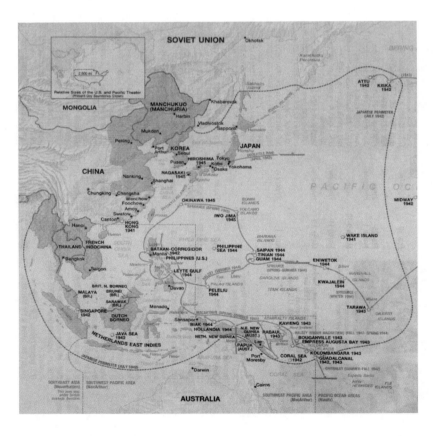

The Pacific Theater, 1941-1945
Map courtesy of the West Point Museum Collections
United States Military Academy
Source: VFW Magazine, November 1991

The Empire of the Rising Sun, 1920 – 1941

The First World War was over, and without question, it had been a great success for Japan. In the years from 1914 to 1920, Japan had doubled its foreign trade and with profits obtained from the postwar annexation of Korea had risen to its first politically recognized role in East Asia.

Many middle- and upper-class Japanese families were financially able to send their sons abroad to such schools as Harvard, Yale, Oxford, the University of Southern California, and the University of California, Los Angeles. The Japanese revered education and made sure that their sons received the best that was possible. In the eyes of the Japanese, education equaled power.

The general populace was enjoying a measure of prosperity not previously experienced. This era of well being would last until 1923, when a series of natural and human-made disasters would cripple Japan's way of life. The results of these events would change the world forever.

The first natural disaster that befell Japan was the great earthquake of 1923. This quake destroyed all of Yokohama and almost half of Tokyo. The already limited housing was severely crippled by the vast damage. Disaster relief poured into Japan from all over the world. The United States sent shiploads of building materials and canned goods and rigged electric lines from its ships to Tokyo to provide emergency lighting. While the U.S. Navy was lending a helping hand, Japanese military experts were secretly taking photographs of, and notes on, U.S. ships.

Rebuilding efforts were slowed by corrupt construction companies, and those with the money to bribe the contractors had first claim to new housing. The remaining housing overflowed with multiple families, forcing people to share limited space. These conditions paved the way for the unrest that was to follow the forthcoming disasters.

The second "natural" disaster was a huge surplus of rice from 1927 to 1930. As the Japanese government struggled to buy the surplus in a vain attempt to keep prices commensurate with the rising cost of living, striking workers marched through the cities in protest over proposed wage freezes. Japan was approaching a critical point of no return.

The human-made, worldwide stock market crash in 1929 was the event that finally broke the backs of the Japanese. Suddenly, many families found themselves not only destitute but also jobless. Tariff barriers imposed on Japanese industrial goods by France, Germany, England, and the United States robbed Japan of the export income it needed to sustain itself. The Japanese government was paralyzed by worker strikes, street riots, and a pervasive air of anger that had never before been displayed by the normally quiet, well-disciplined populace.

When the newly crowned emperor, Hirohito, expressed far more interest in laboratory experiments than in the problems facing his country, a secret society emerged in response. The Kokuhonsha (Society of the Foundation of the Country), composed of civil servants and military personnel of the highest ranks, began to slowly and deliberately wrest control of the government civilian authorities and place it in the hands of the military. This was accomplished through intimidation and assassination of opposing government leaders and several prime ministers. The Kokuhonsha was determined to implement the ancient ideal of hakkō ichiu (the eight corners of the world under one roof) as a way of resolving Japan's most pressing problems.

This ideal is part of the principles of Shinto, the national religion of Japan, and it teaches the origin of the Empire of the Rising Sun. Hakkō ichiu calls for the subjugation of the world to Japan's language, customs, religion, and class system, which was regarded as perfect. This ideal was ingrained in every facet of life and every class of people. It was the very essence of being Japanese.

The Kokuhonsha's implementation of hakkō ichiu became a

cult of blind obedience and violence. The society set in motion events that would lead to death for some of its leaders.

In September 1931 the Japanese Army decided, unilaterally, to invade Mukden, China. Japan had long viewed China as a source of cheap labor and raw materials and an outlet for Japanese goods. The Army concluded that Mukden should be annexed much as Korea had been in 1920. China, however, had no intention of being annexed and retaliated against Japanese forces at Shanghai. Hirohito's direct intervention was the only action that prevented an all-out war.

Hirohito had previously signed pacts with Western nations limiting Japan's expansion into China. He was not about to "lose face" because of the actions of a few renegade military officers. He punished by execution those who had been named responsible for the incident. He considered his actions to be a warning to others and believed the matter resolved.

The results were predictable. While Hirohito continued to pursue his scientific hobby, the Kokuhonsha carried out its plans with the utmost discretion and secrecy. It was not going to be denied hakkō ichiu because of a few executions. By the end of 1936, most of Manchuria, Peking (Beijing), Canton (Guangzhou), and Shanghai had been covertly and effectively consumed through economic and military maneuvers.

By 1937 Japan was a country inwardly smoldering from poverty and choking on a population that had exploded from 52 million to a little more than 80 million. Coal consumption had increased sevenfold, factory production was still stunted by tariffs, and supplies of raw materials were beginning to show critical signs of depletion. The Western nations' political clout kept Japan from further colonization of Korea and China, but clearly something had to be done or Japan would not survive.

The Kokuhonsha, feeling that the time was right to begin the implementation of hakkō ichiu, presented the government with a plan called the "Greater East Asia Co-Prosperity Sphere." This plan showed in detail all of the territory Japan would need to solve its current crisis. Territory from the Kurile Islands (north of Japan) south to New Guinea and from Wake Island west to Sumatra contained the means for solving housing and raw material shortages. This territory also contained the resources necessary to support the well-oiled war machine Japan would need to implement the plan.

The major stumbling block was that most of this territory was in the hands of powerful, well-entrenched Western nations. France, England, the Netherlands, and the United States did not appear willing to share the bounty of such colonies as Guam, Burma, the East and West Indies, and the Philippines with anyone, especially Japan. Negotiation, the Kokuhonsha determined, was not an avenue that would bring the desired results. Conquest was the only path Japan could walk to resolve the overwhelming problems confronting it.

By 1939 successful implementation of the plan depended on two factors: (1) Germany had to keep France, England and the Netherlands so busy fighting for their collective lives that their East Asian colonies would be left vulnerable to invasion; and (2) the United States would have to be attacked in such a way that it would be forced to sue for peace and leave the majority of the South Pacific under Japanese control.

The Kokuhonsha was more certain of the first factor than of the second because it was fully aware that the United States had the ways and means to become a formidable enemy. Many of the society's members had been educated there and knew firsthand the size and strength of the country's economy and industry. Whatever decision was made regarding the United States, the Kokuhonsha was convinced that *any* attack would have to be swiftly executed, deadly and accurate.

When Hitler's war machine began preliminary assaults on France and England, the Japanese began pressuring the Dutch to sell them more oil and rubber and "suggested" to the French-colonial government that they be allowed to station more troops in Indochina to protect their southern flank in Manchuria. These moves would ultimately give them the raw materials and the launching pads necessary for the planned invasions of Burma, Singapore and Vietnam. From these vantage points Japan would be in a perfect position to capture Sumatra, the Indies and the Solomon Islands. The rest of the Pacific would then be caught in a giant web without major opposition.

Meanwhile, in a vain attempt to keep the United States off balance and out of the way during the proposed invasions, Japanese diplomats tried desperately to negotiate a new economic treaty that would allow Japan to obtain more war-oriented materials. The United States refused to sign the treaty because Japan had made a savage attack at Nanking (Nanjing) in clear violation of the pact made between the two countries in 1937. The United States would agree to a new treaty only if Japan agreed to pull all of its military forces back to Manchuria. Japan, of course, refused to give up an inch of what it had taken, and the United States retaliated by turning already existing tariffs into outright embargoes on aviation fuel, scrap iron and steel. When these tactics failed to sway Japan, the United States froze all Japanese assets on July 25, 1941. This action greatly angered Japan and gave it the motive for implementing the second part of the plan.

To reinforce its position, Japan signed the Tripartite Pact with Germany and Italy on September 27, 1941. Article II of the pact held special significance for Japan. Foreign Minister Matsuoba believed that if Japan recognized "...the leadership of Germany and Italy in the establishment of a new order in Europe, Hitler and Mussolini would back Japan's efforts to bring about the new order, in Asia..."[1] The implied meaning was that for the first time Japan was being recognized by other nations as having a "divine right" to its corner of the world. The Ministry of War began to immediately incorporate hakkō ichiu into the formation of Japan's war strategy.

Throughout the autumn of 1941, the Ministry gave the green light for the Army to begin its invasion of Burma. Cutting a path through to Thailand would effectively cut off any future Allied supply lines and make the offensives into the Indies more accessible.

The Ministry of the Imperial Navy began a series of debates over which U.S. targets in the South Pacific would be attacked and in what order. Isoruku Yamamoto, Japan's most respected commander, threatened to resign if Pearl Harbor was not designated as one of the primary targets. The Ministry, bowing to Yamamoto's threat, began planning the method of attacks on Pearl Harbor, Guam, Wake Island, and Guadalcanal.

The Ministry decided that a three-pronged attack, involving the best army and navy commanders, would be carried out against Pearl Harbor, Wake, Guadalcanal, and then the Philippines. The blow directed at the Philippines would ostensibly be enough to force the United States into signing a truce and vacating the South Pacific. Admirals Yamamoto and Nagumo would lead an attack against the U.S. fleet at Pearl Harbor, while Rear Admiral Sadamichi Kajioka headed toward Wake and Guadalcanal. The third strike would be carried out by army commander Lieutenant General Hitoshi Imamura in an effort to trap the U.S. forces in the Philippines.

The success of the entire campaign lay in the absolute annihilation of the U.S. naval fleet at Pearl Harbor. This was made clear in the last message sent by Admiral Yamamoto before total radio silence was imposed: "THE RISE OR FALL OF OUR EMPIRE DEPENDS UPON THIS BATTLE. EVERYONE WILL DO HIS DUTY WITH UTMOST EFFORTS."[2]

The curtain of war was rising. Japan was on a collision course with the United States. Weapons were poised; hakkō ichiu was ready to be launched. Japan was feeling invincible, and for this moment in time, it was.

First Blood

The first uncontested victories in the quest for hakkō ichiu amply justified the confidence Japan's military leaders were experiencing. Pearl Harbor lay in a twisted inferno of ruins, and the American people were stunned and outraged by the seemingly unprovoked attack from a former ally. In the days and months that followed, the United States reeled from one devastating blow after another. Three days after the attack on Pearl Harbor, Japan's army swarmed over an outnumbered and insufficiently armed garrison on the U.S. territory of Guam. In 1941, Wake Island and Guadalcanal were forced into surrender on December 13, and Hong Kong capitulated on December 25; the U.S. Armed Forces in the Philippines were beaten into submission and finally surrendered to the relentless Japanese army on

January 2, 1942.

The citizens of Japan, drunk with happiness over these glorious, unopposed victories, flooded into the streets waving flags and shouting deafening rounds of "banzai" (May the emperor live a thousand years). Borneo, Java, Siam, Truk, Rabaul, and the majority of Micronesia were firmly in the hands of the armed forces of the Empire of the Rising Sun.

The surprise and rapidity of these invasions caught not only the natives off guard, but also the Western nations that had colonized these territories. It seemed that before France, England and the Netherlands could catch their breath from Hitler's assaults, Japan had usurped their East Asian colonies. In four months' time, Japan had managed to conquer territory that had taken decades to colonize and control.

The Ministry of War, knowing the day of retaliation would draw nigh, wasted no time in fortifying every island necessary to secure a perimeter around Japan. Massive numbers of forced laborers and supplies of canned goods, water, ammunition, artillery and concrete were shipped in convoys via pleasure and merchant ships. The territory that had been taken with little resistance initially would not be given up without a price tag written in blood.

Although a majority of Japan's military were enjoying a measure of honor and adulation for their part in these victories, leaders like Yamamoto were not fooled by the exaggerated sense of invincibility that they were currently savoring. Nagumo's failure to finish off the remaining ships of the U.S. fleet disturbed him. He knew, having been educated in the United States, that for Japan to have any hope of retaining what it had taken, it would have to set a trap to draw out the remaining fleet and destroy it once and for all. The Ministry of War, on Yamamoto's recommendation, chose Midway Island as the place to close the chapter on U.S. naval power.

The saving grace for the United States arrived on the heels of the U.S. cryptographers' success in breaking Japan's naval code. Japan had been using an ingenious method of conveying intelligence messages hidden within what appeared to be innocent weather forecasts. The Japanese would refer to countries in these forecasts in the following ways: "EAST WIND – RAIN, was to indicate that Japanese-American relations were in danger.... NORTH WIND – CLOUDY, meant Russo-Japanese relations were threatened.... and WEST WIND – CLEAR meant relations between Britain and Japan were in danger." [3]

Yamamoto, unaware that Japan's code had been broken, set sail with his 120 ship armada toward Midway Island. Once under way, radio transmissions were intercepted by U.S. Intelligence, which alerted the U.S. fleet that Midway was indeed the designated target. Battle forces under the command of Admiral Chester W. Nimitz proceeded to reinforce Midway with every piece of available armament.

Yamamoto believed that this was Japan's last chance to gain complete control of the South Pacific and realize the first stage of hakkō ichiu. U.S. strategists believed that if Nimitz's forces could win the impending confrontation, they could cripple the Japanese beyond repair. The battle was set to begin on June 3, 1942.

The success of the U.S. Navy in the Battle of Midway proved to be a turning point in the South Pacific. Admiral King stated on June 6, 1942 that, "the Battle of Midway was the first decisive defeat suffered by the Japanese Navy in 350 years. Furthermore it put an end to the long period of Japanese offensive action, and restored the balance of naval power in the Pacific."[4]

Yamamoto's desire for a second attack never bore fruit because dive bombers from Rear Admiral Raymond A. Spruance's fleet caught the remaining Japanese carriers at the precise moment when they had their decks loaded with planes waiting for refueling and ammunition. After this devastating attack, Yamamoto turned what was left of his crippled armada toward home. Japan did not launch another major naval offensive for the duration of the war.

The American celebration of the Midway victory did not last long. The Japanese were extremely proficient at breaking into radio transmissions and deciphering U.S. codes. U.S. Armed Forces would have to find a secure method of communications if they were to have any chance of defeating a very clever and intelligent foe. The future of the forthcoming South Pacific campaign was hanging by a slender thread, one that would be strengthened by a most unlikely source: the Navajos.

Notes

1. John Costello, *The Pacific War* (New York: Rawson, Wade Publishers, Inc., 1981), 71.
2. Ibid., 124.
3. Ibid., 645.
4. Ibid., 309.

Ready, willing and armed: *The day after the attack on Pearl Harbor young Navajos reported to the nearest Indian trader seeking information on how and where to enlist to fight the Japanese. Photo courtesy of the Navajo Nation Museum/ Milton Snow Collection, # N07-89*

The Search For Secrecy

Throughout the history of civilization, an aura of mystery and intrigue has surrounded the use of cryptography. Deciphering a code, whether diplomatic or military, has always presented a supreme challenge that only the gifted and clever accomplish. The United States raised the art of cryptography to a new level of distinction during World War I by using a resource no other country had: hundreds of Native American languages so intricate and difficult to learn that few people outside of any one tribe could speak them with any degree of fluency.

A January 23, 1919 report addressed to the commanding general of the 36th Division Headquarters from Colonel A. W. Bloor explained the circumstances involved in transmitting combat information in Choctaw:

> In the first action of the 142nd Infantry at St. Etienne, it was recognized that of all the various methods of liaison the telephone presented the greatest possibilities. It was well understood that the German was a past master in the art of "listening in." Moreover, from St. Etienne to the Aisne we had traveled through country netted with German wire and cables. We established P.C.'s in dugouts and houses but recently occupied by him. There was every reason to believe every decipherable message or word going over our wires also went to the enemy. A rumor was out that our Division had given false coordinates of our supply dump, and that in thirty minutes the enemy shells were falling on that point. We felt sure the enemy knew too much. It was therefore necessary to code every message of importance and coding and decoding took

valuable time.

While comparatively inactive at Vaux-Champagne, it was remembered that the regiment possessed a company of Indians. They spoke twenty-six different languages or dialects, only four or five of which were ever written. There was hardly one chance in a million that Fritz would be able to translate these dialects, and the plan to have these Indians transmit telephone messages was adopted. The regiment was fortunate in having two Indian officers who spoke several dialects. Indians from the Choctaw tribe were chosen and placed in each P.C.

The first use of Indian was made ordering a delicate withdrawal of two companies of the 2nd Battalion from Chufilly to Chadeney on the night of October 26th. This movement was completed without mishap, although it left the Third Battalion, greatly depleted in previous fighting, without support. The Indians were used repeatedly on the 27th in preparation for the assaults on Forest Farm. The enemy's complete surprise is evidence that he could not decipher the message.

After the withdrawal of the regiment to Louppy-le-Petit, a number of Indians were detailed for training in transmitting messages over the telephone. The instruction was carried on by the Liaison Officer, Lieutenant Black. It had been found that the Indians' vocabulary of military terms was insufficient. The Indian word for "Big Gun" was used to indicate artillery. "Little gun shoot fast" was substituted for machine gun, and the battalions were indicated by one, two and three grains of corn. It was found that the Indians' tongues do not permit verbatim translations but at the end of the short training period at Louppy-le-Petit, the results were very gratifying, and it is believed had the regiment gone back into the line, fine results would have been obtained. We were confident the possibilities of the telephone had been obtained without its hazards.[1]

The stage had been set for the use of Native American languages for secure communications during combat. In 1940, based on the limited success of the Choctaws, the Louisiana-based Army Signal Corps field tested Comanche personnel from Michigan and Wisconsin. The problem that had existed for the Choctaws was the same for the Comanches: their language did not contain military equivalents or verbatim translations for such words as "tank," "regiment," "aircraft carrier" and "submarine." These inadequacies in the Comanche language led the Army Signal Corps to label the idea as untenable.

After the attack on Pearl Harbor, the Army recruited fifteen Oklahoma Comanches for duty in language communications. These young men made up the 4th Signal Corps and occasionally substituted Comanche words for military terms during combat in the European Theater of Operations. But these substitutions never developed into a full-scale Comanche-based, specifically-designed combat code.

The use of the Choctaws in World War I and the Army's experiment with the Comanches had been studied with great interest by the Marine Corps. Further research would lead the Corps to a people who had been relegated to obscurity, not only by the United States, but by the rest of the world. Commandant Thomas Holcomb and Major General Clayton B. Vogel would change not only the way the armed forces viewed Native Americans but also the tactics of war. These men would help pour the foundation for the creation of the only unbroken oral code in military history.

Catalyst 1:
Major Clayton B. Vogel

The Army's experiment with the Comanches had been noted with a great deal of interest and curiosity by the Commanding General, Amphibious Force, Pacific Fleet: Major General Clayton B. Vogel. Vogel sought and received permission from Commandant Thomas Holcomb to investigate the possibility of using Indian languages for coded communications. The attack on Pearl Harbor made it imperative that this seemingly impossible task become a reality in some form or another.

Vogel knew that the Marine Corps would bear the brunt of any fighting in the South Pacific, and finding a secure method of communicating was a necessity if the marines were to have a chance of defeating the Japanese. Vogel's concept would be validated through a civilian, Philip Johnston, who contacted Vogel's signal officer, Major James E. Jones.

Catalyst 2: Philip Johnston

Philip Johnston was only four years old when his parents established the Presbyterian Mission at Leuppe, Arizona on the Navajo reservation just outside of Flagstaff. As a young child, having only Navajo children to interact with, he learned to speak a fairly good form of "Trader" Navajo. He could carry on conversations and understand simple directions, much like immigrants who learn to speak pidgin English, but he never mastered the complex Navajo tongue. The nature of the language is such that if it is not learned from birth, fluency is nearly impossible to attain.

His family moved to California during his teen years where he attended and graduated from the University of California, Los Angeles with a degree in engineering. When World War I occurred, he joined the Army and served with an engineering battalion in France.

After the war he often returned to the Navajo reservation, photographing the Navajos, for whom he felt a deep affection. He traveled the Southwest on a lecture circuit, showing his photographs and relating his experiences living among the Navajos. His knowledge and respect were sincere, and in some educational circles he was regarded as an expert on the Navajo tribe.

Johnston was working as an engineer for the city of Los Angeles when he read about the Army's experiments with the Comanches. Intrigued by the idea, he tucked the information away in his memory. After the attack on Pearl Harbor, he contacted the Marine Corps area Signal Officer, Major James E. Jones, concerning the possibility of using Native American languages for combat communications. Jones relayed the results of their meeting to Major General Vogel, who in turn requested that a recruitment proposal be submitted by Johnston for further review.

The recruitment proposal Johnston prepared had general information regarding Native American languages, education and tribal populations in the United States. The majority of the information dealt with the Navajo as this was the tribe he was most familiar with. Section 3(b) contained, however, a serious misrepresentation about the Navajo language: "That such a service would involve the transmission of messages in their own tongue, which is not understood by any other people in the world."[2] (The entire proposal can be viewed in the Appendix.)

Johnston, having grown up around the Navajo reservation, should have known that Navajo trader language was understood by the Apaches, Hopi, Zuni and surrounding tribes. In fact, the Apache language was from the same linguistic stock as Navajo. His statement did not seem to matter, however, because Jones asked Johnston if he could arrange a demonstration to determine if Native American languages could be used for coded communications.

Johnston received Jones's inquiry on February 10, 1942, and sought for possible volunteers from a Los Angeles job placement agency that aided Native Americans seeking work. He interviewed and selected four Navajos for the task and notified Major Jones. Jones replied, "The arrangements in your letter of 18 February are entirely satisfactory. Quarters and meals will be arranged for you and your men as soon as I receive your final confirmation."[3]

Johnston planned to arrive at Camp Elliott, San Diego on Friday, February 27 and give the demonstration the following morning. Jones informed him that Vogel and his staff would be present and that "we're ready for you. A field telephone has been installed in the Headquarters building."[4]

On the morning of February 28, Johnston and the Navajo volunteers walked with Jones to the Headquarters building, where the demonstration was to take place. The Navajos were given the following list of field messages and half an hour to prepare them for transmission:

"Begin withdrawal at 2000 today."

"Enemy expected to make tank and dive bombing attack at dawn."

"Tanks artillery weapon carrying vehicles with ammunition will be landed in next wave."

"Withdrawal will begin at 2000 today as ordered."

"Two officer prisoners enroute to your headquarters."[5]

Because these messages contained words that had no existing equivalent in Navajo, the volunteers requested additional time to work them out. They notified Jones when they were ready to proceed.

It was a tense moment. A lot of expectations would either be realized or shattered in the coming minutes. Two of the volunteers were taken into an adjoining room, and the test began. The messages were dictated in English, sent in Navajo over the field telephone, and then written down in English as received.

Transmitted: From: Commanding General
     To: Commanding Officer, 2nd Marines

     "Begin withdrawal at 2000 today."

Received: From: Commanding General
     To: Commanding Officer, 2nd Marines

     "Will withdraw today 2000."

Transmitted: From: Commanding General
     To: Commanding Officer, 2nd Marines

     "Enemy expected to make tank and
      dive bombing attack at dawn."

Received: From: Commanding General
               To: Commanding Officer, 2nd Marines

                     "Enemy tank, dive bomber expected to attack this morning."

Transmitted: From: Commanding General
               To: Commanding Officer, 2nd Marines

                     "Tanks artillery weapon carrying vehicles with ammunition will be landed in next wave."

Received: From: Commanding General
               To: Commanding Officer, 2nd Marines

                     "Tanks artillery weapon carrying and ammunition will land next."

Transmitted: From: Commanding Officer, 2nd Marines
               To: Commanding General

                     "Withdrawal will begin at 2000 today as ordered."

Received: From: Commanding Officer, 2nd Marines
               To: Commanding General

                     "2000 today withdrawal begins."

Transmitted: From: Commanding Officer, 2nd Marines
               To: Commanding General

                     "Two officer prisoners enroute to your headquarters."

Received: From: Commanding Officer, 2nd Marines
               To: Commanding General

"Two enemy officers sent to your
headquarters."[6]

After the conclusion of the demonstration, Major General
Vogel inspected the results. He was visibly pleased with the translations from English to Navajo to English, especially since the
volunteers had such a short period of time in which to find Navajo words that could be substituted for military terms. He was
confident that sending the results of the demonstration along
with the recruitment proposal would convince Commandant
Holcomb that this idea could succeed. Vogel included a letter of
his own that reinforced his belief in using Native American languages in communications. Paragraphs 3 and 4 stated:

3. Mr. Johnston stated that the Navajo is the only tribe in the
    United States that has not been infested with German stu-
    dents during the past twenty years. These Germans, study-
    ing the various tribal dialects under the guise of art students,
    anthropologists, etc., have undoubtedly attained a good work-
    ing knowledge of all tribal dialects except Navajo. For this
    reason the Navajo are the only tribe available for the type of
    work under consideration. It should also be noted that the
    Navajo tribal dialect is completely unintelligible to all other
    tribes and all other people with the possible exception of as
    many as 28 Americans who have made a study of the dialect.

4. It is therefore recommended that an effort be made to enlist
    200 Navajo Indians for this force. In addition to linguistic
    qualifications in English and their tribal dialect, they should
    have the physical qualifications necessary for messengers.[7]

Vogel's letter and Johnston's proposal were reviewed by Commandant Holcomb and his staff. The idea held a great deal of
promise, but Holcomb decided to undertake further discreet inquiries before making a final decision regarding the use of Navajos for language communications.

Creators of the Navajo Pilot Project: Left: *General Clayton B. Vogel. Right:*
Commandant Thomas Holcomb.

Plans and Policies

After reviewing Vogel's recommendations, Commandant
Holcomb referred the entire package to A.H. Turnage, the director of the Division of Plans and Policies, for further review.
Turnage's perusal of the proposal and proposed project revealed
issues that he felt had to be addressed before the recruitment of
any Native American tribe for transmitting messages in its native
dialect could proceed. He stated his concerns in a letter of reply
to Holcomb:

3. The utilization of Indians to transmit verbal messages would
    seem to have some advantage with regard to the rapid trans-
    mission of information by voice while at the same time main-
    taining security. On the other hand, there would appear to
    be several disadvantages. For instance, as is indicated in the

transcript of messages transmitted and received during the aforementioned demonstration, there were several discrepancies between the message transmitted and the one received. While these discrepancies appear on their face to be of little consequence, it might well be that a false interpretation during battle would be critical. It is possible, however, that with training the Indians could be taught not to make such mistakes. It would also be necessary to teach them to operate technical communication equipment. This imposes a problem which might not be readily solved. Then, too, in the event of casualties, a system carefully built up might possibly collapse. Furthermore, in the smaller units, that is, the regiment and battalion, it is believed that combat action will develop so rapidly that it will be impossible in most instances to transmit messages by voice in plain English without benefit to the enemy, and in such instances the employment of the Indians' dialect would only serve to slow up communications.[8]

Turnage was correct in his assessment that *normal*, everyday Indian language communication would be slow and ineffective. There was no doubt that any Indian dialect would have to be modified to fit combat use. With that possibility in mind, he recommended the idea be given an opportunity to prove itself. Turnage reached the following conclusion:

4. Since the Commanding General, Amphibious Corps, Pacific Fleet, is of the opinion that Indians could be utilized to advantage and since there is no objection to the enlistment of Indians for general duty, there would seem to be no objection to their enlistment and assignment to the Amphibious Corps, Pacific Fleet, for use on the service recommended, if desired. In case this project did not develop satisfactorily, it would then be possible to employ such Indians on the regular duties of a Marine.[9]

On reviewing Turnage's recommendations, Holcomb decided to seek additional opinions before making a final decision. He turned for more advice to the Bureau of Indian Affairs (BIA).

Although all Native Americans had been granted "blanket" citizenship in 1924, it did not include the right to vote, nor did they have control over their own lives. Many tribal treaties contained clauses that forbade tribal members from bearing arms either for or against the government of the United States. Perhaps Holcomb desired a clearer picture of the Navajos' general disposition toward serving in the armed forces.

Holcomb appointed Lieutenant Colonel Wethered Woodworth to hold a roundtable discussion with selected BIA experts and then report the findings to Turnage.

Enforced acculturation had not been 100 percent effective, and those Native Americans who held to their tribal beliefs and traditions were seen as "failures" in the BIA's eyes. Paragraph 3, item 5; paragraph 4, paragraph 6, items 3 and 4; and paragraph 5(2nd paragraph 5) reveal how the BIA personnel believed the Navajos should be "handled." (See entire transcript can in the Appendix.)

3. (5) The Selective Service Board in covering the area of the Reservation has, to a large degree, deferred the induction of many of the tribe on the grounds of insufficient education. This has created a bad feeling in the tribe as on the whole they are most anxious to serve and be treated as other Americans....

4. Some discussion was held as to whether or not the Navaho language would be a fit medium of communication and as to whether or not it would be intelligible to other people. All of the bureau personnel agreed that for ordinary involved communication the Navaho language would be an ideal medium of communication and that messages so delivered would not be intelligible to anyone other than the Navahos themselves. They all agreed that transmitting messages by this method would be exceptionally fast as the individuals could translate as they received and it would do away with any coding or trans-coding of any sort.

6. (3) It should be pointed out to the Tribal Council that the

services required are particularly valuable to the military effort and that the men employed will be in the status of specialists of an unusual order. It is the opinion of the undersigned that if enlistments are made, the Indians should be trained as a group of specialists rather than be put through ordinary recruit training. This opinion [is] based on the ideas put forth by the members of the Indian Bureau, which in the main emphasized the fact that better cooperation and effort might be obtained if the individuals recruited felt themselves to be singled out in an unusual manner for an unusual job.

(4) Mrs. Adam [Chief of Community, Service Bureau and Education, BIA] states that, of course, there were no military terms in the Indian vocabulary and it might be well to employ during the training period two or three of the older Indians (40 to 50 years old) who are expert interpreters and who would be invaluable in helping the recruits develop the proper vocabulary. It will be necessary for them to invent new terms...

5. As a result of the above conference it was felt that the suggestion as to enlisting initially thirty (30) Navahos for training and experimental duty is both practicable and feasible and that the same should be initiated. Before any moves are made, however, it is recommended that someone be detailed to call on Mr. Fryer, the General Superintendent of the reservation, and perfect the general principles under which the program is to be carried out.[10]

J. P. Berkeley was an assistant deputy at the signal section in the Division of Plans and Policies during the time the Navajo proposal came up for review. "The Navajo program first came to our attention in early 1942 when Philip Johnston brought it to our attention via a Marine Corps contact in San Diego," Berkeley recalled. "Johnston, we were told, had been raised in Navajo country where his father had been a missionary. His belief in the Navajo language as a means to secretly communicate stirred quite a bit of interest at Headquarters. Our signal section decided to give the idea a try and I had a heck of a job convincing our commanding general.

"General A. H. Noble finally told us to give the idea a try, but he remarked that it worried him. Noble asked me, 'What can I say at my Court Martial when they ask me why I attacked at that moment and my only answer would be that my Indian told me to?' I pointed out that the idea was not for the Indians to make tactical or command decisions, they would only be handling 'Secret' logistical reports and information. On that basis, he reluctantly endorsed the idea and we gave it a whirl."[11]

Holcomb instructed Turnage to inform Vogel that he had permission to proceed with his Navajo project. Section IV. of that letter spelled out the specific recommendations for the enlistment and employment of the Navajos:

IV. <u>CONSIDERATION OF NONCONCURRENCES</u>:

1. The question of practicability of the proposed use of Navaho Indians was considered in drafting the original memorandum, and the recommendations made therein were based upon the idea of permitting the Command ing General, Amphibious Corps, Pacific Fleet, to try out his proposal.

2. There is no restriction on the enlistment of Indians for general duty in the Marine Corps. It is therefore believed that, all factors considered, the preliminary consideration should be enlistment of approximately 30 Navaho Indians for general duty with a view to their later assignment to the Amphibious Corps, Pacific Fleet, for experiment in the transmission of messages. It is not considered desirable to enlist the above Indians in Class V, Marine Corps Reserve with the promise of special duty or assignment, which might be necessary to revoke if an experiment was unsuccessful.[12]

Holcomb, Turnage, Woodworth and Noble were in total agreement about allowing Vogel's project to commence, but there was one voice of dissension within the Division of Recruiting. He made his feelings known to Turnage in a memorandum dated March 26, 1942.

2. The undersigned, at this time, wishes to express the opinion that the proposed plan has very little practicable value. Action in the field is so fast now that messages sent in the clear usually result in immediate compliance, rendering them of no value to the enemy.

3. For combat directing officers to have to depend on an order which is being transmitted and received in a language unknown to any of the operating forces renders it of very doubtful value as a scheme of communication.

Frank Halford[13]

Halford's opinion might have been secretly shared by Noble, Turnage, Woodworth, and perhaps even Holcomb. Nonetheless, Holcomb notified Vogel that the Western Recruiting Division was being directed to enlist approximately thirty Navajos, under current guidelines for enlistment in the Marine Corps, for his pilot project.

Interestingly, once the decision had been made to recruit the Navajos, the "expert" advice from the BIA personnel was largely ignored. Ultimately, the Navajos that were chosen were not given special or separate treatment. Holcomb believed that the Navajos had to become marines first and specialists second and this approach was not subject to negotiation. The saying, "There is the right way, the wrong way, and the Marine Corps way" was never more true than at this particular moment.

On April 25 D. M. Randall, officer in charge of the Western Recruiting Division, forwarded an inquiry to Holcomb regarding the employment of Navajo interpreters in the Marine Corps. The BIA (also known as the Indian Service), was suggesting the use of these men, and Randall needed a reply.

1. The Officer in Charge, Recruiting District of Phoenix, has

been offered the services of Howard Gorman, age 43, and Henry Gatewood, age 37, both Navaho Indians, to act as instructor-interpreters at the Marine Corps Base, San Diego, California in connection with subject. The U.S. Indian Service will detail these men for this duty for a period of thirty days and pay them their regular salary. These men are at present employed as interpreters on the Navaho agency and are especially qualified for this work.[14]

Holcomb's airmail response was swift and to the point. Interpreters were not acceptable unless they enlisted in the Marine Corps as general duty marines. The generous offer from the BIA was politely turned down. Holcomb was adamant that if the thirty Navajos to be recruited failed boot camp, interpreters would not be needed under any circumstances.

Notes

1. SRH-120 Report, Tab A, pp. 18-19. Military Reference Branch, National Archives, Washington, D.C.
2. RG-127 1535-76, Box 600, Folder 13, Ells-Dran Index, National Archives, Suitland, Maryland Branch; italics added.
3. Ibid.
4. Ibid.
5. Ibid.
6. Ibid.
7. Ibid.
8. Ibid.
9. Ibid.
10. Ibid.
11. Correspondence from Lieutenant General J.P. Berkeley, USMC (Retired) February 25, 1993.
12. RG-127 1535-75, Box 600, Folder 13.
13. Ibid.
14. Ibid.

Navajos report to Ft. Wingate for induction. Photo courtesy of the Navajo Nation Museum/ Milton Snow Collection #N07-45.

Members of the "First 29" are sworn into the United States Marine Corps. Photo courtesy of the Navajo Nation Museum/ Milton Snow Collection #N07-53.

Navajo Recruits

In April 1942, First Sergeant Frank Shinn arrived at Fort Defiance, Arizona to recruit the thirty Navajos requested by Marine Corps Headquarters. His office, near the Navajo Tribal Headquarters, consisted of a simple desk, chair and lamp. He used recruitment posters and assorted Marine Corps paraphernalia to decorate the walls in preparation for the first recruits.

What Shinn did or did not know regarding the reasons behind the recruitment of only thirty Navajos unfolded in an interview conducted by Zonnie Gorman while she was filming a documentary on the code talkers, one year before he died. Shinn guessed that because any potential recruit had to be proficient in English as well as Navajo, something was being designed specifically for the Navajos. Looking back, he said that the recruitments of the first two groups of Navajos for the Marine Corps were the proudest moments of his career.

Shinn's first forays trying to recruit the Navajos for the Corps were unsuccessful, and he was beginning to wonder why they seemed reluctant to sign up. After two days during which he failed to sign a single Navajo, he requested a meeting with Chee Dodge, Chairman of the Tribal Council, to try to discover the reasons for his failure. Shinn enlisted the aid of Dodge's son for the meeting and when Shinn was through explaining the situation and having it interpreted, Chee Dodge answered, in English, that the tribe had not been notified by the BIA that the recruitment by the Marine Corps was sanctioned. Once the situation was clarified, Chee Dodge gave permission for an announcement to be broadcast over the BIA shortwave radio system that the Marine Corps was seeking volunteers.[1]

The broadcast produced a small flow of Navajos to Shinn's office.

First-time enlistment required men to be between the ages of seventeen and thirty-two and in good physical health. Carl Gorman was thirty-five, and William Yazzie, now named Dean Wilson, was only sixteen. Wilson recalled that at the time of recruitment, "I was, according to my parents, only 16 and I remember the day that we were physically examined at Fort Defiance Public Health Service. At noon, the recruiters had gone to lunch, and we were left in the hall. We were mingling around when I saw the stack of folders on the recruiter's desk. Mine was sitting way off to the side, tagged with the information that my parents wouldn't consent to my induction. I gently pulled the folder out and put it underneath the big stack. That's how I got in at age 16 - of course in November I would have turned 17." [2]

When it came to verifying age, recruiters for the most part were forced to believe the Navajos when they said they were between seventeen and thirty-two. The men born in the years that made them eligible to be recruited had no birth certificates, only BIA census numbers. In any case, the recruiters were more interested in the men's linguistic qualifications and fitness to serve than in their true ages.

The recruiters were very careful not to mention the reason for the recruitment, only that it was for "special duty." Carl Gorman was under the impression that they would end up with a desk job in Washington, D.C., and frankly that did not matter. Gorman, like so many other Navajos, joined because there was no work to be found on or around the reservation. Recruitment speeches were a very effective tool, according to Eugene Crawford, as he remembered the one that was given to him on a street in Fort Defiance. "One of the recruiters tried to attract me into signing up by saying that becoming a marine would be much better than staying on the reservation. As a marine I could learn new skills, travel, and meet interesting people. What did it for me was the dress uniform on the poster. Crisp white hat and gloves, brass buttons against the deep blue material, boy he looked sharp! I wanted a uniform just like that." [3]

After approximately two weeks of interviews, twenty-nine Navajos (see Table 1) were notified to report to Fort Defiance for transport to to Fort Wingate for induction. Some of the Navajos returned home to pack and say their farewells. Time was short, but many prayers were offered for the safety and protection of these young men.

Table 1: 382nd Platoon, United States Marine Corps, the First 29.[4]

Charlie Begay	David Curley	Chester Nez
Roy Begay	Lowell Damon	Jack Nez
Samuel Begay	George Dennison	Lloyd Oliver
John Benally	James Dixon	Frank Pete
Wilsie Bitsie	Carl Gorman	Balmer Slowtalker
Cosey Brown	Oscar Ilthma	Nelson Thompson
John Brown	Dale June	Harry Tsosie
John Chee	Alfred Leonard	John Willie
Benjamin Cleveland	Johnny Manuelito	William Yazzie
Eugene Crawford	William McCabe	

On May 4, 1942 the recruits, later known as the "First 29," boarded a bus at Fort Defiance and headed for their induction destination at Fort Wingate. When they arrived at Fort Wingate, they were ushered into the dining area, ate lunch and at the conclusion were duly sworn into the United States Marine Corps. They were then placed on a special bus that would take them nonstop to the Marine Recruit Depot outside of San Diego – 1,200 miles from the Four Sacred Mountains. That bus ride through the southern edge of their land was an exciting occasion for them. As the road melted in the dark, they were filled with conflicting emotions; exhilaration, uncertainty, excitement and pride. The attack by the Japanese on Pearl Harbor could not be left unanswered and this assignment was their chance to protect the land and people they cherished.

They were either too excited or too apprehensive to sleep. They were going where few Navajos had been before, and these were moments to remember. Their plummet back to reality was fast approaching as the bus arrived at boot camp. It was a blessing that they arrived on Sunday, for they would have a day in which to absorb their new surroundings and catch up on the sleep they had refused during the trip.

The first glimpse of the Recruit Depot left much to be desired in their road-weary eyes. One recruit felt as if they had been delivered to the gates of a penitentiary. "After the free life of the reservation, this place looked like a prison with all the guards, gates and barbed wire fences. Were they keeping us in or the rest of the world out?"[3]

The recruits were marched to their barracks, instructed to unpack and relax, and then given orders for the following morning. The itinerary would include a complete physical, a visit to the barbershop, and then a trip to the supply depot for the standard issue of pants, shirts, socks, boots and hygiene kit.

Left on their own, the recruits began to stow away the prized possessions they had brought from home, just as they had done countless times before at boarding schools. The next few days were going to be confusing and demanding, but they liked the idea of going through them together. Eugene Crawford had served in the Reserve Officers' Training Corps (ROTC) and was able to give them a general idea of what would be expected of them in the coming days. Throughout boot camp Crawford would offer advice and solace to those who found boot camp a daunting and lonely experience.

The two basic functions of boot camp are to instill discipline and to secure obedience. Every task performed during boot camp serves these two objectives. Close order drills, eating and sleeping at precise times, long-distance hikes, artillery drills and kitchen duty are elements of obedience and discipline.

Setting aside the individual for the benefit of the whole is how successful fighting units are formed. A soldier's life depends not only on maintaining self-discipline but also on contributing to discipline within the unit. There is nothing precise about war – it is organized chaos at best, and discipline and obedience are necessary ingredients for surviving and winning in combat situations. Boot camp is where these basic tenets are drilled into every recruit, and its ultimate value cannot be overemphasized.

Military discipline is strict and demanding, and there were

some Marine Corps officers who held private doubts as to whether the Navajos could withstand the rigors of boot camp. These young Navajos were as physically rugged as the land they came from. But boot camp is more than just a physical challenge; it is a mental one as well.

For the Navajos, boot camp was a true culture shock. Navajos are taught, for example, not to look someone directly in the eyes; it is considered rude. Their Elders rarely raised their voices to obtain obedience. In boot camp the drill instructor (DI) is forcing the recruit to maintain eye contact while barking orders at the top of his lungs, and all the recruit sees are the instructor's tonsils!

The Navajos who had attended BIA schools were already integrated into the routine of marching. John Benally explained, "We had been exposed to discipline, in some respects, during the old boarding school days within the Bureau of Indian Affairs. We were marched to school, the dining hall and church in formation. We knew how to drill, not in true military fashion, but we knew how to drill."[5]

The truth of Benally's statement was verified less than a week into boot camp when the instructors reported, "These magnificent specimens of 'original American manhood' were already farther advanced than recruits usually are with so few days of training to their credit. All are of sturdy stock and take well to the type of discipline and military instruction offered in the Marine Corps."[6]

George T. Hall, the Commanding Officer of the Recruit Depot, sent a progress report on the Navajo recruits to Holcomb. Paragraphs 4 and 5 of his report stated:

4. This group has done exceptionally well at this Depot. They are very tractable, attentive and loyal. At an early date they developed an exceptionally high Esprit de Corps. They have already fired a pistol record practice; 76% qualified (general average for recruits has been about 70%). They fire rifle record practice 19 June. Preliminary records indicate that a high percentage of qualification will be attained.

5. This group of 29 men is still intact, none has dropped back due to sickness, disciplinary action or lack of ability to keep up with the rest of the group. This is unusual. There is a usual attrition of from five to ten percent in ordinary platoons. Their progress has been highly satisfactory.[7]

Although the grueling schedule left little time for homesickness, the twenty-nine had their moments when they wondered how they had let anyone talk them into joining the Marine Corps. There was one piece of advice from their DI that made an indelible impression on them. Crawford remembered the DI telling them, "If someone orders you to move the Statue of Liberty from the east coast to the west coast, you don't say, 'How?' You say, 'When?' Nothing is impossible in the Marine Corps!"[8] Recognizing the need at this time in their lives to set aside their traditional behavior for the war effort showed how truly remarkable these men were.

There were times when, like all recruits, they were late for a roll call, forgot a piece of equipment during a drill, did not stand up straight enough, or failed to give a proper salute. The resulting demerits could be worked off in a variety of ways. Wilsie Bitsie, nicknamed "Chick" because he was one of the smallest members of the platoon, was known for receiving the most boot camp demerits.

"I was always working off demerits for some offense: not standing up straight, not giving a proper salute, my eyes were crooked, or something!" Bitsie recalled. "I had to work them off by either digging a 6 foot by 6 foot foxhole, do extra KP [Kitchen Patrol] duty, and once by standing on the parade ground with a metal bucket on my head.

"They had a surprise drill one morning, and we all came running to stand at attention for inspection. As I glanced down the line, I realized that I was the only one that forgot my weapon. I leaned out and waved my hand at the sergeant and said, 'Hey, Sarge, I forgot my gun! I forgot my gun!' I then made a mad dash back to the barracks, got my 'gun,' and managed to get back in line before the sergeant reached me. I thought that I had done a real good job, but after the inspection he marched me out to the parade ground and showed me how impressed he was with my actions. He put a metal bucket over my head and made me repeat fifty times, 'Ten thousand Marines have a rifle, but I'm the only shithead with a 'gun'!

"The other way I worked off demerits," Bitsie continued, "was to give Sergeant Duffy a bath every Saturday morning. Oh, he was dirty! I had to wash his ears out, then take a swab and clean his eyes and pull back the folds in his face and make sure all the dirt was out. Then I had to shampoo his head and then the rest of his body. When that was done, I had to sweep out his house, wash it down with Lysol, and then mow and rake the yard. I can still see him leading the review parade. The other guys would poke me and say, 'Hey, Chick, your buddy looks real sharp this morning!' Oh, man, let me tell you! That bulldog was a real pain! He knew me real well, though! I had a lot of fun in boot camp. Fun, work and play. Digging foxholes and bathing Sergeant Duffy. Yes, sir!"[9]

Despite Bitsie's exploits working off demerits, the Navajo recruits were doing the most difficult boot camp drills with relative ease. Standing at attention for hours in the withering heat or hiking five miles with a full field pack was not an undue hardship for them. On the reservation it was not unusual to spend long hours in the sun tending livestock or crops. Walking 30 miles or more to and from the nearest trading post for supplies was a normal occurrence. Sometimes they could not help but laugh when other recruits passed out or fell out during these drills. It was not that they felt superior; it was that they were more accustomed to the rigors of what they were being subjected to. Their stamina did, however, create a certain mystique about Native Americans.

Racial incidents were virtually nonexistent even when the Navajos were referred to as "Chief." Navajos have never had a traditional tribal chief, and the recruits privately considered those who called them that rather ignorant. For the most part, the men trained and played together, admiring and respecting each other's skills.

There was one racial incident that occurred with an instructor from Kentucky who was less than thrilled with the prospect of having to teach "dumb Injuns." His mouth was crude, and his fists were like lightning the day he gave the Navajos their first boxing lesson. Crawford recalled that incident with traces of fear still present in his voice.

"We were told to form a circle around the two men the instructor had chosen to start boxing," Crawford remembered. "Well, they started dancing around each other, throwing punches that wouldn't hurt your little sister. We are not an aggressive people by nature, and fist fighting is something that we were not familiar with. Those two boys looked so silly dancing and ducking each other that we began to laugh. The instructor became so disgusted at the display that he ordered us back in line. He yelled, 'That's no way to box, you #@%*& prairie pea hens!' After we lined up at attention, he told us he was going to demonstrate how a proper boxing punch was executed.

"Starting with the first man," Crawford continued, "he drew back his arm and quick-punched him square in the face. As the instructor worked his way down the line, heads were snapping and some of the boys were knocked off balance. We took those punches just the same, but there was one man who didn't. Carl Gorman had been a boxing champion in high school, and when the instructor reached him, Carl dodged the punch, reared back, hit the instructor square on the chin, dropping on his backside. Carl asked if he had performed the punch in the proper manner, and the instructor just glared at Carl. We went on to other training for the rest of the day.

"It was one of the few times in my life that I was truly afraid. I knew from my ROTC experience that you didn't _ever_ strike someone with rank. I spent a long sleepless night fearing what they would do to Carl. Turned out they didn't do anything to Carl after all, but I have never forgotten how afraid for Carl I was."[10]

Captain McLeod, the officer in charge of drills and instructions, reviewed the incident and decided to forego any punishment for Gorman. The instructor received a verbal reprimand, and future boxing lessons were never conducted in that manner.

While the Navajo recruits were progressing through boot camp, Major General Vogel and other intelligence and cryptographic experts were reviewing the original demonstration transcript. Vogel and his experts would discover that, for the short period of preparation time allowed, the Navajos had been able to come up with some fairly accurate substitutions for military terms. Referring to the transcripts from the BIA discussion and Adam's statement, "It will be necessary for them to invent new terms," they concluded that certain rules would have to be followed to improve the chances of successfully completing the task.

Satisfied with the progress of the intelligence and cryptographic discussions, they decided that the location of the school would be guarded and that only those with a "need to know" would have access. In accordance with military standard operating procedures (SOP), an intelligence officer would be on duty during school hours.

Colonel James L. Underhill, base commanding officer; Lieutenant Colonel Hall, commanding officer of the Recruit Department; and Captain McLeod, officer in charge of drills and instructions inspected the all-Navajo 382nd Platoon on graduation day, June 27, 1942. Colonel Underhill specifically addressed his remarks to the Navajos.

This is the first truly All-American platoon to pass through this Recruit Depot. It is, in fact, the first All-American platoon to enter the United States Marine Corps.

The rest of us in the Marine Corps are American, but our Americanism goes back at most no more than 300 years. Your ancestors appeared on this continent thousands of years ago - so long ago that there is no written record of them. Through your ancestors, you were Americans long before your fellow Marines were Americans.

Yours has been one of the outstanding platoons in the history of this Recruit Depot and a letter has gone to Washington telling of your excellence. You obey orders like seasoned and disciplined soldiers. You have maintained rugged health. You have been anxious to learn your new duties, and you have learned quickly. As a group you have made one of the highest scores on the Rifle Range.

The Marine Corps is proud to have you in its ranks, and I am proud to have been the Commanding Officer of the

Base while you were here.

You are now to be transferred to a combat organization where you will receive further training. When the time comes that you go into battle with the enemy, I know that you will fight like true Navajos, Americans, and Marines.[11]

This was high praise indeed for a group of men whom BIA experts had deemed ill suited to achieve success if treated like "regular Americans." The Navajos were visibly pleased with the respect and affection they were being shown along with the pride of earning the rank of private first class (PFC).

At the conclusion of the graduation festivities, the Navajos were instructed to board a bus that would take them to Camp Elliott for their new assignment. The standard ten-day furlough after completion of boot camp was canceled. In fact, from the day they were inducted until they were either wounded, earned 140 points, or the war ended, the First 29 were never granted leave to go home.

Notes

1. Audio interview with Captain Frank D. Shinn, USMC (Retired), November 16, 1989, Tuscon, AZ by Zonnie M. Gorman.
2. Oral History Transcript VE 25.A1 M37, Marine Corps University, Quantico, Virginia.
3. Interview with Eugene Crawford, June 1991.
4. Quotation is anonymous by request.
5. Carl Gorman, First 29, 2nd Division
6. Oral History Transcript VE 25.A1 M37, Marine Corps University.
7. *Chevron,* May 16, 1942.
8. RG-127 1365-150, Box 333, Folder 7.
9. Interview with Eugene Crawford.
10. Interview with Wilsie Bitsie, May 1993.
11. Interview with Eugene Crawford.
12. *Chevron*, July 3, 1942.

Graduation Day: *Members of the first all-Navajo platoon pose for a traditional graduation picture. Photograph courtesy of Carl and Mary Gorman.*

The Birth of the Code

The ride to Camp Elliott was filled with happy chatter and remembrances of boot camp experiences. Despite not knowing what awaited them, the Navajos clearly felt a sense of pride. On the rifle range they had turned out one expert, fourteen sharpshooters and twelve marksmen. Despite Bitsie's slew of demerits, not one of them had gotten into serious trouble. They were fullfledged members of the United States Marine Corps. The equality and respect they had received helped them understand the essence of esprit de corps. It was a wonderful feeling to be accepted for who they were right along with every other marine.

Upon arrival at Camp Elliott, they were escorted to their barracks with instructions that Sunday would be a "free" day to spend as they pleased as long as they did not leave the compound. They were advised to rest and enjoy this brief respite, for come early Monday morning they would begin their new training. They spent the remainder of Saturday and all of Sunday playing horseshoes and cards, writing letters home, and generally enjoying not having to march, drill or work off demerits.

Promptly at seven o'clock Monday morning their escort arrived, and after roll call they proceeded to the mess hall for breakfast. After the meal was concluded, they were led to the building that would serve as their classroom. Eugene Crawford remembered feeling anxiety flowing through him as he glimpsed the ominous-looking building. It had bars on all of the windows and a barred door that protected the entrance. The thought of being led to the brig flashed through his mind. "If this was the place of our 'special duty,' I began to wonder just what was so 'special' about it."[1]

The escorting officer held the door open until they had all entered, then promptly locked it behind them. He led them down a long hallway that had offices on both sides. They came to a room at the far end and were told to go inside and make themselves comfortable; someone would be with them shortly.

Crawford eyed the sparsely decorated classroom; it reminded him of the ones he had entered in BIA boarding schools as a child. Those memories were far from pleasant. He could almost taste the harsh brown soap the teachers had forced him to use to scrub out his mouth when he was caught speaking Navajo. His thoughts were interrupted when the door suddenly opened and an officer entered. They snapped to attention. "At ease, gentlemen. Please be seated."

The first hour they spent in that building changed their lives forever, and the shock and bewilderment of what transpired are still felt by them to this day. They could never have imagined the project the Marine Corps had recruited them for. In retrospect, some of them believed that had they known beforehand, they might not have enlisted so eagerly.

The memories of what transpired in the next hour are not exactly clear. The Navajos remember the officer saying something about codes, how they are built, used and decoded. He told them that this was the reason the Marine Corps had recruited them.

The Marine Corps believed that a combat code based on Navajo could be developed and employed during battle situations. He turned to the chalkboard and wrote the four rules to be followed in attempting this task:

1.   Construct an alphabet.
2.   Choose words that are accurate equivalents.
3.   Choose short terms for rapid transmission.
4.   Memorize all terms.

He then passed out lists that contained military terms and equipment currently in use, and added that picture charts of planes, ships and weapons would be made available to them. All printed material generated in the classroom would be locked in a safe at the end of each day. The "buddy" system would be in effect at all times. If they needed a break to stretch and get some fresh air, they were to go in pairs. If they needed to use the bathroom, they were to go in pairs. At no time under any circumstances were they to leave the building or the compound without permission or alone. He impressed on them that this project was secret and that they were never to discuss what occurred here with anyone, not their mothers, fathers, girlfriends, wives or fellow marines. To do so would mean spending the duration of the war in the brig.

In closing, he told them to remember everything they had learned in boot camp and apply it to the task now facing them. If they needed any additional material, all they had to do was ask and it would be provided. He thanked them for their attention, wished them good luck, turned and left the room, closing the door behind him.

The stunned, bewildered Navajos stared at the closed door for what felt like a week. Was this some crazy test they were being subjected to? If so, had they passed? They expected the officer to come back any minute, praise them for passing the test, and then tell them what their <u>real</u> assignment was! When that did not happen, confusion and some anger filled their minds.

Many of these men had been punished, sometimes brutally, for speaking Navajo in classrooms similar to this, classrooms in schools run by the same government that included the armed forces. Now this government that had punished them in the past for speaking their language was asking them to use it to help win the war. Bilagáana (white people) were stranger than the Navajos had imagined.

The Emergence of the Code

The silence was finally broken when Crawford asked, "They want us to make a combat code from Navajo? Can we do that?"[1] Recalling how they built the vocabulary was revealed in bits and pieces during interviews with Eugene Crawford in 1992 and Wilsie Bitsie in 1992-1993. To the best of their memories, the following events transpired.

Bitsie said, "My father worked on the phonetics of the Navajo language while teaching school in Mexican Springs. What I learned from him can help us. We should start with the alphabet and see where it takes us. We need to be sure that whatever words we choose, we pronounce them the same way."[2]

Navajo is an intricate, multifaceted language. A slight variation in inflection would mean something entirely different so uniformity was essential.

One man suggested that they use things familiar to their way of life on the reservation when picking words for military terms. If they were going to have to memorize what they were creating, it made sense to memorize familiar things. The first letter, A, was given the Navajo word for ant: wol-la-chee.

As they worked their way through the alphabet, the atmosphere reverberated with school day memories. This time, however, no one was going to beat them or wash out their mouths with lye soap for speaking Navajo. They were free to speak the words without fear, and after a while it became a game of sorts to pick the next letter and then go around the circle until they decided and assigned the complementary term for that letter (see Table 2).

Table 2: The Code Talker Alphabet[3]

Letter	Navajo Word	Meaning
A	Wol-la-chee	Ant
B	Shush	Bear
C	Moasi	Cat
D	Be	Deer
E	Dzeh	Elk
F	Ma-e	Fox
G	Klizzie	Goat
H	Lin	Horse
I	Tkin	Ice
J	Tkele-cho-gi	Jackass

K	Klizzie-yazzie	Kidd
L	Dibeh-yazzie	Lamb
M	Na-as-tsosi	Mouse
N	Nesh-chee	Nut
O	Ne-ahs-jah	Owl
P	Bi-sodih	Pig
Q	Ca-yeilth	Quiver
R	Gah	Rabbit
S	Dibeh	Sheep
T	Than-zie	Turkey
U	No-da-ih	Ute
V	A-keh-di-glini	Victor
W	Gloe-ih	Weasel
X	Al-an-as-dzoh	Cross
Y	Tsah-as-zih	Yucca
Z	Besh-do-gliz	Zinc

Bitsie, being the one with typing skills, hammered out the alphabet while keeping in mind his father's work with the phonetics of the language. Navajo is filled with accents and guttural sounds, and the words as spelled are not the true way they are spoken. Knowing that the code would be memorized, he did not unduly worry about adding accents to the words chosen. Those who would teach the code later would know how to correctly pronounce it.

After reaching agreement on the words and their pronunciations, the men began calling them out, in no particular order, until everyone had them memorized. By the end of that first day, they were feeling much better about the task they had been assigned to complete. That night, long after "lights out," they softly called out the letters to each other saying the words again and again - "wol-la-chee, dibeh, gah, lin, nesh-chee..." until fatigue won over their enthusiasm. Such were the humble beginnings of a code that would baffle and frustrate U.S. cryptographers and eventually the Japanese.

Obstacles

The ease with which the alphabet was created soon evaporated as the twenty-nine wrestled with unfamiliar terms such as "reconnaissance," "amphibious," "right flank," "sabotage." Crawford recalled, "There were days when I thought my head would burst. All the memorizing and frustration trying to find Navajo words that would fit things like 'echelon' and 'reconnaissance.' Sometimes we would spend three or four hours on just one word! It was the hardest thing I have ever been asked to do. Looking back, reservation school was easy compared to building the code. Reservation school did prepare me, in some ways, for what we were faced with, so I guess it wasn't a total waste."[4]

At some point, and none of them could remember exactly when, they hit a wall they feared they could not get over, under or around. Many of the military terms were frustrating their efforts to find equivalents, and they finally asked for help. The requested help came in the form of three Navajos who had preceded them in boot camp: Felix Yazzie, Wilson Price and Ross Haskie. Price and Haskie had college educations, and they, along with Yazzie, entered the project with Vogel's permission.

The addition of these three men resulted in the completion of terms for ships, planes, officers and the remaining military vocabulary (see Table 3). Terms for officers were based on the insignia each rank was assigned. Trying to spell, for example, "brigadier general" broke the rules of short, accurate and easy to memorize. Insignias gave instant identification and were easy to memorize.

Table 3: Code Talker Terminology[5]

Military Term	Navajo Word	Meaning
OFFICERS:		
Major General	So-na-kih	Two Stars
Brigadier General	So-ala-ih	One Star
Colonel	Astah-besh-legai	Silver Eagle

Lieutenant Colonel	Che-chil-getah-besh-legai	Silver Oak Leaf
Major	Che-chil-betah-ola	Gold Oak Leaf
Captain	Besh-legai-na-kih	Two Silver Bars
1st Lieutenant	Besh-legai-a-lah-ih	One Silver Bar
2nd Lieutenant	Ola-alh-ih-ni-hi	One Gold Bar

AIRPLANES: Wo-tah-dineh-ih (Air Corps)

Dive Bomber	Gini	Chicken Hawk
Torpedo Plane	Tas-chizzie	Swallow
Observation Plane	Ne-ahs-jah	Owl
Fighter Plane	Da-he-tih-hi	Hummingbird
Bomber Plane	Jay-sho	Buzzard
Patrol Plane	Ga-gih	Crow
Transport Plane	Astah	Eagle

SHIPS: Toh-dineh-ih (Water Clan Fleet)

Battleship	Lo-tso	Whale
Aircraft Carrier	Tsidi-ney-ye-hi	Bird carrier
Submarine	Besh-lo	Iron fish
Mine Sweeper	Cha	Beaver
Destroyer	Ca-lo	Shark
Troop Transport	Dineh-ney-ye-hi	Man carrier
Cruiser	Lo-tso-yazzie	Small whale

Their collective creativity was one of complete harmony. They were one heart, one mind, one voice and one spirit. The "traditional behavior" that they set aside during boot camp was allowed to radiate in that classroom. The pride of being able to use their language to aid the war effort was almost beyond description. They knew they were creating something that, when implemented in the field, would withstand any and all efforts at decoding. The picture charts of ships and planes showed them the differences between a battleship and a carrier, a dive bomber and a fighter plane. Notice how sensibly the description correlates to the function of each category (see Table 3).

As the terms of the military vocabulary were created, certain safety valves were built into the code. If by chance a Navajo not trained in the use of the code happened to hear any transmission, he would be totally confused by what he was hearing. For example, the following is a simple message transmitted in code as the "normal" Navajo ear would hear it:

> Request artillery and tank fire at 123B, Company E move 50 yards left flank of Company D.

> Ask for many big guns and tortoise fire at 123 Bear tail drop Mexican ear mouse owl victor elk 50 yards left flank ocean fish Mexican deer.

In creating the combat dictionary, these men would have to program themselves to remember that when they said, for example, the Navajo word for "Mexican," it actually meant "Company." This was not an easy task by any means. Along with creating and memorizing the code, the Navajos were also required to learn other aspects of Signal Corps duties. They attended classes on Morse code, panel codes, and radio use and repair.

Three weeks into their training, the man responsible for the initiation of their program, Major General Clayton B. Vogel, was transferred to Australia to help coordinate the first amphibious assault in the South Pacific campaign: Guadalcanal. Vogel was replaced by General H. M. Smith, and it was through his office that 200 additional Navajos would be recruited for this program. He sent his request and the justifications for it in a letter to Holcomb. Smith advised that Navajo recruits be qualified in the same manner as the original group and that additional training in machine gunnery and radio operation be added. Paragraphs 3 and 4 of his request stated:

3. Recommendations in paragraph one (1) are based on the experience and results gained through the three weeks' training of the initial group of thirty Indians received from the Base Depot, San Diego, 27 June 1942. This training consisted of transmitting messages over telephone and over radio from airplanes, reconnaissance cars, and over portable ground sets.

4. The present three weeks' experimental training of the initial group of thirty Indians has proved beyond doubt the value of these men in communication work.[6]

Smith's letter of recommendation was based on field exercises that had taken place around the third week of July. During the first morning that the men field-tested the code, North Island, the security headquarters for the southern California coast, intercepted their transmissions. Wilsie Bitsie recalled the aftermath of those field tests.

"We had been out early that morning practicing and testing the code," Bitsie stated. "Later that day, around four o' clock, a jeep pulled up in front of our barracks. One of the MPs [military police] motioned for me and asked if I was Wilsie Bitsie. I said, yes, I was, and he told me that he was there to bring me in. Bring me where? What did I do? He replied that his orders were to take me to North Island. I thought, my God, what did I do? It's pretty serious to be taken to headquarters under guard. I'd been to North Island before to give suggestions on different things, but never in a manner where an MP had to come after me.

"He asked me where I had been that morning, and I told him that I had been on field maneuvers. He then stated that perhaps I should bring along two of my buddies, and that really killed me! I walked over to John Benally and asked him to go with me. I told him I didn't know what I had done, but since he understood English the best, I wanted him with me to help me understand what was going on. 'What did you do?' he asked. I told him I had no idea, the MPs were here to escort me to North Island, and that I should bring two of my friends with me.

"John rounded up William McCabe, and the three of us were stuffed in the MP car, and we sailed on through downtown San Diego towards the ferry that leads to North Island," Bitsie continued. "My mind was racing with every passing moment we spent on the ferry towards the island. I couldn't think of anything that I could have done that would have landed me in this kind of trouble.

"As we approached the entrance, a large iron gate swung open and closed as soon as we cleared it. We were led to a building that I was not familiar with and escorted to a large barred door. We went through about four sets of barred doors, and John kept asking, 'Son, what did you do?' I had no answer for him.

"We arrived in a small room, and they told John and William to wait in a little vestibule, and I was taken into a large room with the longest table I had ever seen. I only recognized one face among the many that were there, and I was told to take a seat. Next they wheeled in some type of tape machine, and I waited for them to explain why I had been brought there.

"One of the officers finally spoke and said that they had received word from the Coast Guard that strange, and perhaps hostile, radio messages had been intercepted that morning and the entire California coast had been put on 'Red Alert.' They asked me to listen to the tape and identify the source, if possible.

"I sat there and listened, and it was <u>us</u> talking! When they asked if I could decipher what was being said, I told them to give me a pencil and paper and I would try. I wrote down exactly what I heard and then handed it to the clerk.

"Then John and William were brought in and instructed to do what I had done. John was directly behind me, and he had his hand on the top of the chair. When he heard the tape, he tapped me on the shoulder, and they warned him not to make any kind of signs and to keep his hands at his side. When the tape was over, they asked who he thought the voices belonged to. John looked them straight in the eye and stated, 'That is this man, right here, talking!'

"Colonel Beans, the only man in the room I recognized, sat there smiling and said, 'We depend on this type of communication quite a bit over at the base. These men are the ones that initiated this program.' I was so relieved to hear him say that! Later on we had a real good laugh about the whole thing, but that was one of only two times that I was truly frightened."[7]

From that day forward North Island was informed in advance when field exercises involving the code were to take place. By the end of the eighth week, the coded vocabulary contained approximately 263 terms.

The final week of field exercises officers would walk around the pairs of Navajos while sending runners to the receiving locations to ensure that the message sent was the same one written down at the other end. To the officers' utter amazement, they never observed a mistake. To say that it baffled them would be an understatement. William McCabe recalled the final week of review.

"When we sent the message, one of the men would be hiding behind a house with a guard over him to ensure that no one would be able to signal or tell him what the message was before he received it. Then this officer wrote a message that had a dash, comma, and a semicolon and said, 'Let's see you send this!' That was the easiest message they had us send! As soon as it was received and written down, the runner brought it back and compared them. They were the same. The officer exclaimed, 'How in the hell it works, I don't know, but it works! How can they translate in the air?' There wasn't any way to explain exactly how we read a message in English, sent it in Navajo, and then wrote it down in English, word for word, so that they could understand what we were doing. It was a code within a code that only we understood."[8]

The days spent creating, memorizing, and testing were coming to a close. Assignments for overseas duty were approaching, and the men would be divided among the 1st and 2nd Marine Divisions and Raider Battalions (see Table 4). John Benally and Johnny Manuelito, promoted to corporal, were selected to help recruit and instruct the next group of Navajos.

No matter where the men were assigned, they had forged a link – the code – that would connect them to each other for the rest of their lives. Through recruiting, instructing and combat, they would help change the balance of power in the war that was about to take place in the South Pacific.

"I am bringing a distant nation against you. An ancient and enduring nation. A people whose language you do not know, whose speech you do not understand."

Jeremiah 5: Verses 15 & 16[9]
Quoted by Dennie Hosteen

Table 4: Code Talker Overseas Duty Assignments[10]

Signal Company, 1st Marine Amphibious Corps:

Pfc Charlie Begay	Pfc	David Curley
Pfc Samuel Begay	Pfc	Ross Haskie
Pfc Wilsie Bitsie	Pfc	Alfred Leonard
Pfc Cosey Brown	Pfc	William McCabe
Pfc John Chee	Pfc	Chester Nez
Pfc Eugene Crawford	Pfc	Lloyd Oliver
Pfc Felix Yazzie		

2nd Marine Division Communications Personnel:

3rd Battalion, 6th Marines:

Pfc Harry Tsosie
Pfc John Willie

2nd Battalion, 6th Marines:

Pfc Balmer Slowtalker
Pfc Nelson Thompson

Headquarters and Service Company, 6th Marines:

Pfc Carl Gorman
Pfc Oscar Ilthma
Pfc Jack Nez
Pfc William Yazzie

1st Battalion, 6th Marines:

Pfc Frank Pete
Pfc Wilson Price

2nd Signal Company:

Pfc Roy Begay
Pfc John Brown
Pfc Benjamin Cleveland

Pfc Lowell Damon
Pfc George Dennison
Pfc James Dixon

Notes

1. Interview with Eugene Crawford.
2. Interview with Wilsie Bitsie.
3. Copy of vocabulary: Philip Johnston Collection, Museum of Northern Arizona at Flagstaff. The alphabet and vocabulary these men created were not in any archival record group. My efforts to locate the Navajo Communication School records through every Marine Corps channel proved futile. I found the vocabulary and other school documents in a private papers collection that Philip Johnston had deposited with the Museum of Northern Arizona.
4. Interview with Eugene Crawford.
5. Phillip Johnston Collection
6. RG-127 1535-75, Box 600, Folder 14. There seems to be a clerical error in the date in paragraph 3. The first all-Navajo platoon did not graduate from boot camp until June 27, 1942. Platoon members could not have been transmitting messages through any communication devices on *June* 27, 1942.
7. Interview with Wilsie Bitsie.
8. Interview 1171, Doris Duke Collection, Marriott Library, University of Utah, Salt Lake City, Utah.
9. *Holy Bible*, Interview 1158, Doris Duke Collection.
10. RG-127 1535-75, Box 600, Folder 14.

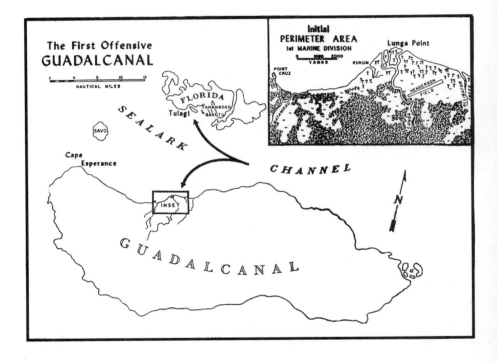

The Enemy Awaits

The Imperial Japanese Army instruction manual stated: "Bear in mind the fact that to be captured means not only that you disgrace yourself, but your parents and family will never be able to hold up their heads again. Always save the last bullet for yourself."[1] These instructions derived from the Bushido, the medieval warrior code of the Samurai, which trained the Imperial soldier to fight to the death for his emperor.

The Imperial Japanese Army underwent the most brutal physical boot camp. Practice patrols were known to cover up to sixty miles in twelve hours on combat rations that consisted of a cup of dried rice and fish, and pickled meat. The five primary rules of conduct when engaging the enemy, reinforced through the intense indoctrination in "death before dishonor," were as follows:

1. Obey without question or hesitation.
2. Always take the offensive.
3. Surprise the enemy whenever possible.
4. Never retreat.
5. Never surrender.

Guadalcanal

The battle for Guadalcanal has been written about many times over the years both from military and personal points of view. It was a bloody, costly, protracted affair that wrenched great losses from Japan and the United States.

The following is a brief background of the U.S. objectives

for the campaign on Guadalcanal and the natural and man-made elements that U.S. soldiers experienced during the first assault into enemy-held territory.

Guadalcanal, the largest island in the Solomon chain, is located south of the equator and is approximately 90 miles long and 25 miles wide. The native population, friendly to the Allies, consisted of 25,000 Melanesians whose livelihood revolved around herds of Tulagai cattle. England had used the island as a seaplane base, communications outpost and outer perimeter defense for Australia.

The Japanese usurped control of the island in May 1942 under the guise of the Greater East Asia Co-Prosperity Sphere campaign, with the idea of using Guadalcanal to launch an invasion against Australia, New Zealand and New Guinea. General Hyakutake and Lieutenant General Mayuyama's 5,000 troops made up the primary occupation force.

Japan would expend thousands of men and numerous ships and planes in a vain attempt to keep control of Guadalcanal. The recent defeat at Midway, still fresh in Japanese minds, was the driving force behind the fight to retain possession of this island. The defense of Guadalcanal would be the first of many battles to the death in the coming conflict.

General Alexander A. Vandegrift was given the task of taking the 1st Marine Division to Guadalcanal to secure Australia's perimeter defense, and to supervise the construction of airfields for Allied use. Stationed in New Zealand at the time he received his orders, Vandegrift had never heard of Guadalcanal. A check of the files revealed very little current data about the island, and most of what was known was based on reports obtained from German reconnaissance patrols during World War I. Vandegrift assigned Colonel Frank Goetgge, G-2 (Intelligence), to fly to Australia and compile an up-to-date dossier from British sources. On Goetgge's return, Vandegrift gathered his staff for a briefing about the island.

Guadalcanal has an 8,000 foot mountain range located in the north-central part of the island and a deep harbor off the northern coast, with flat beaches located near Lunga Point. The Tenaru River, more like a trickle, runs though steep, rocky canyons. The rest of the island is covered in dense vegetation and is dotted with plains covered in razor-sharp kunai grass, scum-covered lagoons and swamps. The swamps and lagoons are infested with crocodiles, lizards, fist-sized spiders, tree leeches and disease-carrying mosquitoes. Rain, intense heat and high humidity characterized weather conditions. All in all, this seemed a nasty piece of geography.

Vandegrift was to exercise overall command, while Brigadier General William H. Rupertus would command elements of the 2nd Marine Division aimed at Tulagi, Florida, Gavutu and Tanambogo, islands that lay northwest of Guadalcanal. Beach Red, near Lunga Point, was designated as the landing area for Colonel Hunt's 5th Marine Regiment and Colonel Cates's 1st Marine Regiment. Their objective was to make a two-pronged assault inward toward the partially completed airfield.

Operation Watchtower, later referred to as Pestilence because of the incessant problems that hampered embarkation preparations, was scheduled to commence on August 7, 1942. After a rather dismal dress rehearsal held July 31 on Fiji, 956 officers and 18,146 enlisted men boarded transports headed for the first amphibious engagement with the Empire of the Rising Sun.

Debarkation Day (D-Day)

The prelanding "softening" of Guadalcanal was highly successful as the landing forces on Beach Red met no enemy resistance. The surprise and ferocity of the U.S. presence panicked Japanese troops, and they fled inland in such haste that they left behind half-cooked meals and valuable maps, artillery, ammunition and radio equipment.

A report from Radio Counter Measures told of a chilling discovery: "It was not until August 1942 that it was positively known that the Japanese had radar. At that time, in the invasion of Guadalcanal, a Japanese radar set was captured. This was a Mark I Model I, intact."[3] The realization that the enemy had advanced communications equipment overshadowed the uncontested landing at Lunga Point.

Guadalcanal objective: *This airfield (Henderson) was a vital target in the struggle to usurp Guadalcanal from the Japanese. National Archives photograph.*

The ensuing battles that took place at the Henderson Airfield, the Tenaru River and Bloody Ridge were complicated by malaria, dysentery, fungal infestations and constant dampness. Add in an enemy that could move rapidly, undetected through the jungle; maintain sniper positions for days without food, water or rest; and intercept and decipher U.S. radio transmissions at will, and the results were heavy casualties and physically impaired U.S. troops. Vandegrift desperately needed fresh food, medicine, artillery, dry clothing, and some form of secure, rapid communications in order to control what territory his forces held.

Seven weeks after the initial landing, Rear Admiral Kelly Turner took an unprecedented risk by bringing a supply convoy to the beaches near Lunga Point. The convoy consisted of fresh supplies plus the 7th Marine Regiment, which included the first group of Navajo code talkers. The arrival of the convoy on September 18 was like an early Christmas to Vandegrift's weary command.

One code talker, William McCabe, remembered the first hours on Guadalcanal as totally confusing. His orders stated that he report directly to General Vandegrift, a task not easy to accomplish in the middle of a debarkation process that resembled nothing but chaos.

"We were assigned as replacements, so we didn't have a regular outfit to report to," McCabe recalled. "Our orders stated that we were to report to the commanding general and no one else, so that is who we went looking for. We didn't know what was going on, we were green, walking around happy-go-lucky and ended up near the front line perimeter. At that point we were stopped and told to return to the debarkation area. We took off and ended up being strafed by a Jap Zero.

"When we finally located General Vandegrift we presented him with our papers and he informed us that we should have reported to his signal officer, Lieutenant Hunt. By the time we found Lt. Hunt it was dark, and he told us to come back in the morning. Hunt said, 'It's night time and we don't do anything at night.'"

McCabe continued, "We were instructed to report to him and start 'talking.' We weren't sent here to fight I informed him, but to talk the enemy to death. That is what our orders stated and that is what we intended to do. Hunt then replied, 'We'll try you out right now!'

"He scattered us to different locations with jeeps that had radios and we began transmitting a routine message. Before we could get through, the whole island was phoning in to ask if the Japanese had broken into our frequency. All the radio operators were trying to jam our message ,and Hunt finally had to get on the radio and tell them to stop. By this time Hunt had more than he could chew so he told us to go to bed and come back in the morning and it would be straightened out then.

"The next morning, Hunt told us he was going to make us compete with a code machine using the same message to see who they were going to keep and use, the machine or the Navajos. I asked him how long it took for a coded message to go out to a unit, decipher it and receive a reply? Hunt replied, 'About four hours. How long will it take you to send the same message?'

'About two minutes,' I said.

"'Are you going to send, decipher and bring a message back telling me it's delivered, give it to a coding officer, have him sign it, and bring it back in <u>two</u> minutes?!' Hunt yelled. 'Yes Sir,' I replied. Hunt just laughed and said, 'Oh yeah! Bullshit! This coding machine will out do any coding machine there is.'"

"To prove it," McCabe continued, "Hunt initiated the message and asked when we were going to start. I replied that I wanted to give them a running start because we could get it done in two minutes. I picked up the field telephone and sent the message. Hunt was standing there timing me with his watch when I got the 'Roger.' 'Two minutes and thirty seconds,' Hunt said. 'You must have already read this message somewhere.'" McCabe replied, "You wrote it just now. I can't explain that we are just a walking code machine. Whatever we send in Navajo comes out properly decoded on the receiving end.' That was the end of the test. Every message that had 'Urgent' or 'Secret' status we sent. The code talkers made a believer of Lt. Hunt."[4]

To keep other radio operators from panicking when the Navajos were transmitting, the tag words "New Mexico" or "Arizona" would precede the transmission. Even if commanders did not understand how the Navajos did what they did, they used the Navajos nonetheless because the speed, accuracy and security of their messages made a vital difference to the men in the field. In October, one incident proved the value of the Navajo radio net for a patrol that was trapped behind enemy lines. Code talker Sam Begay was with the patrol when this occurred. He radioed Bill McCabe to tell him of their predicament and need for food and ammunition. Lieutenant Hunt searched the field map for the location of a secret cache and told McCabe the location. That information was relayed back to Begay in code, secure from Japanese interception and decoding, and made the difference between life and death for that patrol.

While the battle continued, there were short periods of time when rest and recreation occurred. The following account, provided by Sergeant Major Dolph Reeves, USMC (Retired), concerned several different types of activities that unfolded during the Guadalcanal campaign.

"As a young sergeant with Radio Platoon, III Corps Signal Battalion (Radio Intelligence) on Guadalcanal, I had many duties," Reeves stated. "I was a watch supervisor at the radio shack, where we copied FOX schedules, press schedules, and operated an interisland alert radio net. Between major military operations in the South Pacific, everyday life became somewhat boring – an outdoor movie each night regardless of rain and an occasional softball game, with mail call being the great event of the day.

"I was also in charge of atabrine call [dispensing malaria pills containing atabrine]," Reeves continued. "Each evening at a designated time, all sergeants and below reported to my tent for their pill. As each one walked up to my tent with his mouth open, I threw the pill as far down his throat as I could. He had to take a drink of water, close his mouth and swallow before I would let him leave.

"Here's where I immediately became acquainted with our marine Navajo talkers," Reeves remarked. "There were eight or ten in our platoon. I had to watch them closely because they tried to invent ways to fool me, and I'm not sure but what they were successful. After I threw the bitter pill down their throat, they would walk away muttering something in their native tongue that sounded to me like, 'I outfoxed you that time, Sarge.' I could have been mistaken. They might have said, 'Thanks.'

"Now here's the question: how do you train a bunch of Navajo marines to be talkers?" Reeves queried. "I remembered a few sounds that I had picked up during atabrine call but hesitated to use them. I tried one and that night I found something similar to a tomahawk piercing my mosquito net. A mosquito net with holes in it on Guadalcanal was the worst fate that could happen to anyone. Just kidding, but not entirely unrealistic.

"I took morning muster, assigned work details, and marched the platoon to the storeroom where we carried out the daily training schedule. I was probably the most popular marine in our platoon. Our beer ration consisted of two cans per week, if we were lucky. Therefore, the favorite drink on the island was Raisin Jack. It seemed that our talkers always had a friend in the mess hall and had a constant supply of raisins. When a batch became ripe, I didn't have to worry about them for a couple of days. I just kept them in their tents and kept all others away. They even conducted their own training schedule. Even on Guadalcanal there had to be periods of relaxation.

"I became friends with our Navajo marines, and they eventually quit thanking me for their atabrines. They were honorable, dedicated marines who performed a distinguished service for our country."[5]

The Banzai

As the Navajo code talkers settled into their role within the Signal Corps, they encountered their first experience with a banzai attack. Finding the appropriate words to describe this form of Japanese combat is difficult at best. The banzai was used by the Japanese under several conditions: (1) a unit had expended its ammunition, (2) a unit had lost its commander, (3) a unit could not advance or hold its position, or (4) a unit needed a psychological weapon of terror.

The Bushido demanded that a soldier die in battle bravely and honorably. The banzai provided Japanese units faced with any one of the aforementioned conditions with the means to uphold the Bushido. The Japanese saw the banzai as a perfect way to honor their traditions, while the Americans viewed it as an incomprehensible waste of life.

A banzai could happen almost anytime after night arrived, and it made for anxious moments for Americans nestled in their foxholes tensing at every tiny sound, straining their ears and eyes for what they hoped would not happen. The "Don't move after dark, and no lights" orders were passed quietly from position to position. There was no casual chatter, just the quiet checking and rechecking of weapons. The nights on Guadalcanal seemed to last forever.

Then without warning the Japanese seemed to appear from nowhere screaming, "Banzai! Banzai! Banzai!" Rushing the entrenched marines they deployed whatever weapons they had: grenades, mortars, rifles, swords, and in some desperate circumstances, razor sharp sticks. Marines reacted quickly by firing at anything and everything that moved in any direction. Radio calls for naval illuminating shells were transmitted with urgency while marines scrambled to cover their positions. When the shells exploded overhead everyone was cast in a ghoulish green hue that intensified the atmosphere.

The Japanese fought without regard for their own lives or those of the marines, and they did not cease until they were dead. The banzai, which might be brief, seemed to last forever. When it was finally over, the sudden quiet was almost as fearful as the cacophony of the melee. Marines assessed their casualties, tended the wounded, regrouped and waited for daylight. They hunkered down in their foxholes and tried to find ways to compose themselves. Their hands shook, they were covered in sweat and their eyes twitched with flashes of scenes just recently witnessed. Some men were able to shake off the effects of the banzai after resuming their sleep and some never got over the terror these types of attacks produced.

For the Americans, who had been raised with the belief that life is precious, this seemingly useless expenditure of life was beyond explanation or understanding. One code talker observed that "it is not a good thing to make human beings become mindless killing machines. It is not good for the soul, heart or mind. The Japanese forced many a man to become the one thing humans must never become: mindless killers."[6]

The banzai would be used countless times on Guadalcanal and on practically every island U.S. forces set foot on. But no matter how many times banzais occurred, the marines never got used to them.

Navajo Raiders

As the campaign on Guadalcanal marched onward, four Navajos from the First 29 were about to join the ranks of the Raider Battalions. Wilsie Bitsie, Eugene Crawford, Felix Yazzie, and Charlie Y. Begay arrived at the staging area on Noumea, New Caledonia. On debarkation they were told that the Raider Battalions were seeking volunteers and that if they were interested,

Lt. Evans S. Carlson, second man from the left, conducts a casual meeting with medical personnel on Noumea, New Caledonia. Photo courtesy of Wilsie Bitsie.

they should report to Lieutenant Evans S. Carlson.

Raider commanders were well aware of the Navajo code talkers through Colonel Fred Beans and Major James Roosevelt. Colonel Beans had been present during the North Island incident, when the first code talker practice transmissions had raised a coastal alarm, and Major James Roosevelt knew of them from the staff briefings. The code talkers and the Raiders were a perfect blend of unique weapons and warfare tactics. Eighteen Navajos would serve in Raider Battalions as code talkers before they were disbanded in 1944.

How Bitsie, Crawford, Yazzie and Begay came to join the Raiders is not exactly clear. Bitsie was under the impression that they were preassigned, whereas Crawford remembered that they volunteered. According to policy, battalion commanders had the right to request and receive communications personnel. The Raider commanders requested talkers in addition to regular communications personnel. Whether the Navajos would have had any say over the assignment is hard to determine. Either way, both Bitsie and Crawford remembered quite clearly the moment they met Lieutenant Carlson.

Reporting to Carlson's neisan hut, they gave their names and occupations to his aide and were shown inside. They were struck by the quiet strength emanating from the silver-haired man seated behind a bare, makeshift desk. Carlson asked them to be seated and began to explain what the Raider organization represented: the style of training, the objectives during a mission and the all-volunteer nature of the unit. The training period for them would be on a limited basis as they were due to ship out for Guadalcanal in October. He finished by telling them that if they decided to join, they just had to let him know by the end of the day. Not one of them needed any time at all; they joined practically before he finished his talk. If Carlson was surprised by their eagerness, he concealed it. He shook each man's hand, welcomed them, and told them when, where and whom to report to. As they departed the hut, they knew that they had made a good decision.

While training for the Raiders, the Paramarine units were offering anyone who was interested a chance to qualify for this duty. When Crawford heard about it, he asked permission from Carlson; it was granted and he signed up, which left Bitsie in a state of shock. "How far have you ever fallen?' Bitsie asked. 'You've probably never fallen off a chair!' Well, he said that he wanted to try, and off he went to headquarters to sign up. He didn't know what he had gotten himself into. You have to pass a physical and make six jumps in order to earn your Paramarine wings. The day he took his first jump, I could hear his stomach gurgling, and the things he said were just unmentionable! But he made all six jumps, and I thought that was pretty good!"[7]

The days that followed were ones of quiet pleasure for Bitsie. When he reported to Carlson's headquarters, he was assigned a bodyguard. Nearly all of the code talkers were assigned body-guards, but Bitsie was the only one who knew this was being done and why. Carlson instructed "Pappy" Benny Petruso, a member of his signal unit, that Bitsie was a vital instrument for the Raid-ers and was to be treated as such at all times. It was one of the reasons Bitsie felt secure during the war. The other reason was

Carlson himself.

Bitsie fondly remembered just watching Carlson. "I'd watch the way he talked, the way he gave orders. Orders that took precedence were indicated by a slight raise in the tone of his voice. I never heard him yell, swear or lose his temper. If there was a group of men that were ragged, not seeming to be getting very far in their training, but ready to fight, I would hear him calmly point out what they were doing wrong and how to fix it. Then, in the same manner, he would talk to a more advanced group. No difference! I learned a lot from him, just like I did from my elders. I learned how to help, how to get along with people, to know

"My eyes, my ears, my shield." Left *to right, Bill Bailey and Santo "Pappy" Petruso, Wilsie Bitsie's bodyguard. Photo courtesy of Wilsie Bitsie.*

what the word 'love' is. The <u>real</u> meaning, not the mushy, Saturday night low-rider kind of love, but love from deep in the heart. Carlson had that, and that is why I was seldom afraid during the war."[8]

The types of messages Bitsie and Yazzie were responsible for involved relaying operational orders to Raider commanders. Crawford and Begay, on the other hand, went with the forward-echelon positions. Strategy sessions commenced for the impending action on Guadalcanal. The mission was to land just below the Tenaru River and work up the coast toward Matanikau in support of Vandegrift's efforts to squeeze the Japanese off the island. While events on Guadalcanal were reaching a critical point, changes concerning recruitment of the Navajos and the code needed the attention of Marine Corps Headquarters.

Notes

1. John Costello, *The Pacific War*, 216.
2. Exploring the Navajo code talkers' limited involvement on Guadalcanal is in no way an attempt to diminish the role all armed forces played in this relentless, exhausting fight with the Japanese.
3. Radio Counter Measures, Div. 15, Vol. 1, Chap. 15, 311.
4. Interview 1171, Doris Duke Collection.
5. Correspondence from Sgt. Major Dolph Reeves, USMC (Retired), January 1994.
6. Quotation is anonymous by request.
7. Interview with Wilsie Bitsie.
8. Ibid.

Navajo Communication School Instructors: *left to right, Johnny Manuelito, John Benally, Rex Kontz, Howard Billiman and Peter Tracy. Photo courtesy of Camp Pendleton Photographic Section.*

Navajo Code School

The Navajos' success in creating a secure form of combat communications led General A. H. Noble of the Signal Section Headquarters to request permission from Commandant Holcomb for General Smith to recruit an additional 200 Navajos for future use as communications personnel. Noble's letter of recommendation included the standard qualifications for Marine Corps duty, linguistic qualifications in Navajo and English, and on graduation from boot camp, immediate assignment to communications school for further training. Paragraph II, item 5 of his letter reiterated "that no publicity be given this program other than that initiated by the Recruiting Service in the Navajo area."[1]

Four men – John Benally, Johnny Manuelito, Frank Shannon and Frank Shinn – were ordered to report to the Phoenix recruiting station to begin the process of obtaining the requested 200 Navajos. Benally was assigned to cover the western half of the reservation, while Manuelito covered the eastern portion. Shannon would travel to the Phoenix and Tucson areas.

The presence of Benally and Manuelito in Marine Corps uniforms was a recruitment coup de grâce. Their appearance in high schools, chapter houses and street corners left an indelible impression on the Navajos. Seeing one of their own dressed in that uniform, walking straight and proud, sent many a Navajo to enlist on the spot. Kee Etsicitty remembered how impressed he was with how Johnny Manuelito looked.

"I was in my senior year at Fort Wingate High School when Johnny arrived to give a recruitment speech," Etsicitty said. "He told us about the tradition of the Marine Corps, 'First to Fight,' 'Semper Fidelis,' and all that. He told us if we waited until we were drafted, we might not have the choice to join the marines, so it was best to make a decision before that happened. I joined later on, but I made sure the recruiters knew I wanted to be a marine. I wanted to be just like Johnny."[2] Etsicitty joined before graduation and became a member of the second all-Navajo Platoon, 297, in March 1943.

While Benally, Manuelito, Shannon and Shinn were busy enlisting Navajos into the Marine Corps, one man, Philip Johnston, was requesting special permission to join and serve. In September 1942 Johnston, after receiving word that the Marine Corps had developed a Navajo program, made a personal appeal to Lieutenant Colonel Wethered Woodworth asking to join the marines with an eye toward an assignment at the Navajo school. Woodworth forwarded Johnston's request to Holcomb via a mail brief that stated:

PHILIP JOHNSTON DESIRES TO ENLIST AS A SPE-CIALIST TO TRAIN NAVAHOS CURRENTLY BEING ENLISTED FOR AMPHIBIOUS FORCE X BELIEVE APPLICANT IS ACCEPTABLE FOR ENLISTMENT X DO YOU DESIRE SERVICES AS PROJECTED X JOHNSTON IS RESPONSIBLE FOR THE PLAN UTI-LIZING NAVAHOS IN CONJUNCTION WITH A STUDY MADE BY HIM AND LT. COL. JONES X[3]

Johnston followed Woodworth's letter with one of his own stating the reasons he desired to enlist in the Marine Corps. On October 2 Johnston's request was granted, and he was enlisted with the rank of staff sergeant. His only duty was to be an effective administrator for the school. He never created or taught one word of the code, but he did on occasion act as a liaison between the Navajo instructors and Marine Corps commanders.

The second class of Navajo students was set to begin its course studies when Captain Stillwell, a cryptographer charged with monitoring the code, discovered repetitions that needed to be addressed. Repetitive letters, sounds, or terms were keys to deciphering, so two steps were implemented to make the necessary corrections. Step one was the addition of extra terms for the vowels

A, E, I, O, and U. The Navajo instructors and students assigned the following words for these vowels:

A...Belasana...Apple   I...A-chi...Intestines
A...Tse-nihl...Ax   O...Tlo-chin...Onion
E...Ah-nah...Eye   O...A-kha...Oil
E...Ah-jah...Ear   U...Shi-da...Uncle

Step two created additional terms for the most frequently used letters D, H, L, N, R, S, and T:

D...Lha-cha-eh...Dog   R...Dah-nas-tsa...Ram
H...Tse-gah...Hair   S...Klesh...Snake
L...Ah-jad...Leg   T...D-ah...Tea
N...Tsa-a...Needle   T...A-woh...Tooth
N...A-chen...Nose[4]

The second class of students had to learn all of the original alphabet and vocabulary plus the additional terms. Captain Stillwell monitored field exercise transmissions and was satisfied there were fewer repetitions, noting that speed had improved as well. The course lasted about eight weeks, with the last two devoted to field exercises and the use and repair of signal equipment. Four members from this class – Rex Kontz, Peter Tracy, Jimmy King Sr., and Howard Billiman – would be retained as instructors.

Aside from learning the Navajo code and duties related to communications work, the Navajos were ordered to learn Morse code. This was a task filled with frustration for the instructors chosen to teach the complex Morse system. Thomas Randant, of Radio Intelligence, drew this unenviable duty.

"I didn't know anything about their efficiency in combat, but I knew a few things about that bunch of rascals in garrison," Randant recalled. "I believe I lost my temper, health, good disposition and faith in my fellow man over that group of students.

"When the idea of their ability to speak on the radio without giving away secrets came up, someone 'up there' decided that these rustic fellows must first learn Morse code." Randant continued, "For those of you who are not aware of the fact already, let me tell you that it's difficult to teach a Navajo something that he wants to learn, let alone something he's not interested in. Lacking that desire, it's almost impossible.... I could never fault those young fellows for not wanting to listen to the Morse code. It is simply the ability to write, automatically, the letter that is symbolized by the sound in your ear. One who has mastered it could be compared favorably to Pavlov's dog. Reading this code is akin to hitting one's self on the head with a hammer. There is no joy in the accomplishment, but it feels so good when you stop.

"We were assembled in a bunch of rickety huts at Camp Elliott, and the equipment was an insult to modern machinery. The 'troops' did not want to learn, and they were a boisterous (read: murderous; sic: as quoted by Randant) body of men. When they arrived on the scene, they were armed with Springfield .03 rifles. At intervals they were given a break to light the smoking lamp. Upon hearing this, they were wont to fix bayonets and proceed with what they called a 'drill.' Although this was not part of the training schedule, who in his right mind would want to tell a bunch of youths with rifles that they couldn't practice their skills? After a week or more of this practice, they had cut the forearms completely off those rifles and had nicked one another quite a few times too.

"The Corps took great exception to the damage to those antiquated rifles and after cautioning the recipients that they would have great amounts of cash taken out of their pay if the newly issued pieces, the M-1s, were so much as scratched. After the warning they left the firearms in the rifle rack, and when they took a break, they resorted to hand-to-hand physical mayhem to satisfy their need for exercise."[5]

The attitude of the Navajos toward Morse code was not one of any personal animosity toward Randant; rather, it echoed childhood experiences with enforced learning. Many of these Navajos had been treated harshly in their first school experience, and as adults they met forced learning of any kind with hostility. The pressure to learn the code and other duties related to the Signal Corps left them with little desire or energy to learn anything beyond it. But the days were not all work and no play, even for instructors such as Randant. The hand-to-hand mayhem among themselves gave way to a new game called "Let's scare the instructors!"

"If some poor, jelly-headed instructor happened to step outdoors for a smoke, it was not unusual to be buried under several screaming semi-savages," Randant remembered. "All in good fun, mind you. Sorry about the cuts, abrasions and broken bones! The Navajos also thought it great fun to plunge knives through the walls of the huts just to keep the instructors informed of their whereabouts. (Remember, in those days bayonets had 14-inch blades.) They were a lighthearted, not totally unfriendly group, and I'm sure they would have been apologetic if, during their drills, they had wiped out someone they professed to like.

"One of the other instructors told me that on one memorable day he noted that one of the Navajos stayed busy with his copy, not even looking up. His heart swelled up with joy. When his turn at the 'key' was over, he strolled up behind this young fellow, who was just finishing a portrait of a horse."[7]

Despite unruly behavior during break time, classroom behavior in the Navajo school was quiet and intense. Navajo instructors would call out a code term, and the students were required to write down in English what the word meant. Every Friday was test day to measure the progress of the students, and it always produced a great deal of apprehension. "The day of the test was always tense," John Kinsel remembered. "You wanted to do well and print the answers in clean, block letters. The instructors would pound that into our heads: Print! Print! Print! Longhand was not acceptable; the messages had to be clean, neat and readable. I had that pounded so hard into my head that today the only longhand I can write is when I sign my name."[7]

Field tests were even more demanding on the students' memories and depth of concentration. The instructors relayed messages at "combat" speed to acclimate the students to what they would experience under combat conditions. Figure 1 reveals a lot of missing information, but as the students grew accustomed to the code and the speed of the transmissions, their messages became picture-perfect.

Figure 1: Pfc John Alfred's Field Test Message[8]

John Alfred   1-16-43

(1) E_____BATTALION LAND AND HAS SIGNAL THAT BEACH RENDERED IN AFFECTIVE SHORT LOW ANGLE ANTI BOAT GUNS FIVE AEROZ YARDS INLAND

(2) _____IN FAISI AREA TWO CRUISERS TWO DE-STROYER TWO MECHANIC SHIP THREE D_____AT 0100/15

(3) ARTILLERY FIRE HIGH ANGLE___TWO THREE SEVEN POINT FOUR LINE FOUR THREE POINT FIVE FOUR TH. TANK BN._____ALERT AND TAKE AFFEC-TIVE ACTION

(4) LANDING WAVE ON BEACH BUT LOSS HIGH ENEMY MERHANIZE ELEMENTS MANEUVERS

(5) MACHINE GUN FIRE ON RIGHT FLANK I____IN T_____AM_____TO___AD

While the students were busy cramming their heads with the code, Frank Shannon was in the process of recruiting three men he believed could greatly assist in the training of the Navajos. Ellis DeWitt McGee, William Elwood McGee, and John Henry Lee had grown up around the Navajo reservation and convinced Shannon that they spoke fluent Navajo. Shannon, unaware of the decision regarding special status enlistments, forwarded a letter to the Western Recruiting Division officer asking for the authority to enlist the McGees and Lee and appoint them staff sergeants and interpreters.

In Shannon's opinion, these three men were excellent candidates for this duty. Shannon, a former superintendent of a BIA school system, held a biased view that the Navajos' intelligence and proficiency in English were inferior to those of whites. Paragraphs 3 and 4 of his letter stated the reasons for the special status request.

3. These men grew up on the Navajo Indian Reservation, have lived among the Navajo all their lives and speak the Navajo language fluently.

4. It is believed by this officer that the services of these men would be invaluable in connection with the program for which the Navajos are enlisted. With intelligence superior to the Navajos and greater facility in the English language, it is believed that they not only would be able to assist greatly in the training of Navajos, but would also, as stated above, be invaluable in the field.[9]

Whether the Marine Corps believed the McGee's and Lee could speak Navajo was not as important as the response Shannon's request for special status enlistments received. By direction of the Commandant, Shannon was informed:

1. Replying to reference (a), no provision will be made for the enlistment of the subject named men for special duty as requested by reference (a). They may be enlisted as privates for general service and request assignment to communications duties in connection with the program set up in reference (b). However, they should fully understand prior to enlistment that no assurance can be given that their request will be approved as such matters are dependent upon the exigencies of the service. No promise of rank is given.[10]

It seems that the only special status enlistment the Marine Corps was going to allow was that of Philip Johnston. He was granted special dispensation, but he was not given instructor/interpreter status. His role was strictly administrative in nature. As the saying goes, "For every rule there is an exception," and Johnston was going to be the one and only exception.

As to the possibility of finding white people who spoke fluent Navajo, or any Native American language, it was not totally unrealistic. There were many missionary and trading post families scattered throughout the regions of the reservation whose children might have attained a small degree of fluency in Navajo. How probable was it that the three men mentioned in Shannon's letter actually spoke Navajo? The answer can be found in comments by Jimmy King Sr., an instructor in the Navajo school.

"Some of the white boys thought they knew the Navajo language," King recalled. "They were born out here on the reservation and they played with Navajos during their childhood. They picked up the language well, but never well enough to pass the test to become one of the code talkers. They spoke words like coffee, sugar, flour, and the counting of money. But there was always a fraction of a syllable they could not pronounce exactly, and there were some words they had never heard before. They knew the trading post language, but they could not carry on a conversation outside of the trading post language, and we had to eliminate them."[11]

Notes

1. RG-127 1535-75, Box 600, Folder 14.
2. Interview with Kee Etsicitty, April 1992.
3. Philip Johnston Collection.
4. Philip Johnston Collection.
5. Correspondence from Thomas Randant, February 1994.
6. Ibid.
7. Interview with John Kinsel, November 1992.
8. Philip Johnston Collection.
9. RG-127 1535-75, Box 600, Folder 14.
10. Ibid.; italics added.
11. Oral History Transcript VE 25.A1 M37, Marine Corps University.

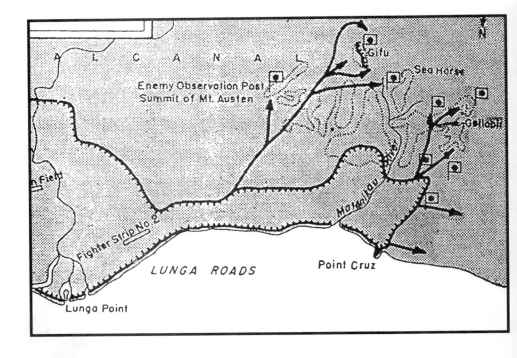

The Final Phase of Guadalcanal

In January 1943 Japan's Ministry of War decided that Guadalcanal was a lost cause and had to be evacuated within the month. Allied Intelligence had no idea the Japanese were planning such a move, but it was aware that the currently entrenched Japanese forces held more than 25,000 men.

Major General Alexander M. Patch figured that three divisions could hold the airfield and clean out the remaining pockets of enemy positions, but he had less than two divisions to work with. The 6th Regiment/2nd Division and selected Army units were due to arrive from Hawaii on January 4. General Patch decided to make use of his current personnel to clean up hot spots located around the jungle perimeter at Point Cruz and delay the attack on Mount Austen, still under enemy control, until the 2nd Division arrived.

Colonel Oka of Japan had two infantry battalions and a mounted regiment firmly entrenched on the summit of Mount Austen, and a ridge to the southwest contained a 1,500-yard pillbox line staffed by 500 soldiers. The Japanese referred to the ridge as "Gifu," a familiar homeland prefecture. This ridge would be defended to the death.

The attack on Gifu was only part of a plan laid out by General Patch. The "Sea Horse" and "Galloping Horse," a series of hills 1 mile west, and the coast west of Point Cruz made up the other two parts of the U.S. battle plan to eliminate the Japanese from Guadalcanal.

On January 1 Colonel Ferry's 2nd Battalion/132nd Regiment jumped off southeast of Gifu while the 1st and 3rd Battalions moved from the east and north to cover a flanking climb of the

2nd Battalion. At 11:00 A.M. two companies of the 2nd reached the summit of Mount Austen but were driven back six times by Colonel Oka's troops. Artillery fire, directed via the Navajo radio net, saved the 2nd Battalion from being surrounded. Gifu was now threatened on every side except the west.

On January 4 the newly arrived 2nd Marine Division and three units of the Army's 25th Division under the command of General Lawton Collins were given the Galloping Horse objective. The 6th Regiment/2nd Division included the second half of the First 29 Navajo code talkers who were to replace the ones assigned to the 1st Division. Pfc William Yazzie (Dean Wilson) remembered using the code for routine, deferred messages marked "urgent." His greatest complaint dealt with the equipment itself.

"We had to use this old clunker, a TBX, a radio unit that had to be cranked by hand. It got to be very annoying, especially at night. It seemed like the enemy could hear you start that thing up and it would give your position away."[1]

As awkward as the TBX was, it was an effective, long-range radio, and it enabled the Navajo radio net to accomplish its transmissions. Navajo radio transmissions from command posts to the destroyer *Reid* sent 360 rounds of 5-inch shells on Japanese positions between Kokumbona and Visale near Cape Esperance. The ability to pinpoint and tag enemy positions for artillery strikes without interference or interception proved that the Navajo code was doing precisely what it had been designed to do: secure communications from the enemy.

On February 9, 1943, near a village on the Tenemba River, General Patch sent a radio communiqué to Admiral William Halsey stating that the Japanese had abandoned Guadalcanal. The operation was for all intents and purposes over and considered by the Joint Chiefs of Staff a "qualified" success – qualified because it had taken more than seven months to be resolved and resulted in thousands of marine and navy casualties which had made the U.S. public uneasy concerning the strategy of the South Pacific campaign.

What the public did not understand about the battle on Guadalcanal was the tremendous tenacity the Japanese displayed during this fight. And Guadalcanal was a mere prelude to what lay ahead. The lessons learned resulted in better equipment and training for soldiers, and the advantage of a secure network of communications. Many commanders came to see the advantages of the Navajo code talkers; only a few felt the code was too risky to use in all but the most urgent circumstances.

Even though the code itself was secure, the men who used it were not. The ostensible physical resemblance between the Japanese and the Navajos created many dangerous situations. The enemy in the South Pacific was clearly defined: dark hair, dark eyes and non-white skin. The Navajos fit all three of these categories, and incidents involving mistaken identities occurred within days after Guadalcanal was secured.

Eugene Crawford recalled an incident that took place on the beach near Lunga Point. "I had been on Guadalcanal for quite some time, and on the day the Army was debarking their supplies, I spied a crate of canned orange juice. It had been a long time since I had a taste of orange, and I decided that I was going to help myself to some before we shipped out. I walked over to their supply depot and started searching when suddenly I felt cold, hard steel in my back and somebody growling, 'Get out of there, you damn Jap!' I tried to explain that I was with the Raider unit located down the beach, but he pushed that .45 in my back, told me to put my hands up and move out.

"He walked me down to the Raider command post and asked one of the officers if I was one of his men," Crawford continued. "The lieutenant asked the man if he was joking and then got real mad and said, 'Of course, he is one of ours! What's the matter with you?' I was released unharmed, but after that I was given a bodyguard that shadowed my every move. If I went to the head, so did he. If I went swimming, so did he. He stuck to me like glue. It still puzzles me that they thought I was Japanese."[2]

Post-Guadalcanal reports concerning the utilization of the Navajo code talkers were forwarded to Holcomb from various field commanders. Their endorsements revealed the value and measure of the Navajos, and these letters enabled Headquarters to evaluate the code talker program.

A letter from G. R. Lockard, of Camp Goettge Signal Company, to General Vandegrift stated:

3. As general duty Marines, the Navajos are without peers. As individuals and as a group, these people are scrupulously clean, neat, and orderly. They quickly learn to adapt themselves to conditions of the service. In short, Navajos make good Marines, and I should be very proud to command a unit composed entirely of these people.

4. The recommendations of the First Marine Division concerning the number of Navajos per Marine Division should be considered a minimum. In my opinion, all voice radio circuits should be manned by Navajos, particularly in the lower echelons which may be in close contact with the enemy. This will eliminate the necessity for authenticating transmissions, and secure all traffic from enemy interception.[3]

Julian Smith, the Commanding Officer of the 2nd Marine Division in the field, wrote a similar report on the use and temperament of the Navajos while on duty at Guadalcanal:

1. In compliance with the following report on the Navajo Indians assigned this Division is submitted:
   (a) In their primary billet as "talkers," they have functioned very well, handling traffic rapidly and accurately.
   (b) When not employed as "talkers," some of the Navajos have been used as message center men, and some as radio operators. They have functioned satisfactorily in both capacities.
   (c) As general duty Marines, they have, in general, been excellent, showing above average willingness to work any job assigned them.

2. It is recommended that the program of supplying Navajo Indians trained as "talkers" to Fleet Marine Force units be continued.[4]

A Breach of Security

While Marine Corps units from Guadalcanal were returning to Hawaii, a dark cloud was surrounding the code talker program. General A. H. Noble, Director of the Division of Plans and Policies, had directed in his letter of recommendation concerning the continued recruitment of the Navajos "that no publicity be given this program other than that initiated by the Recruiting Service in the Navajo area." That policy had been violated. The two offenders were the Marine Corps camp paper the *Chevron* and the *San Diego Union* newspaper.

The January 23, 1943 issue of the *Chevron* and the January 27, 1943 edition of the *San Diego Union* ran similar articles. The *Chevron* stated, "Naturaly, not much can be said about the work they're doing in school and in battle zones. But it takes advantage of individual intelligence, military training and heredity, and is distinctly annoying to enemy forces." The *San Diego Union* stated, "Little reference may be made to the nature of their training at the Marine Corps training center at Camp Elliott, but their job requires individual intelligence and military training. It combines the warfare of the Indian with that of the White man."

While on the surface these articles seemed vague and harmless, they constituted a breach of security that Marine Corps Headquarters took seriously. The Navajo program was on confidential, restricted status, and no article concerning it was considered harmless. On February 5, 1943, K. E. Rockey fired off a mail brief that warned:

IT IS NOTED THAT THE <u>CHEVRON</u> HAS CARRIED ARTICLES RELATIVE TO THE NAVAJOS. PLEASE CAUTION PUBLIC RELATIONS OFFICERS THAT THIS PROGRAM IS TO BE GIVEN THE MINIMUM OF PUBLICITY. NOTHING THAT INDICATES THEIR CONTEMPLATED EMPLOYMENT SHOULD BE GIVEN TO THE PRESS.[5]

Every Navajo who attended the code school, whether he

Break time: *Navajo Communication School students take a break from the rigors of learning the code by playing with one of the camp mascots. Museum of Northern Arizona Photo Archives.*

passed or failed, was told, in no uncertain terms, that what was taught and learned in their classroom was never under <u>any</u> circumstances to be revealed or discussed with anyone. To do so would result in severe consequences. Thomas Begay remembered being told, "If you talk about what this school is about to anyone, the Marine Corps will put you before a firing squad! They might have said that just to scare us, and they might not have meant it, but we definitely believed them!"[6]

Instructor Jimmy King Sr. related how he would drill the importance of keeping the code a secret under any circumstances, including the possibility of being captured by the Japanese. "You think you love your country enough that you would lay down your life?" King would ask. "Suppose that you were captured tonight and they had a Samurai sword at your throat, starting to cut inch by inch. The officer would ask you what a word meant, and you begin to bleed. The minute you see your own blood, are you going to tell? Of course not! You'd give your life before you would tell!"[7]

The Next Class of Code Talkers

Reactions to their first day in the Navajo code school ranged from surprise to logical acceptance. Harold Foster recalled his first moments as confusing. "As we sat in the class, two Navajo instructors passed out blank sheets of paper with the instructions to write down every word we were about to hear. Then they fired off a message in what sounded like Navajo but made no sense to me at all. I wrote down in English the Navajo words I thought they were saying, but the speed that they rattled them off lost me completely. Then they gathered the papers, set them aside, and began to explain the purpose of the school. It surprised me at first, but then as we learned the code, it made perfect sense to me. I was happy and proud to be able to use my language in the service of my country."[8]

Thomas Begay felt the same way. "I thought that using our language was a good idea. I had other Navajos to talk to, and it was a simple assignment, except that memorizing all the vocabulary was difficult at times. Using the Navajo language as a disguise was very clever."[9]

Secrecy was only one concern the instructors had while teaching this intricate form of military communication. Accuracy was emphasized above all else. If a Navajo sent a message that contained coordinates for an artillery or bombing strike and relayed the wrong numbers, disastrous consequences would follow. A student had to pass the final exam with a grade of at least 75 percent before he could qualify as a code talker. With each successful graduating class of code talkers, King Sr. felt a deep sense of satisfaction and pride about his students.

"I'll bet my life on these men," King said. "I can trust them. These are the kind of men the Marine Corps wants. They are the only kind because there are thousands and thousands of lives involved. I want to be sure, and then sure on top of that, before I

297th Platoon, *second all-Navajo platoon, graduates from boot camp with honors. Photo courtesy of the Navajo Nation Museum, # NO7-54*

pass a man and say, Yes, this man is capable of being a code talker! That was the extra precaution we took. When that man went across, he was number one. Whether there was another Navajo next to him or whether he was alone, I knew that this man could be depended upon 100 percent."[10]

During preparations for the formation of the 3rd Marine Division, a potential disaster loomed over the Navajo program through the unauthorized publication of an article that revealed the Marine Corps's utilization of the Navajos.

The *Arizona Highways* Incident

The second all-Navajo Platoon 297 (the third group of Navajos to enter the code school) had graduated from boot camp. They were just entering school when the *Arizona Highways* incident occurred. It seems that the orders for minimal publicity involving the Navajo program had been seriously breached for the second time.

The June 1943 issue of the magazine *Arizona Highways* contained an in-depth, five-page exposé on the Navajo people ("The Navajo Indian at War" by James M. Stewart, General Superintendent, Navajo Indian Service, Window Rock, Arizona), including the work of the Navajo code talkers. Those five pages went far beyond what the *Chevron* and *San Diego Union* had intimated about the marine Navajos. This article came right out and exposed what the Marine Corps Navajos were doing in conjunction with the war effort. Pages 22 and 23 of the article stated:

> The U.S. Marine Corps has organized a special Navajo signal unit for combat communication service. A platoon of thirty Navajos was recruited in the spring of 1942. Its members were trained in signal work using the Navajo language as a code, adapting a scheme tried with considerable success during World War I, when the enemy was completely baffled by the employment of an Indian language in front line communications. The thirty Navajo Marines performed their duties so successfully that the plan was expanded, a recruiting detail was sent back to the Navajo Reservation in the early autumn, and by early December 67 new boys were enlisted. Two members of the original detachment went back corporals to assist in explaining the work to eligible Indians. Corporals John A. Benally and John R. Manuelito have made good in the Marine Corps, a fact which almost anyone would guess at first sight. The boys look extremely competent. They are neat, poised, keen eyed and fit. In movement and manner they give the impression that they understand their business, the business of making trouble for the enemy.[11]

Prior to the publication of the June issue, Philip Johnston had received a letter of inquiry from Dover P. Trent, the assistant superintendent of Indian Affairs for the Navajo Service, requesting information regarding the part the Navajos were playing in the war. Johnston replied that "we are maintaining complete silence on the whole Navajo subject."[12] That was not quite true.

Johnston had given extensive information about the Navajo program to General Superintendent James M. Stewart of the Navajo reservation which Johnston believed had been given "off the record" but was passed along to Raymond Carlson, editor of *Arizona Highways*.

In any case, it was not long before all hell broke loose. J. P. Sullivan, the commanding officer of the Field Signal Battalion Training Center, obtained a copy of the magazine from Johnston and sent it post haste to Commandant Holcomb. Sullivan's letter was followed by one from the Office of the Commanding General, Fleet Marine Force, stating, "It is believed that the subject article is in violation of the directive which stated that no publicity was to be given to the training program for Navajo Indians."[13]

Although *Arizona Highways* did not enjoy a large national circulation, what it exposed endangered not only the Navajo code program, but also the Navajos serving in combat areas. The United States might have felt secure, but spies abounded everywhere, and an investigation as to who was responsible for leaking vital information began in earnest. Philip Johnston, Frank Shannon, John Benally, and Johnny Manuelito would be questioned and deposed by Robert M. Dergance, the Post Intelligence Officer, with the results forwarded to Commandant Holcomb.

While these inquiries were beginning, the Army was trying to ascertain whether the code talkers actually existed. Colonel George L. Townsend, an Army Signal Officer, sent a letter to Major Charles H. Hiser, Chief Signal Officer of the South Pacific Security Intelligence Corps (SPSIC), concerning the Navajos:

1. Information received by this office indicates that during the Guadalcanal operations American Indians were used in some instances as "talkers" on telephone circuits when secret or important messages were to be transmitted.

2. It is requested that any information regarding this subject be sent to this office, with the thought in mind that perhaps such a procedure could be used in the Alaskan Theatre if such is feasible and the personnel is available.[14]

Whether Marine Corps Headquarters was aware of the Army's interest in the Navajos is not known as there are no documents to indicate any damage control concerning the Army's interest. The reply that Colonel Townsend received from Major Hiser, however, is amusing to say the least: "No information is available to this office except in rumor form. However, investigation is continuing and results will be forwarded if they seem worthy of consideration."[11] It is rather clear that neither Colonel Townsend nor Major Hiser were aware that the Army had a unit of talkers comprised of Comanches who were serving in the European Theatre of Operation. The Navajo code talkers were fact and not "rumor," and their program had come under considerable duress.

When Johnston was giving his deposition, he placed the blame for the breach of security on Frank Shannon and falsified his relationship with General Superintendent Stewart. Johnston knew Stewart from his involvement in the infamous stock reduction program that had been enforced against the Navajo sheep and cattle herds in the 1930s. Johnston's deposition included the following statements:

1. I do hereby certify that none of the material in the article "The Navajo Indian at War," which appeared in the June 1943 issue of Arizona Highways was furnished by me, either directly or indirectly. I am not acquainted with James M. Stewart, the author of the article, and at no time have I ever been interviewed by any of his employees or agents....

5. On October 14, 1942, I arrived in Phoenix, Arizona, and reported to Major Frank L. Shannon, Officer in Charge of Marine Corps recruiting for that district. While I was standing by awaiting further orders from Major Shannon (a period of five days), I showed him a file of correspondence relative to the Navajo communication project, containing a letter from Colonel Jones with the sentence ... "For your information there is to be no publicity on this program."...

11. The foregoing facts and personal experience with regard to publicity on the Navajo program have given me a most profound cognizance of the fact that it is highly confidential. I have missed no opportunity to make this point emphatically clear to anyone who mentioned the matter to me. In short, I have spared no pains, not only to comply with the Commandant's orders myself, but also to ascertain that same be observed by others.

12. I took the magazine at once to my commanding officer, Major J. P. Sullivan, C.O. Field Signal Battalion, Training Center, Camp Pendleton, Oceanside, California, and recommended that action be taken without delay to learn how so flagrant a violation of orders had been perpetrated, and, above all, *to make sure that such a thing would not happen again.*[15]

Shannon's deposition, however, implied that Johnston was the likely culprit. Paragraphs 1 and 5 stated:

1. I hereby certify that I have at no time released any publicity, either magazine, newspaper or radio concerning reference....

5. It is noted that Sergeant Philip Johnston, USMC, Headquarters Company, Camp Elliott, San Diego, California, was assigned to the Recruiting District Headquarters, Phoenix, Arizona for a period of several weeks and assisted in the Navajo country in the procuring of Navajos. It is further noted that Sergeant Johnston is a writer.[16]

Benally and Manuelito testified that they suspected a potential Navajo recruit who was turned away might have been responsible for the leak. With all the accusations and counter accusations, Headquarters could not ascertain who was responsible for the breach of security and eventually decided that strong letters of warning to all of those involved would serve the purpose. Headquarters thereafter considered the matter closed.

The dust had settled, and everyone went back to their duties with a heightened sense of caution. The Navajo code program was still intact, and recruitment was stepped up to fill the demand of 100 code talkers per division. The 1st and 2nd Marine Divisions were busy training in Hawaii, while the 3rd Division was preparing to embark for a trip to the next objective in the South Pacific: Bougainville.

Notes

1. Oral History Transcript VE 25.A1 M37, Marine Corps University.
2. Interview with Eugene Crawford.
3. RG-127 1535-75, Box 600, Folder 18.
4. Ibid.
5. Ibid.
6. Interview with Thomas Begay, November 1992.
7. Oral History Transcript VE 25.A1 M37, Marine Corps University.
8. Interview with Harold Foster, September 1991.
9. Interview with Thomas Begay.
10. Oral History Transcript VE 25.A1 M37, Marine Corps University.
11. RG-127 2185-20, (folder number not identified in file.)
12. Ibid.
13. Ibid.
14. SRH-120 Report, p. 056 A.
15. RG-127 2185-20; italics added.
16. Ibid.

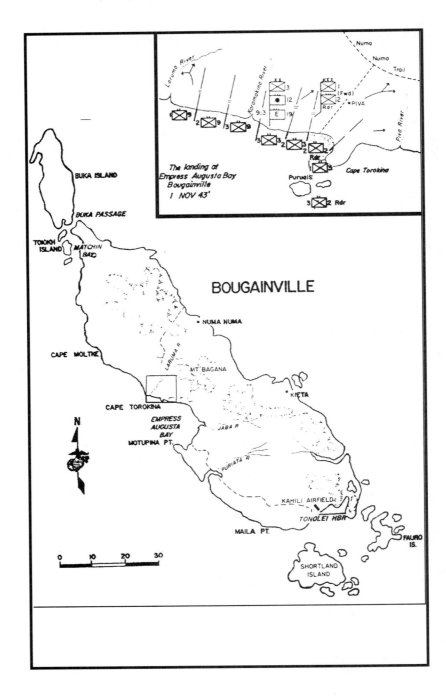

Bougainville

Operation Cartwheel

Bougainville was part of the main Japanese defense headquarters located in the Solomon Island chain. Thirty miles wide and 125 miles long, Bougainville contained large airfields near the Tonolei Harbor on the southern tip of the island. Around the perimeter were large tracts of cultivated land and coconut plantations. The only dry ground on the entire island was from the shore to about 250 yards inland. Allied forces needed Bougainville as an air base for their plans to destroy the Japanese command located at Rabaul, New Britain.

Japanese defenses included 35,000 troops under the command of General Haruyoshi Hyakutake and Major General Nabor Sasaki. Pillboxes were entrenched five feet deep in the coral ridges around the island; they were twelve feet square, roofed with crisscrossed layers of coconut logs and camouflaged with grass and leaves. Only a direct hit from a tank could destroy these entrenchments.

Reconnaissance missions informed the Allied command that the best place for landings would be at Cape Torokina at the entrance to Empress Augusta Bay, which was lightly defended. Lieutenant General Alexander Vandegrift Jr. would be in charge of ground troops; Rear Admiral Theodore S. Wilkinson would be in charge of the Amphibious Corps. Operation Cartwheel was to commence on November 1, 1943, with a diversionary landing to be carried out at Choiseul and Treasury Islands.

The 3rd Division, commanded by Major General Allen H. Turnage, and the 2nd Raider Battalion, led by Lieutenant Colonel Alan Shapely, would land and secure the beaches. The diversionary attacks on Choiseul and Treasury worked as planned, and the landing forces secured the beaches with little resistance. Although they met no Japanese, securing the beachhead was complicated by the high surf and the steep, sloping beaches. Richard Bonham, 3rd Battalion/9th Regiment described the landing.

"We had been dumped on a very steep part of the beach, and it was utter chaos. The Higgins boats were swamped by the high waves and tossed sideways on the beach. By noon, the beach was littered with boats that couldn't get off in order to be used later to resupply our units. It was pretty disappointing because the whole exercise was to have been completed by noon and the fleet had moved out.

"We had been strafed several times that morning, and the area we were in provided little cover. The trees began at the top of the sand line, and just beyond that was nothing but swamp. Trees and swamp, roots and swamp! There was nowhere to dig in; it was miserable! If command knew about the terrain beforehand, we certainly weren't prepared for it. Everybody was confused."[1]

Confused or not, by late afternoon, Cape Torokina was secured. The marine defense perimeter ran 2,000 yards from the Koromokino to the Piva River. The forces of nature, including the eruption of Mount Bagana, were making up for the lack of Japanese resistance. It rained daily from noon to dusk, and there was not one square yard that could remotely be considered dry. Marines who had experienced the soggy terrain on Guadalcanal decided it could not compare to the miasma of Bougainville. Tropical birds dove at soldiers' heads, bats whirled around them in swarms, and there were too many snakes, lizards and insects to keep track of. The dense overhang blocked the sun and inhibited the use of transmitting equipment.

For Bill Toledo, a code talker in the 3rd Battalion/9th Regiment, the weather, terrain and Japanese were not the only hazards he was subjected to. Richard Bonham, Shackle cipher specialist and soon-to-be body guard, recounted the incident that almost cost Toledo his life.

"Early in the afternoon of landing day, a rifle company

Bougainville Talkers: *front row, left to right, Privates Earl Johnny, Kee Etsicitty, John V. Goodluck and Pfc. David Jordan; back row, left to right, Privates Jack C. Morgan, George H. Kirk, Tom H. Jones and Corporal Henry Bahe, Jr. Marine Corps photo.*

brought Bill to Battalion Headquarters at gunpoint," Bonham recalled. "They were saying, 'He says he is a Marine, but he doesn't look like one to us, and we almost shot him. Is he for real, or do we shoot him on the spot?' Colonel Walter Asmuth, Battalion Commander, affirmed that Bill was indeed 'for real' and then turned to me and said, 'Bonham, he is yours.' No more than that, but I knew exactly what he meant.

"Bill and I, from that point on, stayed as close as possible," Bonham continued. "If I went out on patrol, I assigned someone else to watch him. He was never to go outside the front lines alone, and he was <u>not</u> to be captured. We didn't want anything to happen to Bill.

"While we were training in New Zealand, we didn't have the chance to get acquainted with the code talkers. What communication practice they had was strictly on the telephone and maybe only a short time on the radios for short distances, but nothing long and nothing that was important. We had been informed that the code talkers were a valuable weapon, and their safety was first and foremost. That incident with the rifle company is how I came to be assigned Bill's bodyguard, and we remained together until the end of the war."[2]

Cape Torokina

On D-Day the command post for the 3rd Division on Cape Torokina was established approximately a quarter of a mile from the entrance to Empress Augusta Bay. Messages concerning operational orders were sent and received via the Navajo net. Kee Etsicitty, a code talker at Headquarters and Service (H&S), was one link in the Navajo chain. "The commanders," Etsicitty recalled, "would tell us when and where the units were going to move. We would relay the orders to the rear echelon, and then they would relay it to the forward echelon. We referred to the Japanese as 'mouse'–na-as-tsosi–. Because we couldn't use the word 'bastard,' we nicknamed them 'mouse.' Anytime we sent a message that dealt with where the enemy was located, we used mouse in the message.

"We called them mouse because of the way they could travel through the jungle without detection," Etsicitty continued. "They had great skills in the jungle and knew how to fight and survive. The commanders knew this about the Japanese, and that is why when they told you, 'Don't move after dark,' you obeyed without question. One man, Harry Tsosie, chose not to obey that order, and it cost him his life.

"About the third night on Torokina, word was passed to dig in for the night, set the watches, no lights, and stay put until morning," Etsicitty remembered. "That means you don't stand up to stretch your cramped legs, you don't leave your foxhole to go to the bathroom, you don't light up a cigarette. Harry Tsosie made the fatal mistake of leaving his foxhole and paid for it with his life. He wasn't killed by a sniper; he was killed by a navy medic. Of course, the medic didn't know until the next morning that he had shot a marine instead of a mouse. I don't think he ever got over it."³

Harry Tsosie, the only member of the First 29 killed in action, became one of eleven verified code talker fatalities during the war. He was the only code talker killed by friendly fire.

Code Rescues the Shackle

Not all operational orders for units were handled through the Navajo nets. Some units still depended on the Shackle cipher, and it was a prolonged, complicated process to decode. The Shackle consisted of a combination of letters and numbers, with fixed grids changed every twenty-four hours to keep them secure. Take this example: "XB6T7YJL9P2MDX4Z HP6GWQ8U4RINL2T9 VD5A8SWK6FBM4YQL BR8DCZ8RFP6QLK9D." This simple-looking series might contain only one word of a message that might consist of perhaps three lines: "Jump off at 0600; move 50 yards left flank of C Company. Proceed 200 yards and report your position." It could take up to four hours to decode the entire message before it could be relayed to the commanders. Richard Bonham related the frustration of having to decipher this laborious code.

"In the middle of the fourth night, we received orders from Regimental Headquarters concerning what we were to do the next day," Bonham recalled. "It was a long message sent in the old Marine Corps code, the Shackle. During my training, I was told that this was the same type of code used during the Civil War. It had been refined over the years, but basically it had not changed since that time. I was called out of my foxhole, and I crawled over to a covered tent, where lights could be used, and started to decode this long message.

"What a mess!" Bonham continued. "It had been poorly relayed, poorly transmitted, and I could not get the full context of the message. I crawled back to my foxhole and asked Bill if he could get on the radio and try to help me figure out just exactly what we were supposed to do the next morning. Bill got on the radio, requested and received our orders, and transcribed, by himself with one flashlight, in less than five minutes! And it was correct! Later that night he tried to explain to me that it was a code

Corporal Henry Bahe, left, and Pfc. George Kirk operate from a portable radio set in the dense jungle on Bougainville. Marine Corps photograph.

within a code where words were used to describe other words. All of it was memorized and verbal. They wrote the message down as they received it, perfectly decoded. It was a wonderful code! It was faster and more efficient, and as the battle went on it became our way of communication forward and back.

"The efficiency that the Navajos developed themselves, to write it down immediately and exactly, was something we marveled at," Bonham remarked. "When you needed an artillery strike, you want it to start <u>now</u>! You don't want to wait for a complicated code to be broken down, certain parts relayed again, and perhaps not even get it right. Bill's method was efficient, and he got it right the first time. During combat, anytime that you can get an immediate message and response, you save lives. No question about it, the Navajo code saved lives. We made sure that nothing happened to Bill."[4]

Toledo was often puzzled by the appreciation he received from

Bonham. "I felt that learning and using the code was my job, and I didn't need to be thanked for doing it. I was happy to help Richard whenever he needed it. I was happy to be alive and have the privilege of Richard's friendship and company in the foxhole every night. We watched out for each other like good marines should, and I always felt safe when he was around. I didn't learn until 1988 that he had been assigned to be my bodyguard, and frankly I was a little surprised when he told me. Looking back over my experiences during the war, I was most grateful for his watchful eye."[5]

The Numa Numa Trail

On November 11 the 9th Regiment advanced, unmolested, to the Piva Village and set up a command post to serve in reserve and protect the 2nd Battalion/21st Regiment's northern advance toward the junction at the Numa Numa Trail. The 2nd Battalion/21st Regiment's objective was to clean out the last of the Japanese resistance located in a coconut grove and expand the marine defense perimeter 16,000 yards inland.

D-ah a-kha ta-a-tah da-az-jah: Beh na-ali-tsosie gah-tso dineh-ba-shoa-blehi da-ne-lei ya-ha-de-tahi tsa-na-dahl nas-nil do ehl-nas-teh. Ba-ha-this.

To all units: Japanese are booby trapping personnel equipment, installations, and bivouacs. Over.[6]

Toledo received and relayed this message, in less than thirty seconds, to the rear-echelon units that were following the retreating Japanese on the northern track of the Numa Numa Trail. It was only seconds after he sent that message that he encountered his first narrow escape from enemy retaliation.

"I had received the warning message and passed it along to the rear units, shut off my radio, and only moved about 10 yards when a Japanese mortar hit the exact spot that I had just sent the message from," Toledo recalled. "One of the first things they teach you in the field training exercises is to send, receive, 'Roger' the message and move! To stay on the radio one second longer than necessary could cost you your life. We were told that the Japanese had very good tracking equipment that could pinpoint the location of radio signals and deliver a strike to that location. You don't quite believe the enemy can do that until it actually happens to you. I'll tell you, once it does happen, you never forget it, and you never stay on the radio one second longer than absolutely necessary!"[7]

While the 9th Regiment was proceeding up the Numa Numa Trail, Kee Etsicitty was busy directing an artillery strike with a 105 mm weapon intent on cleaning out Japanese positions in a canyon located near Mount Bagana. "They couldn't take the larger artillery in the canyon because they needed a gun that was easy to move like the 105 mm," Etsicitty said. "When a message was marked 'urgent,' you sent it in code; if it was general information, other radio operators handled it. Using the code for an artillery strike made me proud, and I never questioned why I joined the Marine Corps. Bougainville was a bad place, but I learned valuable lessons that stood me well for the rest of the war. George Kirk, an experienced code talker, taught me to carry the radio in the front so that if the enemy started shooting at you, the radio would give you some protection. A radio could be easily replaced, but we could not. You put your combat pack on your back, carry your rifle in the 'ready' position, and use whatever you need to survive. George also warned us never to touch anything that belonged to the enemy because the enemy often booby-trapped their dead.

"The only close call I experienced on Bougainville," Etsicitty continued, "was on the day our sergeant took a group of us out to spray DDT on the standing water surrounding our bivouac area. He didn't say anything about bringing our rifles, and he wasn't aware that there was an enemy company less than 300 yards in front of the area we were to spray until the point man spotted them and alerted the sergeant. The point man didn't fire on the Japanese because he didn't have his weapon with him. It was probably a good thing because it would have been our last day on earth if he had because none of us had our weapons.

"When we got back from the DDT duty, the sergeant got busted for failing to take an armed point man, failing to arm the detail, and for taking code talkers without permission. A few days into the campaign, orders came down that code talkers would be assigned bodyguards. That was when I realized that we were just a little bit important to the war. Looking back, I feel that we were one spoke in the Marine Corps wheel, no more important than the contributions of the Navy, the people back home that bought war bonds, collected scrap metal, or sent their sons to fight."[8]

Piva Forks

On November 19 the 3rd Battalion/3rd Regiment along with the 1st Battalion/21st Regiment launched a frontal assault near Japanese barriers located at what would become known as the Battle of Piva Forks. Lieutenant Steve Cibik's 21st Regiment was assigned the task of securing a 440-foot ridge that dominated Empress Augusta Bay. The fight for control of the ridge would ping-pong for four days before Cibik's men took final possession. Cibik recalled his reaction to the capture of the ridge, which enabled the marines to direct artillery strikes at the heart of Japanese defenses.

"I walked to the edge of the ridge and almost gasped," Cibik stated. "What a view of Bougainville! We were on the tip of a thumb of earth 500 feet high, an oasis in a sea of mist-covered jungle, the only high ground for miles around.... From here, we could spot Jap positions and direct our heavy-artillery fire; from here, we could drive down into the valley, engaging the Japs while our main forces fought their way across the river. On the other hand, were the Japs in control of this ridge, the tables would be turned. This ridge could be the key to success or failure in this phase of the Battle of Bougainville."[9]

On December 6 during the final attempt to secure a 2,000-yard defense perimeter around Piva Forks, a powerful earthquake struck. Reaction to this unusual phenomenon ranged from fear to puzzlement. John Kinsel, a code talker in H&S 9th Regiment, remembered feeling unsure as to what defensive action to take during the earthquake. "I heard a deep rumble coming up from the ground and and then, all of a sudden, everything was rolling and shaking. Snipers were falling from the swaying trees, and I was afraid to move or get down on the ground because I wasn't sure there was going to be any ground to lay down on! I rode out that quake standing and swaying from side to side, just like the trees, until it stopped. Nothing that happened during the rest of the war scared me as bad as that earthquake did!"[10]

Bill Toledo could not figure out what was happening until Richard Bonham explained it. "That earthquake was something strange! If Richard hadn't told me what it was, I wouldn't have known. He was from California and knew right away what was happening. The only earthquake I had experienced was in a movie. I was thinking that the earth was going to open up and swallow everything. Richard just laughed while the trees were swaying, the ground was rumbling and rolling, and I was shaking."[11]

Final Days on Bougainville

By December 26 the majority of the Japanese forces had been defeated and Bougainville had been declared secure. While the marines were packing up equipment and supplies, the need for code talkers on the radio nets ceased. This period of rest gave the Navajos a chance to relax, read letters from home, take baths, don fresh clothes and visit with each other. Some of the Navajos packed their combat fatigues, unwashed, and sent them home. Their families would use this clothing in protection ceremonies as a representative of their sons to ensure that they would re-main safe until they returned. These rituals were an important part of the men's spiritual and tribal beliefs, and they swore they could feel the exact moment when their families were perform-ing ceremonies for them. It was a great feeling of comfort and security for the Navajos a long way from home.

During the last few days on Bougainville, an event took place that has stayed with Kee Etsicitty to this day. "One day we went out near the airfield to see a group of Navy Corsairs that had landed. They were waiting for ground crews to service them be-fore flying on to Rabaul. A couple of service crewmen came over to our bivouac and asked if we wanted to look at the planes. Ray Dale and I went over and looked at the planes and met the men who were flying them.

"One man in this group was an ace called Boyington," Etsicitty continued. "He told us they had been training on New Zealand and were due back later that day. Boyington was a very friendly man, and we asked him silly questions and he answered them. He talked about what the good Lord had in mind for him and asked us where we were from. He shook our hands, wished us Godspeed and got into his plane. He scored a lot more than the rest of us did, and I was proud to have had the chance to meet him. I was saddened when I heard the news that he had been shot down in January 1944. He seemed like a fine man."[12]

Colonel Gregory "Pappy" Boyington, of the famed Black Sheep Squadron, was shot down during a raid over the dreaded "Dead End," located at Rabaul on the eastern tip of New Britain. He survived but spent the duration of the war in Japan as a Prisoner Of War (POW).

While the marines were embarking for their journey back to their staging area on Guadalcanal, the next battle target, Cape Gloucester, New Britain, was being planned. The plan would be executed by the 1st Marine Division.

Notes

1. Correspondence from Richard Bonham, 1993.
2. Ibid.
3. Interview with Kee Etsicitty.
4. Correspondence from Richard Bonham.
5. Interview with Bill Toledo, November 1992.
6. Ibid.
7. Ibid.
8. Interview with Kee Etsicitty.
9. S.E. Smith, *The United States Marine Corps in World War II* (New York: Random House, 1969), 461.
10. Interview with John Kinsel, July 1991.
11. Interview with Bill Toledo.
12. Interview with Kee Etsicitty.

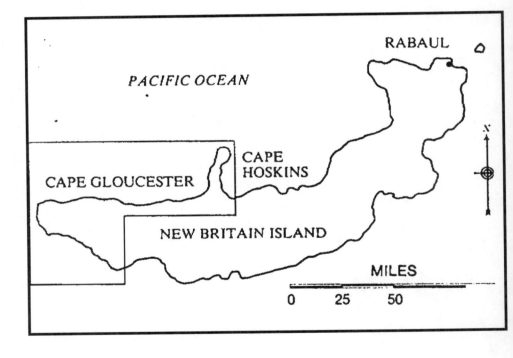

Cape Gloucester, New Britain

Operation Dexterity

New Britain, a crescent-shaped island 370 miles long and 40-50 miles wide, belongs to a group of islands in the Bismark Archipelago. This part of the Pacific Ocean, lying between New Britain and the Solomon Islands, was known as "the Slot." The purpose of Operation Dexterity was to capture and secure the airfield located on Cape Gloucester at the tip of New Britain.

The north shore of Cape Gloucester was the designated landing area for the 1st Marine Division under the command of General William H. Rupertus. This would be the first action in which the division participated since Guadalcanal. A two-pronged attack on Borgen Bay at Silimati Point and Tauali was set for December 26, 1943.

The Japanese defenders consisted of 9,500 men of the 65th Brigade under the command of Major General Iwao Matsuda, the commander of the forces that had fought on Guadalcanal. A large number of Matsuda's men were already on half-rations and suffering from malaria, dysentery, and numerous fungal infections. Monsoon rains had destroyed their primitive shelters and their health. Matsuda's troops, as physically depleted as they were, would put up a desperate fight to the death to keep the United States from taking another Japanese-held island. The main defense on Aogiri Ridge was laced with 37 bunkers that were mutually supported with interconnecting tunnels.

Colonel Julian N. Frisbie's 7th Regiment landed on Yellow 2 Beach at Tauali, wheeled left, and made their way toward the edge of the airfield. Colonel William J. Whaling's 3rd Battalion

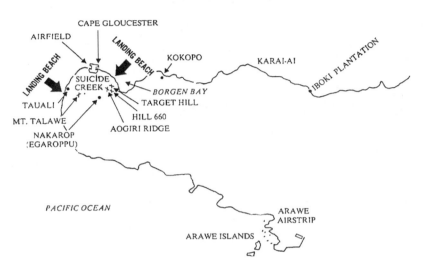

landed on Yellow 1 Beach and headed toward Target Hill. By noon of D-Day, the 450-foot Target Hill had been secured without opposition, and by nightfall the marines had established a 1,000-yard defense perimeter.

Matsuda's troops counter attacked with Major Shinchi Takabe's infantry against the center of the perimeter held by the 2nd Battalion/7th Regiment. Amid a torrential rain, Lieutenant Colonel Odell Conoly's company managed to hold off the attack until reinforced by the men of Battery D.

During this attack, Alex Williams was running a message to the 2nd Battalion because its radio was out. On the return trip he became lost and barely escaped being shot by a fellow marine who mistook him for a Japanese defender. "It was raining and the first order of the day was, 'No lights.' Not even a match for a cigarette. I was lost, crawling around trying to feel my way back when I ran into this marine. He asked me for the 'password,' and I thought it was lame duck, so I said it. He asked me to say it again. 'Lame duck.' I guess I didn't say it too well because he said, 'You son of a bitch!' and stuck a bayonet in my back ready to kill me when I tumbled backwards into a foxhole. That foxhole just happened to have Sergeant Curtis in it. He asked, 'What the hell is going on?' I told him that this marine thinks I am a Jap and wants to kill me. Curtis cleared up the matter and I stayed in his foxhole the rest of the night. Our jobs didn't always involve the radio or telephone. If an urgent message needed to be delivered, right or wrong, we delivered it. We risked being questioned and shot at by our own men, but we got those messages through."[1]

The next day the 2nd Battalion began its forward advance from Tauali to Mount Talawe. It met with fierce opposition that lasted five days. James Nahkai, a code talker in the H&S Battalion, relayed artillery strikes in support of the 2nd Battalion's advance. "Whatever the Colonel wanted to relay to the battalions we sent in code," Nahkai recalled. "If they wanted a certain sector hit we relayed the coordinates and strike time in code to each battalion. We directed the fire of the 105 mm weapons and we never sent a wrong coordinate during the entire operation."[2]

Aogiri Ridge

On December 28 Brigadier General Lemuel Shepherd was ordered to clear the area from Borgen Bay to Aogiri Ridge. The ridge served as the Japanese supply route, and to keep it open they would defend it to the last man. At the base of Aogiri Ridge, the second code talker of the war was killed. William McCabe witnessed Ralph Morgan's death.

"It was funny [strange] the way he got killed. The men were in a foxhole under a tree when a shell landed but didn't explode; it just fell apart and a large piece of schrapnel hit him right on the chin and split his head clean off. He never knew what hit him. We just stood there and looked at him, we didn't know what to do. It didn't seem real."[3]

General Rupertus began planning assaults on three targets that surrounded the Japanese defenses around Borgen Bay: Target Hill, Hill 660 and Aogiri Ridge. On December 29 the Japanese launched their strongest attack near the Cape Gloucester airstrip. Captain Buckley's company fought and attained control of Hill 660, which enabled them to direct artillery barrages against the entrenched enemy and aid the 2nd Battalion/7th Regiment in securing the airfield.

The advance of Shepherd's units toward Aogiri Ridge crossed through swamps that led to a stream 300 yards inland. The forward scouts crossed first. Nothing untoward

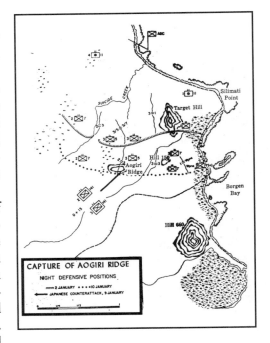

CAPTURE OF AOGIRI RIDGE
NGHT DEFENSIVE POSITIONS

happened. Then the first platoon began to cross.

"Suicide Creek," as it came to be known, was a swift, shallow, twisting waterway that ran between steep banks 10-20 feet high. The marines did not know that the Japanese had created a moat-like stronghold laced with pillboxes and machine gun nests that were fortified with dirt and coconut logs and could easily sweep both banks.

When the Japanese opened fire on the exposed marines, utter chaos erupted. Men were pinned down with no room to withdraw. Scouts eventually managed to creep across undetected and locate the entrenched Japanese. After the positions were relayed to headquarters via Navajos assigned to Shepherd's communication post, bulldozers were ordered to move into position to begin cutting down the banks, thereby making a path for tanks. It took the bulldozers two days of working around the clock before the tanks could advance and begin the task of demolishing the Japanese strongholds. This action effectively ended the marines' futile attempt to cross Suicide Creek.

As the Japanese were desperately fighting to keep the marines from taking further ground, a replacement commander was giving Jimmy King Sr. a difficult time. "When a replacement battalion commander came in that didn't know all of the forward echelon personnel, they questioned what we were doing," King recalled. "They would ask us, 'What is the message, what are you saying?' I told him not to bother me or talk to me because our orders were clear. No one with less than two stars had any business asking us about messages or what we were doing. I would say, 'Well, Mr. So and So, I hate to tell you this but I'm not authorized to tell you what this message is about or what that man is saying over the air. May I have your name, Lieutenant, or Captain, or Major So and So?' I answered directly to the message center Chief and to those with two stars and up, those below two stars didn't interfere with us."[4]

Last Gasp

January 9 and 10 marked the last of the Japanese efforts to keep the supply route along Aogiri Ridge from being severed by the marines. Captain Buckley's weapons company massed a huge Navajo-directed artillery barrage that broke the Japanese defenses surrounding the base of Hill 660. Five days later Cape Gloucester was declared secure.

The successful campaigns on Bougainville and Cape Gloucester gave Allied forces important territory with which to strike at the heart of the Japanese Defense Command at Rabaul. The Navajo code was beginning to make its mark in combat situations, and Headquarters was duly notified. John Kinsel, Kee Etsicitty, Bill Toledo, James Nahkai, William McCabe, Jimmy King, and others proved that they could send vital information without making a mistake or being deciphered. The Japanese made every effort to disrupt and distract the Navajo transmissions. They would scream, swear, bang pots, and yell, but they never succeeded.

When the code talkers returned with their units to their training areas on Hawaii, they spent long hours learning new terms that had been added to the code as well as long hours doing field exercises. It was hard work, but they knew firsthand the true value of the contribution they were making toward winning the war in the South Pacific.

The success of the code generated a request from Commander Air, South Pacific (ComAirSoPac) Lieutenant Commander L. R. Hird to transfer 10 Navajo code talkers to his command for six to eight weeks of temporary duty. The Air Corps was having an extremely difficult time getting pilots safely through the Slot. A Radio Counter Measures report stated; "Japanese land-based, fire-control and search-light-control radars, admittedly four years behind Allied developments, were instrumental in permitting the Japanese to shoot down our aircraft under unseen conditions. As such, they constituted a serious Air Force problem."[5]

The ability of the Japanese radar to detect and decipher Air Corps flights and transmissions led to Hird's request. Paragraph 3 of his letter, dated January 7, 1944, stated:

3. These talkers are to be used on a voice air operational radio circuit at various Solomon Island air bases. While giving valuable assistance to ComAirSoPac they will be obtaining valuable experience on actual operating circuits during a period of time when this Corps does not require them for operational use. It is planned to send other groups to relieve this initial group at approximately six week intervals until they are required for Corps operations.[6]

The staffing of the ComAirSoPac circuits with Navajo code talkers reduced the pilot fatality rate from 53 percent to less than seven percent in a very short period of time. If the Japanese intelligence command in the field was feeling thwarted by the unidentifiable language traveling through radio and telephone circuits, personnel at Intelligence Headquarters in Nagasaki were feeling hopeful. During the last month of the winter of 1944, the Japanese could positively identify who was sending the messages they could not decipher. They were the Navajos, and the Japanese had one.

Joe Kieyoomia, POW

Joe Kieyoomia joined the Army in March 1941 with the idea that he would serve his two years and then return home. One week after he had been stationed in the Philippines, Pearl Harbor was attacked. The morning the Japanese raids began on the Bataan Peninsula, he knew that his hitch would probably be more than just the standard two years.

He survived the Bataan Death March only to be moved from camp to camp, finally ending up in Japan itself. The day he was removed from Camp O'Donnel, Philippines, his family was notified that he was "missing, presumed dead." He spent 1,240 days as a POW, moving from the Philippines to Hatashi, Matishuma and Nagasaki, Japan.

Kieyoomia believed one of the reasons he was moved to Japan was because the Japanese thought he was of Japanese ancestry. The pronunciation of his name, Key-oh-me, convinced them they could make him see the "light" and return to his true people. They would find out later just how wrong they were.

"One evening," Kieyoomia stated, "I was brought to the commander's quarters for questioning, and they asked me again, for the hundredth time, if I was an American. I told them I was an American Indian, but that only made them angry. 'You are American Japanese! Why are you fighting against your own people?' the commander shouted. The interpreter, a guy named Goon, understood that I was American Indian, but the interrogator didn't. When I refused to confess that I was Japanese, the interrogator hit me with a club, broke my ribs and then my wrist. When I refused to confess again, they dragged me back to the barracks and threw me in a cell.

"We had a British doctor named Whitfield who examined me," continued Kieyoomia, "but all he could do was bind my ribs and give me aspirin. Later that night the pain was so intense they took me to the infirmary. It wasn't much better there. They laid me flat on the floor with only a thin straw mat under me and checked me every four hours.

"Sometime later that month, Goon must have figured out

that the talkers on the radio who couldn't be identified must be Indians," Kieyoomia said. "They were having a tough time deciphering the code, and they finally figured that I might be able to help them. When they first made me listen to the broadcasts, I couldn't believe what I was hearing. It sounded like Navajo, just not anything that made sense to me. I understood my language, but I could not figure out the code they were using. That made the interrogators very angry!

"They stripped off all my clothes and threw me out on the parade ground to coax me into cooperating. It was very cold out there, and my feet began to freeze to the ground. They left me out there about half an hour, then clubbed me back into the radio room. My feet were bleeding from being torn from the ground, but I still couldn't help them. They were trying to keep me alive to get something out of me. I liked hearing the Navajo language: it gave me hope. It told me that American forces were getting close, and I felt like I would be liberated the next day. If it hadn't been for the code talkers, I would have been put before a firing squad."[7]

The torture and daily beatings Kieyoomia endured showed the value the Japanese placed on breaking the mysterious transmissions. They became obsessed with trying to force him into giving them something he could not, and he endured these sessions with the same quiet strength that had enabled him to survive the Bataan Death March. As the days and months dragged on, a decision was reached to relocate him to a different POW camp.

"I was transferred to Matishuma," Kieyoomia continued, "60 miles south of Nagasaki. This happened the day before America dropped the atomic bomb. When Japan surrendered, Red Cross officials thought I was from Singapore. I told them I was an American Indian. They asked me from what state, and I said, Arizona."[8]

Joe Kieyoomia's official service record simply stated; "Prisoner of War, 9 April 1942 to 4 September 1945." After Red Cross officials matched Kieyoomia to Army records, they placed him on a hospital ship bound for Hawaii. The next four years Kieyoomia spent in a variety of veterans' facilities recovering from malnutrition, dysentery, and multiple operations to mend his damaged arm. He finally made his way home to Shiprock, New Mexico, in 1949.

What would Marine Corps Headquarters have done if it had known the Japanese had a Navajo who spoke and understood the language? The code talkers believed that because theirs was a code within a code, Kieyoomia would have needed firsthand knowledge of the code to decipher it. To effect any advantage from the network, Japanese field command would have needed an entire complement of cooperative Navajo code talkers able to translate on the spot. This was not even a remote possibility. The code talkers agreed that if trying to force Kieyoomia to break the code helped keep him alive, then the code was a blessing. The code, after all, was designed to save lives.

Notes

1. Interview 1162, Doris Duke Collection.
2. Oral History Transcript VE 25.A1 M37, Marine Corps University.
3. Ibid.
4. Ibid.
5. Radio Counter Measures Div. 15, Vol. 1, Chap. 15, p. 313.
6. RG-127 76-30 F5, Box 1 9/13-49-6-3.
7. Interview 664, Doris Duke Collection.
8. Ibid.

Johnston's Betrayal

Training progressed, and commanders were planning the next tactical and strategic ways to implement campaigns for the second phase. Philip Johnston, in the meantime, had set in motion the final breach of security in the Navajo code talker program.

On March 10, 1944 a letter arrived for Colonel William F. Friedman from Carl Wheat, of Wheat and May, Attorneys at Law, on behalf of Philip Johnston concerning a proposal to create an Indian code program for the Army (see Appendix for entire letter).

The following excerpts reveal Johnston's reasons for approaching the Army with an eye toward starting a code program similar to the one the Marine Corps was using:

1. Right on the heels of the foregoing news comes a dispatch from the Italian front proving beyond all doubt that the Navajo system would be of inestimable value to the Army. It has been revealed that a critical situation on the Anzio Beachhead was further complicated by the fact that the commander of our forces was unable to transmit information regarding his plight without, at the same time, revealing his weakness to the enemy. Mountain passes were closed by blizzards, barring the passage of couriers, and any attempt to make use of radio communications would have apprised the enemy of his predicament. Here, then is a classical illustration of how a method of radio communication which is <u>absolutely secure</u> against enemy interception would be of <u>priceless</u> value.

2. At present time I have eleven Navajos in my school who are either acting as instructors, or who are competent to do so. Two or three of these would be ample to finish the training program authorized for the Marine Corps. The balance, say eight men, might be loaned to the Army for a limited period (about eight weeks) if such a request were made by the proper authority. Each of these men could instruct a class of twenty. Assume that eighty percent of this group of 160 men qualified, as trainees have done here, and we would have about 128 men ready for communications duty. A few of these could be retained as instructors, and the balance sent to the locale where they are most needed.[1]

Johnston's offer to share a proven method of secure communications to save U.S. soldiers in Europe sounded very noble indeed. The problems with this gesture were (1) Johnston disregarded the direct order concerning the confidential, restricted status of the Navajo program, and (2) the Marine Corps would never have allowed any branch of the armed forces, especially the Army, access to marines or a marine program.

The official Marine Corps response to this, the most serious breach of security about the Navajo code program, was surprising, but the Army response was predictable. Colonel Carter W. Clarke, Assistant Executive Officer of G2, offered the following opinion concerning the use of any Indian dialects for coded communications:

a. The use of Indian dialects as a substitute for authorized military code and ciphers violates the rules of security.

A further source of insecurity in the use of Indian dialects lies in the fact that code words must be improvised to fill in deficiencies of the Indian dialects with respect to modern military and technical terms. It must be acknowledged that the use of Indian dialects cannot be assumed to provide security for even a few hours in communications where transmissions can be picked up by enemy intercept facilities.[2]

The Wheat and May letter ended up on the desk of Major J. M. Marzloff, Air Corps Chief of the Cryptographic Branch, whose reply was almost identical to that of Colonel Clarke's. Paragraphs 4 and 5 illustrated, again, the Army's opinion that any Indian dialect within coded communications was without merit:

4. Mr. Wheat indicated that the system is "absolutely secure against enemy interception," but it is not evident to this Headquarters how such use of a known native tongue transmitted by radio can afford security over any appreciable length of time.

5. Although the plan has a certain amount of merit as a "stopgap" or an emergency system of communication, this Headquarters feels that the low-grade security afforded by such a plan would be dangerous to the operations for the AAF, whereas authorized War Department cryptographic systems offer better security than the recommended procedure. It is felt that there are too many "loop holes" in the plan to justify its usage by the AAF.[3]

Major Marzloff was correct in stating that a known Indian dialect would be useless for coded communications, but the Navajo language was recognized by very few people outside the tribe. Marzloff's conclusions concerning the use of any Indian dialects for coded communications did not put an end to the inquiry. On April 1, 1944 a secret conference took place at the Arlington Annex, Room 2126 between Marine Lieutenant Colonel Smith and an unidentified Army lieutenant. The surprising content of the meeting appears to be a carefully constructed smoke screen to deflect the Army's curiosity concerning the Marine Corps code talker program. Paragraphs 1, 4, 7, 11 and 12 give the impression that the men trying to explain the use of the Navajos were careful not to expose their true mission.

1. The training of Navajo Indians for security purposes in radio voice transmission has been a Marine project for some time. Up to the present writing approximately 250 of these Indi-

ans have been trained in this respect. This training has been under the guidance of T/Sgt. Johnston at Camp Pendleton, California.

4. The use of Indians is not a theory, it is an actuality. These Indians have been used on the combat front at Guadalcanal, Bougainville, and Tarawa. The 1st, 2nd, 3rd, 4th and 5th Marine Divisions have these Indians in their Division Signal Companies and Lt. Col. Snedaker (Arlington Annex) Lt. Col. McGill (Arlington Annex) and Lt. Col. Nelson (Quantico) can give accounts of their use on the combat front.

7. In general, the Navajo vocabulary does not suffice for military purposes, but the Marines augment or supplement the regular parent tongue with original phonetic words coined expressly in the Navajo tongue for military purposes.

11. Both officers concerned agree that the more Navajos employed in this type of signal communication the less secure the system will be, which is a natural deduction, but not necessarily a true one.

12. Code books used in this type of communication are never taken far enough forward to place in danger of capture and the men are definitely trained to develop their memories. Retentiveness of learned material is outstanding in the Navajo.[4]

One of the most fascinating pieces of misinformation discussed during the meeting concerned the code books. To say that the "code books used in this type of communication are never taken far enough forward to place in danger of capture" was an understatement. The code books were signed in and out of the only two training areas in existence; Camp Pendleton, California and Pearl Harbor, Hawaii. It is highly unlikely that any code book ever made its way to a combat area.

If Marine Corps Headquarters intentions were to deflect the Army's curiosity concerning the Navajo code program, it worked.

In a letter to the Army Ground Forces 1st Lieutenant Charles E. Henshall, Director of Communications Research, reiterated the Army's mistrust of using Indian languages for communications. Henshall states:

> <u>Army Ground Forces:</u> Lieutenant Colonel James M. Kimbrough, Jr. of the Signal Section of Army Ground Forces informed the writer that Colonel G. B. Rogers and Colonel O. K. Sadtler took this matter up with G-2 and obtained their feelings and opinions on it. Apparently, G-2 was dead set against the adoption of the plan to use Indians, since it was felt that the security features inherent in the Navajo tongue were not sufficient enough to warrant development for general radio telephone transmissions. It was further objected to that the enemy could obtain translators and after the recordations of sufficient plain test had been obtained, the entire language be subjected to successful analysis and compromise.
>
> Therefore, the Army Ground Forces did not feel justified in screening the entire army in search of Navajo linguists.[5]

If Marine Corps Headquarters punished Johnston in any way for this incident there is no official record of it.[6] The scuttlebutt around the Navajo code school was that Johnston was in deep trouble with Marine Corps command, but no one knew, or was willing to tell what had caused the problem. Paul Blatchford was given the impression, when he was assigned to the school, that he was specifically chosen to replace Johnston. Blatchford had a background in radio broadcasting and electronics and was assigned to teach radio repair, switchboard and telephone set-up operations. When he arrived at the school, Johnston refused to talk to him or explain his duties. "When I got to the school, I was introduced to Philip Johnston, and he acted like he didn't even want to talk to me. He looked the other way and just shook me off. The next day I went to his office and asked him for my assignment, and he said to go to the end of the hall and take charge of the department. Shortly after that he disappeared from the school and I never saw him again."

Whatever transpired between Marine Corps Headquarters and Johnston took a back seat to what was about to take place during the second phase of the South Pacific campaign.

Notes

1. SRH-120 Report, p. 92-94.
2. Ibid.
3. Ibid.
4. SRH-120 Report, p. 100-103.
5. SRH-120 Report, p. 104-105.
6. I was unable to obtain his service serial number and so could not obtain a copy of his military record to determine if he had indeed been charged with any form of misconduct.
7. Interview with Paul Blatchford, October 1991.

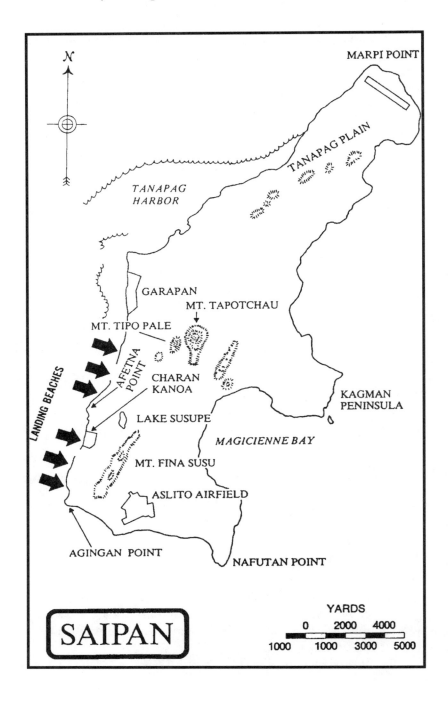

MARPI POINT

N

TANAPAG PLAIN

*TANAPAG
HARBOR*

GARAPAN

MT. TAPOTCHAU

MT. TIPO PALE

LANDING BEACHES

AFETNA
POINT

CHARAN
KANOA

KAGMAN
PENINSULA

LAKE SUSUPE

MAGICIENNE BAY

MT. FINA SUSU

ASLITO AIRFIELD

AGINGAN POINT

NAFUTAN POINT

SAIPAN

YARDS

0   2000   4000

1000

1000   3000   5000

Saipan, Tinian, Guam and Peleliu

The tenuous toehold the American forces held in the South Pacific would become a firm footing through the next phase of campaigns. The target islands of Saipan, Tinian, Guam and Peleliu would, once they were out of enemy hands, provide solid stepping stones to the eventual attack on mainland Japan.

As allied forces began preparations for this second phase, the Navajo dictionary was again being revised and enlarged from 265 terms to over 508. These additions included new weapons and military terms. A few examples can be seen in Table 5.

Table 5: Additions to the Navajo dictionary

Term	Navajo Word	Meaning
Armored	Besh-ye-ha-da-di-teh	Iron protected
Camouflaged	Di-nes-ih	Hid
Code	Yil-tas	Peck
Ordinance	Lei-az-jah	Under ground
Torpedo	Lo-be-ca	Fish shell
Tracer	Beh-na-al-kah-hi	Tracer
Pontoon	Tkosh-jah-da-na-elt	Floating barrel
Robot bomb	A-ye-shi-na-tah-ih	Egg fly
Sniper	Oh-behi	Pick off

The tempo of training increased in every section from artillery to field communication tests, and if the marines were heartily sick of constant practice landings, combat drills and classroom instruction, they were not ready to die unnecessarily. Code talkers that had served in combat zones often visited the code school and gave advice to the students about what to do and not do before, during and after a battle. One of the strongest warnings the veterans could give the students was that souvenir hunting could get you killed – <u>never</u> touch anything that belonged to the enemy dead. Once in combat, this advice was rarely disregarded.

Operation Forager

The Joint Chiefs of Staff formulated a plan for the invasion of the Mariana Islands, which were the key to Japan's "Inner South Seas Empire." Allied control of the islands Saipan, Tinian, and Guam would provide bases from which to attack the island of Japan. Admiral Nimitz was in charge of the major invasion convoy which would include two army divisions and three Marine Corps divisions. The commander of the marine forces would be Lieutenant General Holland "Howling Mad" Smith.

Operation Forager called for the Northern Task Force, comprising the 2nd and 4th Marine Divisions, to attack Saipan

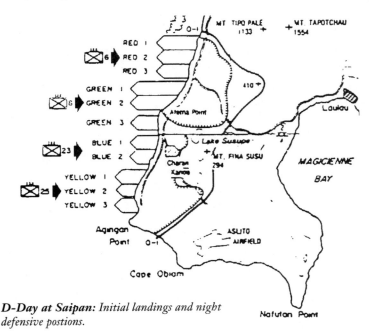

D-Day at Saipan: Initial landings and night defensive postions.

and Tinian, while the Southern Task Force, made up of the 3rd Marine Division and the First Army Brigade, would concentrate on Guam.

Saipan

Saipan had been under Japanese domination since 1920, when the League of Nations awarded Japan a mandate to develop Saipan's sugar, wine, lumber and cattle industries. The population was a blend of Japanese, Chinese, Chamorro and Filipino, and was considered the heart of the Mariana Islands.

Saipan is 14 miles long and five miles wide and is fringed with beaches, high plateaus, rolling hills and an extinct volcano, Mount Tapotchau. The terrain would present a new set of logistical barriers for the marines: caves.

Lieutenant General Yoshitsugu Saito commanded the 43rd Division and the 47th Independent Mixed Brigade, while overall naval command was exercised by Vice Admiral Chuichi Nagumo and his 6,000 men. Saipan's defenses consisted of four 8 inch, eight 6 inch, nine 5.5 inch, and eight 5 inch dual-purpose guns along with four 200mm mortars and several concrete pillboxes located at Agingan and Afetna.

Air and naval bombardments began on June 11, 1944, and ended just before D-Day, June 15. The Marine Corps plan of action was as follows: Beach Red 1, 2 and 3, and Beach Green 1, 2 and 3 were assigned to the 6th Battalion/2nd Division. Beach Blue 1 and 2, and Beach Yellow 1, 2 and 3 were assigned to the 23rd Battalion/4th Division. The target of the Army's 27th Infantry was the Aslito airfield. A part of the 2nd Division, acting as a floating reserve, would create a diversionary attack at Tanapag Harbor.

D-Day carriers began a series of air strikes along with naval gunfire that lasted from 4:30 to 6:30 A.M. just above the designated landing areas. This was done to knock out any coastal defenses the Japanese had in place. This tactic was, for the most part, ineffective because when the landing forces hit the beaches, General Saito's forces opened fire from the well-concealed pillboxes and marines began to die everywhere.

Finding a place to dig in became the priority of Dan Akee, code talker for the 23rd Regiment/4th Division. He and his foxhole partner, Robert Holmes, dug in as quickly and as deeply as they could. Japanese shells were raining down all around them when Akee believed he had been hit by shrapnel. "I was with Robert Holmes in the foxhole," recalled Akee, "and we were both scared. The shells, coming very close to us, shook everything and a part of the bomb came right on my helmet. I said, 'Robert, look, I've been hit!' He started to laugh because what had landed on my helmet was a big frog!"[1]

By midmorning the reserve units, led by Colonel J. M. "Jumping Joe" Chambers, had landed on Yellow Beach 1 just below Charon Kanoa. They moved behind an embankment near the railroad tracks and dug in for the night. Their next day's objective was to cross a large field, skirt the north edge of the airfield, and secure it. Surviving the night would become a test of alertness and skill.

> D-ah a-kha t-a-tah da-az-jah: Tses-nah tlo-chin tsah ha-ih-des-ee ma-e ne-ahs-jah gah ne-tah al-tah-je-jay. Le-eh-gade do who-neh bihl-has-ahn.

Big guns: *an artillery batalion takes aim and lets the Japanese feel the might of the 2nd Marine Division during the Saipan campaign. Photo from the private collection of F.D. McClain, USN, Retired.*

To all units: Be on alert for "banzai" attacks. Dig in and report positions.

Akee received a similar message from Regimental Headquarters and passed it to the forward echelons. The moment it got dark, the night attacks began. Japanese flares lit up the beaches, and units braced themselves for the first wave of banzais. When the Japanese came, the marines dispatched them with relative ease, but the fighting lasted all night. Wilfred Billey, a code talker for H&S Company 2nd Regiment/2nd Division, remembered that first night and the peculiar events that took place the next morning.

"Our foxhole was right on the beach and we had barbed wire strung not too far from where we were," Billey recalled. "We had been fighting all that night and the next morning it was so quiet that one of the gunnery sergeants decided to investigate. By the shore there were these rock formations that had big holes in them where the surf shoots up and the Japanese would hide in them. He wanted to find out what it looked like so he went over there. He got shot right through the seat, just as clean as could be. Some of the fellows were laughing, can you imagine? Later on that morning was probably the only time I had to use my .45. One lone Japanese, with a gun, was walking out of the water. The tide was down and he came right towards us and began to fire. The company commander ordered everybody to shoot, so everybody fired. That was about the only time I had to shoot and it was not a pleasant experience."[2]

Having survived the night, Colonel Chambers's next objective was to secure Hill 500, a collection of jagged peaks that afforded an overview of the entire southern portion of Saipan. Following an artillery barrage, Chambers and his men worked their way up the hill and gained possession near nightfall. The next day they moved through the gullies beyond Hill 500 toward a support position at the base of Mount Tapotchau. As they worked their way through, they were ambushed and put an urgent call through for tank support:

A-woh a-kha: N-kih Ashi-hi
Bi-tsan-dehn: Moasi A-woh N-kih tseebii
Jo-jayed-goh chay-da-gahi ba-ah-hot-gli
a-la-ih ashdla nos-bas a-del-tahl Dibeh
a-kha shi-da a-woh cha a-la-ih ashdla dii.

To: 2nd Division
From: CT28
Ask for tank support 50 yards South 154.

A tank battalion was dispatched toward Mount Tapotchau and saved Chambers's unit. The tank also blew up a Japanese ammunition dump, which allowed the marines to advance to the base of the mountain. On day nine Chambers's unit was ordered back to Hill 500 for a rest period.

During the final phase of the operation, the 2nd Division was positioned on the left flank, the 4th Division was on the right, and the 27th Infantry Division in the middle. Their objective was to proceed forward, in a wedge-like fashion, to force the Japanese into the northern part of Saipan. The attack was set to commence on June 22, and would be directed from General Smith's headquarters at Charon Kanoa. He was protected by 120 men of V Amphibious Corps (VAC) Reconnaissance Company, commanded by Captain James L. Jones.

By the end of the day, the 2nd Division had advanced 1,000 yards, and the 4th Division had covered nearly 2,000. Digging in and preparing for the night meant that all there would be to eat was C rations. However, the Navajos had a better idea. Dan Akee shared this story.

"Samuel Holiday had a sling-shot and killed some chickens that belonged to the Saipan natives. He cleaned one and we got a big can, put some water in it and started boiling this chicken. Everybody was watching us and asking, 'What are you doing Chief?' 'Well, we're going to make chicken stew.' And we did. Everybody wanted a taste and to help kill the chickens. Even the colonel said, 'Grab me one, Samuel.' He was a good shot, you know. Everybody was boiling chicken soup."[3]

On July 6, Japanese forces started their last counter attack on

Watchful eyes: Pfc. Carl Gorman, code talker, 2nd Division, mans the Garapan, Saipan outpost. Tracking enemy movements was just one of the many functions of a code talker. National Archives photograph.

the Tanapag Plain against the 27th Infantry. The 1st Battalion/ 29th Regiment, commanded by Lieutenant Colonel R. M. Tompkins, along with the support of the 3rd Battalion/8th Regiment helped break the backs of General Saito's forces. Garapan and Mucho Point had been secured by the 2nd Marine Division, while the 4th had captured Mount Petosukura. For all intents and purposes, Saipan was now in the control of the U.S. forces, and the flag was raised at General Smith's Headquarters on July 10. Mop up would continue for another two weeks, but the marine divisions could now return to their staging areas in preparation for the next battle.

During the last days of the battle, Carl Gorman, code talker from H&S Company, 2nd Division, and another marine were carrying a wounded man on a stretcher to the shore for transportation to the hospital ship when a mortar shell exploded close enough to knock them off their feet. They dropped the stretcher and the man they were carrying, but they were not hit. When they recovered, they placed the wounded man back on the stretcher and ran with him to the boat.

On July 26 Gorman was assigned to serve during the battle on Tinian despite the continuing and increasing effects from the concussion he received from the mortar shell. The shock from the mortar shell brought on another attack of malaria, and by the time he returned to Saipan he was physically debilitated. Gorman was evacuated to Pearl Harbor on September 19 but remembers little of that trip. When he regained consciousness he found himself in a white gown tucked into white sheets in a bed. He thought he had died and gone to heaven.

"There was a pitcher of water by the bed and I thought, people drink water in heaven," Gorman recalled. "Then I saw a window and thought, there are windows in heaven. On the opposite wall was a picture of a battleship firing a cannon and knew that this was not heaven. There are no battleships in heaven."[4]

Gorman recovered fully and was discharged later in the fall of 1945. He is now 86, and the oldest living code talker.

With the end of the battle for Saipan, the next target for the marines and the army was Tinian. Elements of the 4th Regiment and the 27th Infantry were set to debark on July 24, 1944.

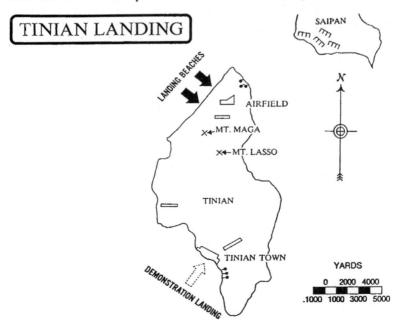

Tinian

Tinian, located across a 3-mile-wide channel from Agingan Point, Saipan, was defended by 9,000 crack army and navy troops under the command of Colonel Hiyoshi Ogata that included veterans from the 50th Infantry/29th Division which had seen action on Guadalcanal.

Navy frogmen had reconnoitered the shores around Ushi Point and reported that this was the best location to effect the landings. This area was designated White Beach 1 and 2, and marine command decided that a diversionary landing at Tinian Town would enable everybody to get ashore. Prelanding bombardments expended 30,000 rounds of ammunition on July 23 to avoid what had happened on the D-Day landings at Saipan.

Major Clifton B. Cates left Tanapag Harbor headed toward Ushi Point, while the diversionary force headed toward Tinian Town. General Ogata fell for the fake landing and rushed the main body of his forces toward that target. By the time he realized he had been fooled, he was helpless to prevent the landing of Cates's 15,000 troops.

Ogata decided the only course of honorable action left for him was a banzai. He commenced this attack about 2:30 A.M. and recommenced it again near dawn. The marines opened up with bazookas, antitank guns, and half-tracks, which quickly ended this futile act. By August 1, 1944, all of Tinian was in U.S. hands.

Guam – Operation Stevedore

Guam was the last of the U.S. objectives in the Mariana Island chain and a sore spot on American pride. Guam had been a U.S. territory since 1900, and when it was usurped by Japan on December 10, 1941, reclaiming it became imperative.

Guam's Chamorro population had secretly remained loyal to the United States during the occupation and rendered aid to the marines during the invasion. Japan had renamed Guam Omiya Jima and given the Chamorro people a choice of enforced slave labor or death.

Guam is 30 miles long and riddled with limestone ridges, ravines, dense, impenetrable jungles, rice paddies, large airfields and an excellent deep water harbor at Apra. The Japanese had reinforced the island with 19,000 troops under the command of Lieutenant General Takeshi Takeshima. Their weapons included nineteen 8-inch, eight 6-inch, six 3-inch, and twenty-two 5-inch dual-purpose guns plus eight 75mm anti-aircraft guns and eighty-one field artillery pieces lending support to two tank companies with eighty-six antitank weapons.

Pre-invasion bombing began on July 8 and continued for thirteen days. During that time, a number of entrenched Japanese defenses were disabled or destroyed. Commander Draper L. Kauffman's underwater demolition team (UDT) detonated mines and cleared underwater obstacles along the proposed landing beaches near Asan Point.

Operation Stevedore called for the 1st Provisional Brigade, under the command of Brigadier General Lemuel C. Shepherd Jr., to land on Asan Point just north of the Apra Harbor. Major General Allen H. Turnage's 3rd Marine Division along with Major

General A. D. Bruce's 77th Infantry Division would land at Agat just south of Apra Harbor. On D-Day, July 21, 9,072 rockets plus 22,000 rounds of naval gunfire were unleashed on the designated landing beaches, but stiff Japanese resistance kept the marines fighting for every square inch of ground.

Dennie Hosteen, a code talker for Headquarters Company, 2nd Battalion/9th Regiment/3rd Division, recalled the D-Day landings. "It was a hot day. The weather and the firing," Hosteen said. "When we hit the coral reefs you could see a lot of mortar shells and artillery shells hitting the water. My commander, Lieutenant Colonel Robert E. Cushman, got word that we were needed to help the 3rd Marines because they were having trouble on their left flank near Fonte Plateau."[5]

The 1st Brigade had made great progress in reducing the Japanese forces on the Orote Peninsula. Then the brigade linked up with the 3rd Division to reach the town of Asan before nightfall. During that night, one of the wildest banzai charges of the war took place. Japan's 38th Infantry launched a counter attack against the 3rd Division, a second wave hit the 21st Regiment, and a third wave hit the 2nd Battalion/9th Regiment. The Navajo radio net lit up like a Christmas tree, and messages were flying as fast as they could be sent: "2nd Battalion in desperate need of mortars....3rd Division requesting ammo and grenades....Need night flares....Requesting machine gun reinforcement." The night seemed to last forever, and the carnage was unbelievable. Although the marines suffered minimal fatalities, the Japanese dead littered the landscape. The wounded marines were tended to, and the dead were registered for burial. One of those was code talker Johnson Housewood of the 21st Marines.

"John Goodluck was supposed to relieve Johnson. The 21st Marines was on a small hill, and when he raised his head he got shot," Kee Etsicitty remembered. "You think at first your drill instructors are crazy when they tell you how and when to move, go this way, go that way, zigzag if you can, and don't stand up! This is where the protection comes in. Johnson didn't intentionally stand up. He didn't mean to get killed, but his cover wasn't enough to protect him if he moved one inch. The one good thing

I learned from his death is when you hear a shot, you duck for cover. You might be scared, and some men might make fun of you for that, but at least you are alive."[6]

On July 30 the battle for a vertical bluff called "Sugar Ridge" began in earnest. Sugar Ridge was a perpendicular, 500-foot crag peppered with interconnecting caves, pillboxes, and spider traps that held an overview of the landing beaches located directly below Adelup Point. Inch by inch the marines, under the command of Lieutenant Colonel Wendell H. Duplantis, managed to blast out the enemy, and at midday Duplantis was able to establish his command post halfway up the ridge. From this position he was able to coordinate the logistics of securing the rest of the ridge. Sugar Ridge was under marine control by July 31, and the 3rd Division was able to move its outpost to the edge of Guam's largest city, Agana. Ensuing artillery, mortar and naval barrages destroyed many of Agana's structures, and when the fire was lifted, the marines discovered that the city had been abandoned.

Just hanging around: left to right, Eugene Roanhorse Crawford, Wilsie Bitsie and Edmund John pose outside their quarters. These three seem happy to still be in one piece after two years of combat duty. National Archives photograph.

Command posts, kitchens and bivouac areas were set in and around the town. Many of the Chamorros who had fled before the bombing now began to leave their hiding places in the jungle and give information about the Japanese to the marines. One native in particular touched the hearts of these war-hardened troops. His name was Johnny, he was seven years old, and he was an orphan. Wilsie Bitsie told how he came to know Johnny and what he learned from this little boy.

"The town of Agana had been completely destroyed, and he was hiding in the woods with other people from the town," recalled Bitsie. "The people came over to our camp and started talking with us. He spoke beautiful English. We took him over to the galley with us to eat. A lot of times we did that – we'd take the natives and put them in our chow lines.

"One day," Bitsie continued, "he taught us a song:

> *On the eighth day of December the Father above took my father and took my mother. He took my sisters and he took my brothers, he took baby Jer who was only a month old, he took them all. He left me by myself and I have no one to turn to.*

He asked if he could stay with us because he didn't have anyone to call Father," Bitsie said. "I said, 'Well, if you want to, you can call me Father. I'd be glad to father you; I'll help you in any way I can.' Later on he said, 'I want to sing you a song we were learning after the Japanese invaded our island:

> *Early Monday morning they dropped their bombs. Eighth of December 1941. Oh Mr. Sam, Sam, my dear Uncle Sam. Oh won't you please come back to Guam.*

"I learned those two songs from Johnny, and I've never forgotten them," Bitsie said. "We taught each other a lot of things. He stayed in our tent when we went out on patrol, and he was always there, with a smile on his face, when we returned."[7]

The bond that Bitsie and Johnny formed grew from the fact that Johnny was totally alone. Navajo children are surrounded by loving parents, uncles, aunts and grandparents from the moment they are born. These relatives are responsible for raising and teaching the children traditions and ceremonies that are vital to the Navajo way of life. It pained Bitsie to know that Johnny had no one to look out for him, and the man felt a certain obligation to do what he could for the child. They would be good for each other at a place in time that was anything but good.

Even though the island was far from secure, there were moments when the radios weren't being used for operational purposes and the Navajos could use them to contact other Navajos to see how everyone was faring. "Sometimes when we were finished sending messages from the ship, we would talk to each other, in regular Navajo, about home," Kee Etsicitty said. "Once headquarters moved ashore, we slept in the same place with General "Howling Mad" Smith, so we felt like we had extra protection. One day Admiral Nimitz, General Shepherd and General Smith came to the tent. They would discuss battle plans while we sat in a corner. Then they would give their orders to the G2 colonel, who then brought it to us to send. That is the way it worked. An incoming message was handled the same way. It had to go through two or three hands before anything was decided. In my situation we used the code the way they wanted us to."[8]

Although Etsicitty might have been feeling secure at headquarters, code talkers in the field were anything but safe. When radio equipment failed or was destroyed, messages still had to get through; then code talkers often became runners between units. It was a dangerous but necessary job that code talkers as well as other communications personnel performed. For the men assigned to protect the Navajos, however, it became a nightmare.

"Our radio and telephone had been knocked, and the sergeant gave me an urgent message to deliver to Regimental Headquarters," recalled Bill Toledo. "I took the message and took off without thinking anything about it. I got away from Richard Bonham that day, which I didn't know I wasn't supposed to do. I began working my way through the front lines towards a road that was jammed with trucks. When I came out into the open, a sniper hidden in the hills above the road started shooting.

"I started running, zigzagging, and the marines along the bank hollered for me to get off the road," Toledo continued. "The bullets were hitting into the mud, but all I heard was the shots, and when I finally realized I was the sniper's target, I jumped down the bank to get out of the way. A marine sharpshooter was called in, and he nailed the sniper. After that everybody started to return to their duties, and I made it to Regimental Headquarters. I gave them the message and returned to my unit.

"When I got back Richard was really upset. He grabbed me by the shirt and started shaking me, asking me where I had been. I told him that I had an urgent message that needed to be delivered to Regimental Headquarters, took off, and delivered it. 'When did this happen?' Richard asked. 'A couple of hours ago,' I said. He wanted to know who the Sergeant was and what his name was, so I told him. He was very upset and said, 'You know this is a very serious thing that happened. If anything had happened to you and my commanding officer found out about it, I could have been court-martialed! Don't ever do that again!'"[9]

Ambush

On August 7 the Japanese abandoned their Tumon Bay defenses in the jungles along the eastern cliffs of Guam. Marines moved in quickly and secured the Tiyan airfield. This conquest, however, was not accomplished without fatalities. Moving through the area on patrol, code talker Charlie Begay and his unit were ambushed and cut to pieces. A few hours after this happened, Wilsie Bitsie and his unit moved through the area and discovered the remains of the forward patrol.

"We came into an opening in the jungle and spied what was left of the forward patrol," Bitsie remembered. "Making sure that there weren't any Japanese left alive, we began to care for the wounded and dead. I came upon this one body, and my heart stopped. It was Charlie! I couldn't believe that he was dead. My heart was just breaking. We had been with each other from the beginning, through the Raiders, and now he was gone.

"Charlie had a huge gash that ran from the top of his right shoulder straight across his neck and chest. His lips were blue, and there was no sign of breath in his body. The graves registration hadn't begun yet, so I took one of his dog tags and put it in my pocket. I straightened out his body and placed the other dog tag in his mouth and tied it shut with a piece of cloth. That way when the graves registration people came by, they would be able to positively identify him. I placed him near a log and covered his body with leaves and bark, said a prayer, and went back to camp. I gave the one dog tag I had to the CO (commanding officer) who then packed Charlie's belongings, wrote a letter to his family, and sent all of it back home. I never felt such sadness."[10]

Final Days

On the final night of fighting, at 10:30 P.M., three heavy Japanese tanks made a last-ditch charge down the road from Dedo, but they were easily repelled. By the morning of August 8, 1944, Guam was again a U.S. possession. Embarkation for part of the 3rd Division began, which gave Bitsie time to place Johnny with a Red Cross delegation that promised to find a good foster family for him. Bitsie promised to keep in touch with Johnny and bade the boy good-bye. The trip back to Guadalcanal was doubly sad for Bitsie. He had to leave a child he felt an obligation to, and he had to deal with the loss of Charlie.

Two weeks after returning to Guadalcanal, Bitsie received a surprise that, for one of the few times in his life, left him utterly speechless. "One night when we were sitting around the tent, we heard a jeep pull up. I was lying on a cot by the tent flap, and Leslie Cody was on the opposite side facing the opening. We saw a sea bag fly out of the jeep, and I thought, 'This must be Charlie's replacement.' All of a sudden Leslie stood up and said in Navajo, 'Have you been to hell?' When everybody turned around to see why Leslie had said such a thing, we all just about jumped out of our skin! Standing there, in clean khakis, was Charlie! I didn't know whether to shake hands with him or not! He wasn't breathing when I found him! He laid there all morning and half of the afternoon. Never a breath! I couldn't figure out how he got back.

"When I asked him what happened," Bitsie continued, "he

said he didn't remember much of anything at all except he could feel his feet twitch. Then he heard his own heart beat, and he started moving his body. He saw that he was covered by leaves and bark, so started moving to shake it off. When he rolled out from his cover, he wasn't pleased about the dog tag tied in his mouth. He just started to stand up when the graves registration unit came by. They evacuated him to the hospital ship, and that is where he had been for the last two weeks. He lost a lot of blood, and the scar was clean around his neck. It was the most amazing, scary thing I ever witnessed. Once I got over the shock, I was truly happy that Charlie was alive."[11]

While Bitsie, Cody, Begay and the other code talkers were enjoying a brief respite and reunion, there was work being done in preparation for the impending battles that would take place on Peleliu, Iwo Jima and Okinawa. Staging areas on Hawaii, Guadalcanal, New Zealand, Australia and New Caledonia were busy training for the final phases in the South Pacific war.

Pre-invasion briefing: code talkers on Pavuvu in the Palau Island chain, receive instructions at the staging area. Colonel James G. Smith (kneeling) instructs the men on what will be expected of them during the campaign. Front row, left to right, Pfc.s James T. Nahkai, John H. Bowman, Ira Manuelito, Jimmy King, Andrew Calledito, Lloyd Betone and Cpl. Lloyd Oliver. Back row, left to right, Pfc Preston Toledo, Cpl. John Chee, Pfc.s Sandy Burr, Ben Manuelito, Don Bahiya, Edward Leuppe and brothers Del and Ray Cayedito. National Archives photograph.

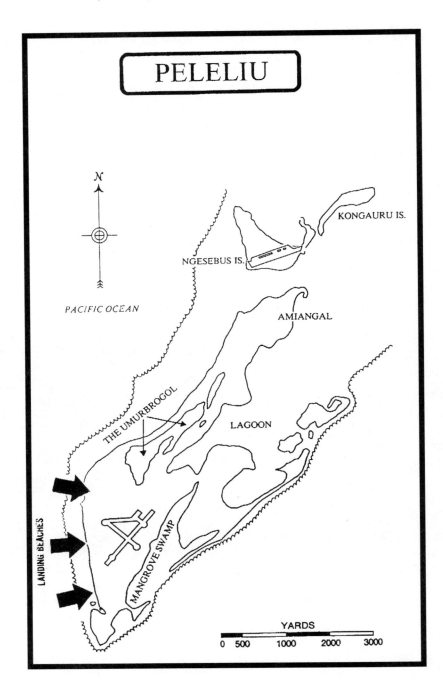

Peleliu

The victories on Saipan, Tinian and Guam gave the Joint Chiefs of Staff a tremendous boost of confidence that the war would soon be over. The decision on what island to target next led to heated debates among the Marine Corps, the Navy and the Army. General Douglas MacArthur was anxious to fulfill his "I shall return" promise to the Philippines, and his voice carried a great deal of weight. MacArthur decided that Peleliu had to be neutralized to pave a smooth path through to Leyte. The airfields on Peleliu would be utilized to launch fighter plane assaults in advance of the planned attack on Leyte.

Reconnaissance photographs revealed little about the Japanese defenses on the island. Whenever a plane was detected on radar, the Japanese simply melted into the dense vegetation until the plane had passed over. The failure of these reconnaissance flights to give an accurate picture of the defenses, as well as troop strength on the island, would lead to a disastrous landing for the marines.

Peleliu, part of the Palau Island chain located 470 miles east of Mindanao, Philippines, is six miles long and two miles wide. Peleliu lies in a coral reef, volcanic in origin, that is covered in dense vegetation. It also contains a concealed coral ridge, the Umurbrogol, that runs north to south in the center of the island.

Peleliu's tactical command was in the hands of Colonel Kunio Nakagawa and his 10,700 troops. He had constructed a network of tunnels through the Umurbrogol, in some places six stories deep, with fire ports and steel doors that would be impervious to prelanding bombardments.

General William H. Rupertus, looking over the reconnaissance photographs of the island, mistakenly pronounced that the battle would be "a quickie. Rough but fast." General "Howling Mad" Smith would exercise overall command, while Rupertus would direct field command of the 1st Marine Division along with the 321st Infantry.

Rupertus's plan of attack was to land three regiments abreast over five beaches that paralleled the airfield. Colonel Puller's 1st

Regiment would land on Beach White 1 and 2, and wheel north up along the coast. Colonel Harris's 5th Regiment would land on Beach Orange 1 and 2, cross the island, and secure the airfield. Colonel Hannekin's 7th Regiment from Beach Orange 3 were assigned to clean out any resistance around the southern tip of the island. Operation Stalemate was set for September 15, 1944.

Pre-invasion meetings were taking place when William McCabe, a code talker for the 7th Regiment, received his landing day assignment. "They were assigning landing beaches to the different officers, and ours was Orange Beach," McCabe recalled. "Suddenly I hear my name, 'McCabe, front and center! Here is the Division flag, take it and go in on the fourth wave. Pick an area on the beach and plant it.' Then everybody started coming up to me saying, 'Good-bye McCabe, it's been nice knowing you!' Jesus, I thought. What the hell did I do to get that assignment!?"[12] If the commanders thought they were bestowing an honor on McCabe by giving him the Division flag to carry and plant, they were not. Any man carrying that symbol was an obvious, prime target for enemy fire.

Prelanding naval bombardments began in the early morning hours of September 15. When the fire lifted, little damage had been done to neutralize the Japanese beach defenses. Preparing for debarkation, McCabe's "luck" took an unexpected turn for the worse.

"On board the transports I was responsible for debarking the communication personnel in proper order," McCabe said. "After making sure everyone was in place, I went below to get my gear and some of it was gone! I didn't have any ammunition! My bandoleers were gone. The ammunition I had was assigned to me before we left and there wasn't any place to get more. We were about to land and I only had one clip for my weapon. I had my radio and message center gear and one clip."[13]

There were many unpleasant surprises awaiting the marines headed for their designated landing areas. Colonel Nakagawa had given strict orders not to fire on the marines until they reached the beaches. Once the marines landed, Nakagawa unleashed a firestorm that sent marines every which way desperately seeking any kind of cover.

Jimmy King Sr., code talker for H&S Company, 5th Regiment, described landing day and the death of Tom Singer, a fellow code talker. "Before we landed Tom told me, 'If you get home first, Jimmy, you tell my folks that I'm all right,' King recalled. "He gave me a picture and said, 'This is my family. Tell them I'm all right. Don't tell them that I was wounded once already and recuperated and we're going into another fight. This may be my last one.' And sure enough it was. When we hit the beaches, Tom got hit right in the throat and it cut him from ear to ear. He was bleeding but I couldn't reach him, couldn't cross to where he was because the fire was so intense."[14]

Casualties were mounting at an alarming rate, and commanders were frantically calling for air strikes to neutralize the pillboxes and the powerful 70mm artillery that was pounding them from the southern tip of the island. Peleliu was the first island to have a grid map used for artillery and air strikes. The grids enabled the coordination of the Navajo radio net to keep the strikes confined to enemy positions away from the marines. The grid map of Peleliu was used extensively throughout the battle.

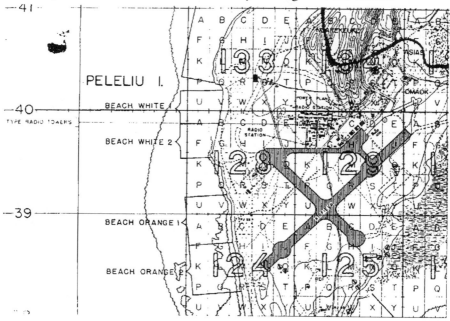

"HqLanFor [Headquarters Landing Force] message to AirObserver. K plus 20 to K plus 40, bomb and strafe 1220, 128MHC, 133XSN." William McCabe headed for his destination at Beach Orange 3 and after several futile attempts to land was redirected around the island to land on Beach Purple where there was less opposition. Once landed, his first order of business was to set up a message center. "Command decided to use the Navajo code 100 percent during the landings," recalled McCabe. "I had to keep the communications line open and make sure that everybody checked into the net every thirty minutes to make sure that everything was all right. I had my job cut out for me and Division flag is just laying there. Colonel Hannekin turned to me and said, 'Bill, let me take the flag, I'll put it up for you. You're too busy, you take care of everything right here.' We were in some kind of crater or something, and he stuck the flag near the entrance. When he planted that damn flag, machine guns opened up from both sides, in a criss-cross manner, and cut him in half. If that had been me, I would have been killed."[15]

By the end of first day, the marines held a mere 25 feet of the beaches, a situation that would remain so for the next ten days. On day two, Captain George Hunt's K Company/3rd Battalion beat off repeated attacks and captured many enemy machine gun nests near grid square 124 O. On day four, Colonel Puller's 1st Regiment were nearing the first ridge of Umurbrogol; they crossed a road and came right up against a sheer cliff. From the base of the cliff, they inched their way up, fighting the entrenched Japanese cave by cave.

The other serious threat facing the marines was in trying to get supplies from the ships to the shore. The Japanese coastal guns were keeping the ships, Higgins boats and LSTs at bay, and until those guns were silenced, the marines would have to make do with what they had. The most serious shortage was water. "We had been without a taste of fresh water for a long time," recalled Jimmy King. "They had to throw the water barrels into the water about a half a mile from shore and let the surf bring them in. A lot of the barrels hadn't been cleaned; they still had fuel oil in them. There weren't enough stretcher bearers either. We were stretcher bearers and water boys."[16]

Taking care of the wounded was not a problem for the Navajos, but for some, tending to the dead was. The Navajos who held to their traditional ways did not feel comfortable being around or handling dead bodies. Tradition teaches that once someone is dead, his or her spirit does not depart at the moment of death. To touch or move the body is to interfere with the spirit, an action that should be avoided at all times. Setting aside these beliefs to do what was necessary was another illustration of the dedication the Navajos displayed during the war.

On day seven, the northern peninsula and the coral ridges of the Umurbrogol were still in enemy hands. The 7th Regiment were committed to fight the high ground, while Puller's unit inched its way up the first ridge. Lieutenant Colonel Spencer Berger's 2nd Battalion/7th Regiment managed to establish a command post on a coral cliff directly above Horseshoe Ridge.

"At the message center when runners were being sent," King said, "the commander would say, 'King, come here. I need you to send somebody that you are sure can get through.' I considered my men and I valued their lives just as much as I valued my own. I wouldn't ask a man to do something I couldn't do myself. I was the senior code talker of the group so often times I would run the message myself."[17]

After a brief holding period while waiting for the 321st Army to move up the west coast road, two battalions of the 7th moved along the ridge. Berger's unit went up the east coast road, while Lieutenant Colonel Gormley's unit traveled west and then cut inland behind Horseshoe Ridge.

By October 3rd a junction of the 2nd and 3rd Battalions/7th Regiment captured a prominent hill located between grid 156Y and 157U in the northeastern region of the Umurbrogol. On October 6 the 321st Infantry along with the 5th Marines advanced to Garekoro, while the 7th Marines fought on the ridge.

As the marines advanced north, they came under heavy fire from pillbox positions located on Ngesebus Island. Naval gunfire was directed at grid 161V and cracked the enemy defenses in northern Peleliu. On October 12 the 1st Marine Division was relieved by the 81st Army Division and Peleliu was declared secure. The cost in American lives had been enormous, and it had taken an average of 1,589 rounds of heavy and light ammunition to kill one Japanese defender on Peleliu. MacArthur wanted it, the marines took it, and yet Peleliu was never used in any way as a fighter plane base for the invasion of the Philippines.

The 1st Marine Division returned to Australia for a rest and retraining, and the Joint Chiefs of Staff began the initial planning stages for the next amphibious campaign. While the strategy sessions were taking place, Marine Corps Headquarters sent letters to every commanding general within the Fleet Marine Force eliciting opinions concerning the Navajo code talkers. The training program was running short of students, and Headquarters needed to know if an additional recruitment order would be necessary.

Command Endorsements

From: The Commanding General
To: The Commanding General, Fleet Marine Force, Pacific

Subject: Navajo Code Talkers, SSN 642

1. The experience of this Division indicates the continuance of the Navajo recruiting and training program is justified.

> C. B. Cates
> Fourth Marine Division

From: The Commanding General
To: The Commanding General, FMF, Pacific

Subject: Navajo Indian Code Talkers

1. Navajo Indians (SSN 642) have been extensively used in training within this Division and such employment has proven to be of value in the training phases. Their po-

tential value in combat appears to make the continuance of the program worthwhile.

2. Successful employment of Navajos as Code Talkers requires constant drill on the Navajo vocabulary. In order to make such training similar and effective throughout Fleet Marine Force units it is recommended that all Navajo Code Talkers be pooled under FMF control and assigned to Corps and Divisions for specific operations as required.

> Ray A. Robinson
> Chief of Staff
> Fifth Marine Division

From: The Commanding General
To: The Commanding General, Sixth Marine Division

Subject: Navajo Indian Code Talkers, SSN 642

1. The use of Navajo Talkers for sending messages requiring security has proven much quicker in the field than to encode the messages at point of origin and then decode at point of receipt. However, in regiments and below most messages sent by radio are over circuits formed with sets SCR 300, which to date have been thought secure enough that all messages are sent in plain English with little use of Navajo Talkers. For higher echelons with more powerful and different types of sets the Navajo Talker should be of value. Situations in regiments and below may arise where Navajo Talkers could be used effectively where it is necessary to encode messages for security reasons.

2. The Navajos have proved to be excellent Marines, intelligent, industrious, easily taught to send and receive by key and excellent in the field.

3. The continued use of Navajo Talkers is recommended.

F. D. Beans
Sixth Marine Division

From: Division Signal Officer
To: The Commanding General, Sixth Marine Division

Subject: Navajo Indian Code Talkers, SSN 642

1. Experience has shown that the use of Navajo talkers on voice circuits has been definitely advantageous in the past, and with the new equipment (SCR-600 series), that is being placed into use now, it is believed that the Indians will be employed even more on the voice circuits, between Division and the Regiments, and between Regiment and Battalion.

2. These talkers provide a reasonable security to transmissions and the employment of them considerably reduces the time of delivery of messages which otherwise would have to be encoded if sent by C.W. radio transmission.

3. It is recommended that the program of recruiting and training Navajo code talkers be continued.

E. D. Martin, Jr.[18]

Division Signal

These letters of recommendation made quite clear that the Navajo code talkers were a vital, still-needed communications tool. In the formation of the battle plans for the next campaign, commanders would consider the best way to use the special skills of the Navajo code talkers. At this point in the war, the Navajos had proven that they could be an accurate, dependable source of security. The Navajo Communication School would continue to train men who would be incorporated into the 6th Marine Division, and the field school in Hawaii was four weeks long and incorporated new terms and skills in telephone wire circuit function, message delivery and wireman duties. The upcoming battle on Iwo Jima would require that all the skills the Navajos possessed be sharpened to perfection.

Notes

1. Interview 1159, Doris Duke Collection.
2. Interview 1161, Doris Duke Collection.
3. Interview 1159, Doris Duke Colleciton.
4. Correspondence from Carl Gorman, June 8, 1994.
5. Interview 1170, Doris Duke Collection.
6. Interview with Kee Etsicitty.
7. Interview with Wilsie Bitsie.
8. Interview with Kee Etsicitty.
9. Interview with Bill Toledo.
10. Interview with Wilsie Bitsie.
11. Ibid.
12. Interview 1171, Doris Duke Collection.
13. Ibid.
14. Oral History Transcript VE 25.A1 M37, Marine Corps University.
15. Interview 1171, Doris Duke Collection.
16. Oral History Transcript VE 25.A1 M37, Marine Corps University.
17. Ibid.
18. All four memoranda are from 62A:2086 Loc 02/35-38-3, Box 14, "Navajo Code Talkers," Marine Corps Historical Center Indexes, Washington Navy Yard, Washington, D.C.

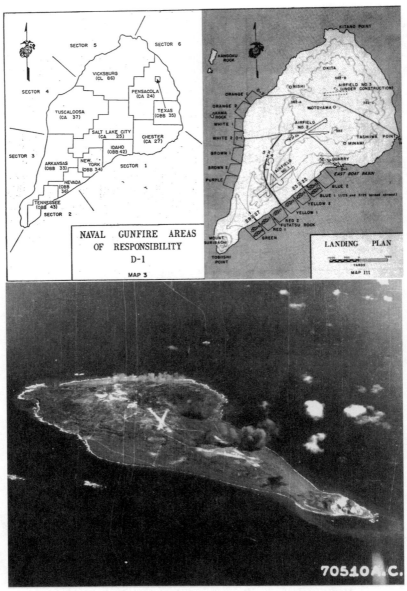

Pre-invasion bombing run: *over Iwo Jima, October 21, 1944. Dark puffs just above the island show flak from anti-aircraft guns that damaged and shot down many American planes. Photo courtesy of Air and Space Museum, Smithsonian Institution.*

Iwo Jima

By December 7, 1944, the third anniversary of the bombing of Pearl Harbor, U.S. Armed Forces in the South Pacific were beginning to recognize that the war against Japan was nearing final stages. The victories on Saipan, Tinian, Guam, and Peleliu gave Allied forces bases from which to launch bomber attacks against mainland Japan. On paper such attacks looked like a good plan, but the round-trip distance from Saipan to Japan proved to be a dangerous stretch for the B-29's fuel capacities. Fuel distance was not the only obstacle that planes faced: their flight patterns carried them directly over a Japanese anti-aircraft base whose deadly accurate guns created enormous damage.

This base was located atop a volcanic island in the Nanpo Shoto, a chain of islands 750 nautical miles south of Tokyo Bay. The Nanpo Shoto comprise three major island groups: the Izu Shoto, the Ogasawara Gunto (Bonin Islands), and the Kazan Retto (Volcano Islands). Iwo Jima, located 660 nautical miles from Japan, lies within the Kazan Retto, and it was here that many a U.S. pilot met withering fire from anti-aircraft guns mounted on Iwo Jima's Mount Suribachi. Pilots referred to it as "Mount Sunovabitchi," and the Joint Chiefs of Staff realized Iwo would have to be neutralized for the attack on the Japanese mainland to have any measure of success.

While the Joint Chiefs of Staff were consulting about the proposed invasion of Iwo Jima, the 3rd, 4th, and 5th Marine Divisions were busy training at Guam and at Parker Ranch and Camp Tarawa in Hawaii. Al Mertz, of 5th Division Reconnaissance, became a close friend of code talker Samuel Tso and described some of the activities the Navajos enjoyed during periods of rest between training exercises. "One of their favorite pastimes was horseshoes," Mertz recalled. "While on maneuvers they would practice their code talking, and I was always amused with the way they handled it. They would get a call on the radio, answer it within a minute or two, and then resume the game as if nothing had happened. Pitching horseshoes was a strange sight to see in the backwoods of Hawaii."[1]

The scuttlebutt around Hawaii was that the marines were preparing to attack the Japanese homeland, but the code talkers, serving with reconnaissance, knew differently. Because they were present at many of the commanders' planning sessions, in order to send messages when needed, they knew what the true target was: Iwo Jima. Many code talkers would be involved in sending vital information via Navajo code so that the commanders could develop their beach assault plans.

Target: Iwo Jima

Iwo Jima, colonized by Japan in 1830, was considered essential to that nation's inner island defense perimeter. In 1937 Iwo Jima was placed off limits to all unauthorized personnel. On the east boat basin a sign in both Japanese and English announced, "Trespassing, surveying, photographing, sketching, modeling, etc. upon these premises without previous official permission is prohibited by the Military Secrets Protection Law. Any offender in this regard will be punished to the full extent of the law."[2]

Iwo Jima is two and one-half miles wide and five miles long, covered in coarse gray-black volcanic sand, and shaped like a pork chop. There is no natural water source or animal life, and a constant dry wind blows from all directions. Mount Suribachi, located at the southern end, holds an overview of the entire island. The northwest part of Iwo is crisscrossed with interlocking ridges of lava rock. Just below Mount Suribachi were two large airfields and just to the north a large sulfur plant.

The man who converted this somewhat desolate island into a formidable fortress was Lieutenant General Tadamichi Kuribayashi, a former chief of the Japanese Imperial Guard and a Deputy Military Attaché in Washington, D.C. from 1928 to 1930. While in the United States, he had been invited on a number of occasions to tour U.S. military facilities and was liked and esteemed by those he met. He returned to Japan with a great deal of respect and knowledge concerning U.S. military and industrial capacities. He used this information in constructing the defenses on Iwo Jima.

When Kuribayashi arrived to take command of Iwo Jima on June 10, 1944, he found the 22,000 troops and conscripted Korean laborers in dismal shape. Installations had not been built according to design, discipline was lax, and the general disposition of the men was unacceptable.

Kuribayashi wasted little time whipping his charges into military shape. Six months later Kuribayashi's men had finished building 150 concrete, reinforced, bomb-proof pillboxes around the airfields. In the northern sector, 16 miles of interconnecting tunnels with multiple entrances and exits had been excavated. This tunnel system would contain approximately 800 positions, including 120 75mm guns, 90 large mortar and rocket launchers, 130 howitzers and 68 antitank guns. The beach defenses comprised 21 block houses, 92 concrete pillboxes, 32 camouflaged artillery emplacements and five freshwater distilleries, which supplied the entire island.

Kuribayashi also drilled his men to execute an inner island defense plan: let the enemy land and make small progress on the beaches, then open up and hit the enemy's troops where they stood. "Above all, we shall dedicate ourselves and our entire strength to the defense of this island; we shall grasp bombs, charge enemy tanks and destroy them; we shall infiltrate into the midst of the enemy and annihilate them; with every salvo we will, without fail, kill the enemy; each man will make it his duty to kill ten of the enemy before dying; until we are destroyed to the last man we shall harass the enemy with guerrilla tactics."[3]

Kuribayashi continued reinforcing Iwo. In August 1944 Allied reconnaissance missions commenced. Aerial photographs of Iwo revealed a large number of fortified installations throughout the island. The photographs showed the type and location of the

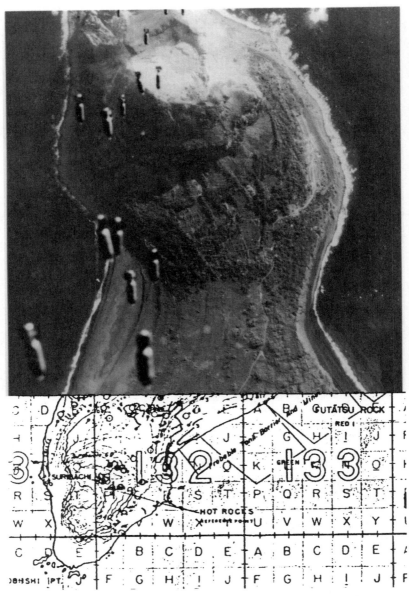

Bombs away! *Top, fighter and bomber planes pound Iwo Jima prior to the designated landing day of February 17, 1945. Photo courtesy of Air and Space Museum, Smithsonian Institute. Bottom, Iwo Jima grid map of Mt. Suribachi.*

various emplacements that would become targets during bombing runs. From October 1944 through January 1945, daily bombing sorties pounded the island but with little result. The only effect these raids produced was to interrupt the sleep patterns of the Japanese defenders.

While Allied bombing continued, meetings were taking place concerning the planning and execution of the invasion of Iwo Jima. The Central Command South Pacific (CinComSoPac) studied a Joint Chiefs of Staff report that advocated gaining control of Iwo Jima. The purpose of this action was:

- To maintain unremitting military pressure against Japan
- To extend U.S. control over the Western Pacific
- To establish a base from which U.S. forces could attack the Japanese empire, protect bases in the Marianas, cover naval forces and conduct search operations in the approaches to the Japanese empire, and provide fighter escort for long-range operations.

Admiral Spruance would exercise overall command of the Iwo Jima operation, while Lieutenant General Holland Smith would command landing forces. Even though these men understood the objective and the reason behind it, Smith held serious concerns about the execution of the battle plan. The acrid taste of what Peleliu had cost his marines was still with him, and he wanted to make sure that Iwo would not become a repeat performance. Smith agreed that Iwo, its location, and its airfields would aid the effort to end the war with Japan; he just was not convinced that the price his marines would have to pay would be worth it. As the CinComSoPac meeting ended, Smith's parting statement expressed his mind-set about the impending campaign: "This will be the bloodiest fight in Marine Corps history. We'll catch seven kinds of the hell on the beaches, and that will be just the beginning. The fighting will be fierce, and the casualties will be awful, but my Marines will take the damned island!"[4]

Operation Detachment

Scheduled to commence on February 19, 1945, Operation Detachment would involve the 3rd, 4th, and 5th Marine Divisions. This would be the largest, most ambitious campaign of the entire South Pacific conflict. The logistics of coordinating three full divisions of marines and equipment toward a single goal were daunting. CinComSoPac decided that the island should be divided into three parts, with the 3rd Division minus the 9th and 21st Regiments placed as the floating reserve. The 4th and 5th Divisions, scheduled to land on the western beaches, would be responsible for securing Mount Suribachi and the airfields. The beach designations for each of the divisions were as follows:

3rd Marines (division reserve): To be ordered later as necessary
9th Marines: Yellow 1 and Yellow 2
21st Marines: Red 1 and Red 2

4th Division
23rd Marines: Yellow 1 and Yellow 2
24th Marines (division reserve): Blue or Yellow as ordered
25th Marines: Blue 1

5th Division
27th Marines: Red 1 and Red 2
28th Marines: Green 1
3rd Battalion/28th Marines (division reserve): Red or Green
1st Battalion/26th Marines (division reserve): Red or Green
26th Marines: As ordered.[5]

Mount Suribachi, the first major D-Day objective, was assigned to the 28th Marines, led by Colonel Harry B. Liversedge. Motoyama, the second objective, was assigned to the 4th Division/23rd Regiment, led by Colonel Walter W. Wesinger, and the 25th Regiment, led by Colonel John R. Lanigan.

The marines were to proceed in six waves, five minutes apart; effect their landings; and move forward to their designated targets. Division artillery units would be used to support these assaults from selected positions on the various landing beaches. While the landing preparations were nearing completion, marines were nearing the end of their training exercises on Hawaii and Guam.

Embarkation

On January 4, 1945, the 4th and 5th Marine Divisions embarked on the ships that would carry them to Saipan, the last place supplies would be loaded before their departure for Iwo Jima. The 3rd Division, stationed on Guam, would join the convoy on the designated day of departure. Reconnaissance teams would be dispatched from Saipan to provide last-minute details for the D-Day landings.

During the trip from Hawaii to Saipan, Lieutenant Colonel J. P. Berkeley, recently promoted to Chief Operations Officer of the Signal Corps, 5th Division, decided to prove that the code talkers not only were prepared for this battle but also would be instrumental in sending urgent traffic accurately, rapidly and securely.

"Enroute to Saipan, I put on a demonstration for the 5th Marine Division senior officers," recalled Berkeley. "I put two Navajos in the lower bowels of the ship and two topside with their radios. At the same time, I had two pairs of white marine radio operators located likewise. I had the G4 section prepare a typical logistical report, such as would be sent from the front lines to the rear echelon, that was about two and a half paragraphs of typed information. The lower-deck Navajos and the white operators sent the message to the upper deck, where the general and his staff were.

"The test took about twenty-five minutes," Berkeley continued. "The Navajos sent their transmission topside with very few errors; the text of the message was not lost. The white operators did very poorly and never completed the entire message. This demonstration convinced a number of senior officers that the Navajos could be accurate and efficient with these types of messages and should be used without hesitation."[6]

As the ships neared Saipan, the code talkers and other communications personnel were brought to planning rooms and shown the relief map of Iwo Jima. They were instructed where to place their communications posts and what frequencies to use, and they were advised that Morse code would be used as a "dummy." In other words, the marines would force the Japanese to waste precious time decoding messages that were meaningless, while the Navajo radio transmissions carried the valid orders.

Arriving in Saipan, the troops debarked to practice landing maneuvers for Iwo Jima. On February 16 reconnaissance teams along with navy underwater demolition teams (UDTs) performed operations aimed at clearing landing beaches of mines and other obstacles. Among the UDTs were code talkers Paul Blatchford and Samuel Tso.

Code talker Sam Billison of the 5th Division tried to volunteer for one of the missions but was turned down. "Before we got to Iwo Jima, we had three Marine divisions and each of them had reconnaissance companies." The reconnaissance companies were assigned to gather and relay information back to command. Billison continued, "The officer in charge asked for volunteers, and I raised my hand. He said, 'No, you are a special program,' so I was left behind. Only a third of our company came back, most of them were all shot up. Most of them were sent back to the States right away."[6]

Al Mertz and Samuel Tso were paired with one of the UDT launches designated to measure surf and wind conditions on the landing areas. "There was always at least one Navajo for any team that went in," Mertz remembered. "They were usually the form of communication used from shore back to whatever clandestine transportation, such as a ship or submarine, that was being used. Information about beach conditions, installations, and obstacles were always transmitted in code back to the code talker onboard the vessel. Their efficient form of communication could be transmitted quickly, with practically zero probability of being broken. It was a distinct advantage that reconnaissance used to the fullest extent."[7]

Although the UDT examination of the western beaches happened under constant fire from the Japanese, all of the teams returned intact and unharmed. The UDTs on the eastern beaches, however, were not so fortunate. Japanese defenders, believing that this was the beginning of the actual invasion, opened fire and accidentally revealed beach fortifications not previously known to exist. Out of the twelve UDT craft involved, nine were seriously damaged, and a number of men were wounded and one was killed.

The USS *Nevada*, standing by to offer watchdog services during the reconnaissance, leveled its 14-inch guns on the newly revealed Japanese positions as well as laying down a smoke screen until the UDTs could safely return. The information was worth the risk because CinComSoPac commanders now had a clearer picture of what to expect on D-Day.

On completion of the final landing rehearsals, the landing force convoy lifted anchor off Saipan and departed for Iwo Jima on the evening of February 15, 1945. Below decks, soldiers were busy checking and rechecking combat packs, equipment and weapons; writing letters home; playing cards; and in general doing anything and everything to keep their minds off the impending battle. As the convoy silently sliced through the Pacific toward Iwo Jima, prayer services of every denomination were conducted on every deck and every ship. If ever there was a time for prayer and reflection, this was it.

The convoy arrived at 1:00 A.M., 4,000 yards from Iwo Jima, and settled in to await the first waves of prelanding bombardments. Around 4:30 A.M. some code talkers quietly made their way to the top decks to perform the ritual greeting to Father Sun. They reached into their pouches and retrieved small dabs of sacred corn pollen, placing it on their tongue then the top of their head and, finally, making an offering to the east. This would give them clear speech, clear thought and a safe path to walk. They recited this ancient ritual with the echoes of the voices of the Diné filling their hearts, minds and souls. When they finished, they made their way down to the galley for the traditional landing day breakfast of steak, eggs, biscuits with gravy and coffee.

"Before a landing they always fed you a big T-bone steak and eggs," recalled John Kinsel, a code talker with the 3rd Division. "The navy cooks would tease you by saying, 'Enjoy your last meal, Leatherneck.' Of course, we knew that it would be the last hot food we would have for a while, so you learned to eat everything your stomach would hold. I couldn't finish all of the steak, so I put what was left of it between two pieces of bread, wrapped it up, and put it in my combat pack. Once you've been in combat, you learn to stash food. There might come a time when you are pinned down, your C rations are gone, and your grumbling stomach reminds you about your stash."[7]

The time between breakfast and embarkation into the LSTs was tense. The wait seemed endless. Marines were loaded down with equipment but had to wait patiently below decks for the order to start moving topside. The air was stale and filled with the unspoken question, "Is this the day the bullet with my name on it finds me?"

D-Day, February 19, 1945

As darkness gradually dissolved, the silhouettes of the 450 ships of the 5th Fleet sharpened in the dawn's first light and seemed to dwarf the tiny island. As the ships took form on the horizon, so did Iwo Jima. Thomas Begay and Johnny Manuelito, code talkers for H&S Company, 5th Division, were at their communication post on the top deck when they caught their first glimpse of Iwo Jima. "I couldn't believe how ugly and forbidding that place looked," recalled Begay. "It made me very uncomfortable, and then something happened that confirmed that feeling. Johnny and I had our radio net operating when a shell, fired from the island, bounced off just below where we were standing. It bounced off the next deck below and exploded on the third bounce. We would have been the first casualties of Iwo Jima if that shell had exploded on impact. Things like that made you glad that you performed your ceremony."[9] Shaking off the near miss, Begay and Manuelito settled into their station and began relaying naval gunfire requests for prelanding bombardments.

At 6:30 A.M. guns from the heavy support ships *Nevada*, *New York*, *Tennessee* and *Idaho* boomed into action to silence the Japanese emplacements that dominated the proposed LST lanes and beaches. This intense, overwhelming fire storm lasted until 8:05, when 72 fighter and bomber planes from Admiral Mitscher's Fast Carrier Force assaulted the eastern and northern slopes of Mount Suribachi and the designated landing beaches. These attacks were followed by 48 Marine Corsair F4Us, led by Lieutenant Colonel William A. Millington, which ravaged the same targets with napalm, rockets and machine gun fire.

At 8:30 the first wave crossed the line of departure and headed in a straight line for the shore, following gun boats that poured rockets and 40mm shells into the beaches. Commanders had allotted thirty minutes for each assault wave to travel the 4,000 yards, and naval gunfire was shifted 500 yards inland once the first LSTs neared the beaches.

By 9:05 the first troop-carrying waves hit the 3,500-yard strip of ugly beaches. The LSTs lowered their ramps, and marines from the 4th and 5th Divisions swarmed ashore. The minute they hit the beaches, the volcanic sand sucked them in ankle deep and reduced their run to a slow plodding trudge. Moving forward under protective cover of naval barrages, marines stumbled, staggered, and dragged themselves up the incline of the first terrace. Both divisions were reporting little or no enemy resistance, which led some commanders to entertain the idea that the softening barrages had been more effective than expected. They also thought that perhaps the estimates of enemy strength had been exaggerated and that this island might be more easily secured than had been first believed. This false sense of security lasted until 9:30.

Seven Kinds of Hell

Kuribayashi had monitored the forward progress of the marines, and when he guessed that more than 6,200 had landed, he sprang his trap. The beaches themselves were not heavily defended, but his gun emplacements on Suribachi and the northern plateau between the airfields were arranged to execute deadly fire on the unsuspecting marines. When they began to advance beyond the first terrace, intense machine gun, mortar and rocket firepower erupted from the concealed Japanese defenses.

The effect was like being on top of a volcano and having it erupt without warning. There was not one square yard of that terrace that was safe to move on. Marines were sent flying down the incline to escape the maelstrom being unleashed. The only error Kuribayashi made was allowing tanks, bulldozers and artillery pieces to land before he opened up. This equipment enabled the marines to eliminate the pillboxes and blockhouses that were responsible for pinning them down on the beaches.

Samuel Billison, Thomas Begay and Johnny Manuelito remembered how quickly and furiously the Navajo radio net reacted from shore to ship when Kuribayashi unleashed his attack.

Deliver to Green Beach 1: 500 rounds 81HE 56; 500 rounds 60HE; 5,000 rounds .30 caliber belted; 5,000 rounds .30 caliber clips.:

Estimated battalion casualties at present 50 killed and injured undetermined.

Receiving mortar fire.

We have lost four radiomen and one telephone man. Unable to estimate equipment damage as yet.

Need bulldozer on Green Beach immediately.

Receiving steady machine gun and rifle fire from 132B.

"On D-Day the marines went in, but I was kept on the ship to help coordinate naval gunfire," Billison said. "We were supposed to work in six-hour shifts with four hours off in between, but the first two days at Iwo there were no shifts. We were sending message after message for hours on end. Just about the time they told us to lay down or eat, they would come and get us to go back on the radios because more traffic was coming in. I thought that it was rougher duty being on the ship than being on shore. The third day we went in with the 5th Division on the third wave. Once we landed, I found out what rough really was."[10]

The effectiveness of the Navajo Code was described by Major Howard Conner, signal officer of the 5th Marine Division at Iwo Jima. "During the first 48 hours, while we were landing and consolidating our shore positions, I had six Navajo radio nets operating around the clock," he recalled. "In that period alone, they sent and received over 800 messages without an error."[11] If the first few days were any indication of how much the Navajo radio net was going to be used in the coming days, the Navajos were in for the talking of their lives.

Zigzag

The 6,200 marines pinned on the beaches were not the only ones facing the wrath of the Japanese weapons. The first assault waves had landed virtually untouched, but the following waves were under constant barrage before they could land. Part of the problem was that the Landing Vehicle Transports (LVTs) and LSTs followed a straight path from ships to shore, and this made them perfect targets from gun emplacements on Mount Suribachi and the northern plateau.

Paul Blatchford, Reconnaissance, 5th Marine Division, was slated to go in with the third wave when he made a lifesaving observation. "The first wave made it in with very few problems, but the second wave got all shot to pieces. I could hear our commander yelling, 'Where is that chief? Find him and tell him to come over here. I want to talk to him!'" Blatchford remembered. "I went over to him and he asked, 'Hey Chief, what are we doing wrong? We're getting the hell kicked out of us!' I said, "You're taking a straight beeline that makes it easy for the Japs to shoot you. They could shoot and hit you if they were blind; they don't even have to aim. That's what you are doing wrong, and it's a mistake. You need to make it harder for the Jap guns to hit those transports; zigzag a little, and they will make it to shore in one piece.

"The commander, 'Stormy' Davis, got on the microphone and told the cockswains to make a zigzag pattern to the landing beaches," Blatchford continued. "The cockswains told him they had orders to make a straight-line approach, and if that was to be changed, it would have to go through their commanders. Davis got on the radio to the flagship and got the orders changed and had it announced over the PA [public address] system that all cockswains taking the third wave would execute a zigzag pattern to the landing areas.

"We loaded onto our transport and took off, zigzagging all the way! Shells were hitting all around us, but not on us, and when we debarked, we heard men yelling from all the boats, 'We made it! We made it!' Yeah, we made it just in time to get pinned down like everybody else."[12]

Not all units remained pinned on their landing areas. Lieutenant Colonel Chandler W. Johnson, of the 2nd Battalion/28th Regiment, maneuvered his troops off the beach toward the target objective – the base of Mount Suribachi. They would cut across the narrow strip, wheel south and begin to eliminate Japanese positions cave by cave.

The 25th Regiment, led by Colonel John R. Lanigan, hit the beach, turned right, and headed toward the quarry, while the 23rd Regiment moved toward Motoyama 1, with the 27th lending rear-echelon support. The Japanese forces that lay in wait were Captain Osada's 800-troop 10th Independent Infantry Brigade and Major Matsushita's 10th Antitank Battalion located on the northern plateau just above Motoyama 1.

As the marines advanced, the enemy was forced to retreat north of Motoyama 1, and when the 27th followed, it ran smack into Major Tasumi's 311th Independent Infantry. By the time the fight was over, only 23 of the 800 Japanese defenders were alive to retreat to the northern plateau. As the day slowly faded into night, all units were ordered to report their positions and the number of wounded in action (WIA), killed in action (KIA) and missing in action (MIA). Then they were to dig in and relay the password for the coming night. The passwords that were chosen always contained L's and R's because the Japanese had extreme difficulty in pronouncing these two letters. Combat call signs were changed every day to provide security.

Digging in for the night became a real problem for many units because the loose volcanic terrain made it impossible to dig in very deeply or widely. Marines would scoop out the sand, only to have it cave in on them. The shifting sand was not the only problem they faced: Iwo Jima was laced with underground steam vents that produced intense heat.

"The first night on the island was very uncomfortable," John Kinsel remembered. "When you tried to dig your foxhole, the sand just poured back on top of you. The heat coming up through the ground was intense. You had to constantly shift your position to keep from getting seared by it. But the heat and shifting sand weren't the only problems we faced that first night: the Japs shelled the beaches all through the night, so sleep was impossible for any length of time."[13]

D-Day had been an uneven struggle, with the advantage of terrain and troop positions heavily in favor of the Japanese. D-Day advances had fallen far short of projected positions, and the landing beaches were cluttered with smashed equipment, wounded, and dead. However, communication posts had been established and were operational, and the loss of life was well below the five percent commanders had expected: 548 killed in action and 1,775 wounded. The next four days would test every man and piece of equipment currently on the beaches.

Day Two Through Day Five

Radio traffic between command ships and beach commanders started around 4:30 A.M. so that troop movements and air, artillery and naval gun strikes could be discussed and relayed. As the Navajos began sending and receiving, two curious events transpired. "While off the assault beaches at Iwo, I had Navajos, and other radio nets, operating just above the flag bridge," Lieutenant Colonel J. P. Berkeley recalled. "The closeness of the radios did cut into the ships radios from time to time. At one point Commodore McGovern caught a Navajo transmission on his TBS and thought the Japanese had broken into his circuit. He grabbed the microphone and yelled, 'You goddamn Jap, get the hell off this circuit!' Immediately a Navajo voice replied, 'I'm no goddamn Jap; I'm a Navajo. You shut up!' The astounded commodore backed away from the radio and left the bridge."[14]

Peter Sandoval, a code talker of the 4th Division, recounted another incident in another radio room, this one involving an admiral who had knowledge of the Navajo code talkers. "I was on a battleship talking to my partners on the beach when the messages started coming in pretty fast. I started writing messages and acknowledging them and there was a runner standing beside that would take it to the message center and then on to the Admiral.

"The messages were coming in really fast, I was tearing off one sheet after another handing them over my head to the runners. At this time, though I wasn't told until later, the admiral just happened to be standing right behind me. I tore off the next message sheet and said, 'Here take this to the old man.' Well it was the 'old man' that was standing behind me. He said, 'Well son, it's been quite a long while since I did this.' I didn't pay any attention to the comment because there was another message coming in that I had to receive and acknowledge. After I finished, the crew informed me that the Admiral had been standing behind me. I guess he wanted to see us in action and was amazed at the talking we were using on the radios. I heard that he was satisfied with our results, and not upset that I had referred to him as the 'old man.'"[15]

The second day's plan of operation consisted of two major objectives: capture the base of Suribachi, and clear the airfields in preparation for taking the reminder of the island. The job of securing Suribachi belonged to the 28th Regiment/5th Division. The airfields were assigned to the bulk of General Harry Schmidt's VAC.

Colonel Liversedge, the 5th Division commander, planned to move the 28th Regiment in position to attack the base of the mountain, surround it, secure it and search for suitable routes to the summit. The proposed timetable for this action was two days; it took nearly four days to accomplish this task. A grid map was used to pinpoint artillery and air strikes in the pre-attack bombardment support action before the 28th was due to jump off.

Bi-tsan-dehn: Ashih-hi Na-ha-tah-ba-hogan D-ah a-kha:
Moasi A-woh N-kih Tseebii Nilchi nay-dal-ghal bilh a-la-ih
nos-bas nos-bas ne-zhoni a-kha shi-da tsah be a-ye-shi a-la-
ih taa a-la-ih Ah-jah Dibeh tsa-na-dahl a-la-ih taa n-kih Ma-
e Ba-goshi tsa-na-dahl a-la-ih taa n-kih Tsah tsa-na-dahl a-
la-ih taa a-la-ih Tsin-tliti Moasi tsa-na-dahl a-la-ih taa n-kih
Yil-doi da-ahl-zhin Be-al-doh-cid-da hi ah-di a-la-ih taa a-
la-ih Tsah-as-zih Klesh.

From: Division Headquarters
To: CT 28
Air strikes with 100 pound bombs at 131E S, 132F C, 132N,
132M C, 132J. Mortars at 131Y S.

Regimental Combat Team (RCT) 28, with the 2nd Battalion
on its left and the 3rd Battalion on its right, jumped off at 8:30
A.M. following the air and mortar strikes. This advance was met
with the most horrific crossfire from Japanese positions in, around
and above the base of Suribachi. RCT 28 could only manage to
move 50 - 70 yards toward the base. Aircraft, ships and 37mm
guns fired round after round into the Japanese positions, but stiff
resistance continued.

"I don't even remember that day," Teddy Draper, a code talker
for RCT 28, stated. "I can remember what happened on February 19th, but the 20th is a total blank to me. The fire was so
intense, men were being killed all around me, and we were pinned
down and couldn't move. I kept wondering if I was going to live
through the day or be killed in my foxhole."[16]

Assault demolition teams using flame-throwers and explo-
sive charges were called in to support RCT 28's position. At 11:30
A.M. tanks moved forward from pillbox to pillbox to pave a path
for the 37mm guns and the 75mm half-tracks. When the attack
halted around 5:00 P.M., the forward position was 200 bloody yards
closer to the base of Suribachi.

While elements of RCT 28 were fighting to gain small foot-
holds near Suribachi, two assault battalions from the VAC were
encountering pillboxes and land mines as they advanced toward

Motoyama 1. Direct mortar and artillery barrages from the Japanese made support from the 5th Battalion necessary, and the marines were able to advance 800 yards toward the northwest edge of Motoyama 1 by the end of the day. They dug in for the night and waited for counter attacks, but these never developed. Naval illumination shells filled the skies over Iwo with an eerie light, while exhausted marines strained their eyes toward the south searching for hostile activities.

Progress for the first two days had been laborious, but the front lines were firmly established at the base of Suribachi and Motoyama 1. The morning of February 21 saw a forty-plane strike on targets within 100 yards of the front of RCT 28. Two hundred yards in front of the 4th and 5th Divisions' lines, 68 carrier planes delivered rockets and bombs in advance for the move toward the north end of the airfields. By that night, the regimental lines of RCT 28 extended 650 yards on the left, 500 yards in the center, and 1,000 yards on the right of the base of Suribachi. The 4th Division had advanced 500 yards toward the center of the island. The night was characterized by harassing counterattacks and enemy infiltration of both the 4th and 5th Divisions' positions. The beaches continued to receive mortar and artillery fire, which made sleep impossible except for very brief periods of time. Watches were set, passwords were relayed through the ranks, and the standard "Do not move after dark" order was issued.

During the first two days, Paul Blatchford was at a command post on the beach when the Navajo radio net became operational. "My job was to interpret the incoming and outgoing messages the Navajos were sending. My commander told me to get over there with the radios and interpret what was going on. They were talking about his company making a 100-yard advance, another company calling for ammunition, and so on. I was interpreting all of this. I had been assigned to the Navajo Communication School as a radio repair and Morse code instructor. I never attended the school to learn the code. I learned it at night from Wilson Price, Johnny Manuelito and Rex Kontz. I guess that I am the only one that understood Navajo better than I spoke it. My discharge papers state, 'Interpreter 642' because of the duties I performed on the beaches those first few days on Iwo Jima.

"While the Navajos were sending and receiving and I was interpreting," Blatchford continued, "runners would arrive from other communication posts with 'dummy' messages. I really felt sorry for those boys. By the time they arrived, I had already given the 'true' message to the commanders, and the runners were just waved off and told they already had what they needed from the Navajos. The runner looked really puzzled but gave them the message anyway and then went back the way he came. I saw one of the messages, and it didn't mean a thing! It was just a decoy to keep the Japanese off balance, and it worked."[17]

Merrill Sandoval, a code talker with General Rockey's 5th Division, recalled how he used the code on Iwo. "We would send reports of missing in action, wounded and killed in Navajo so the Japanese wouldn't know how many men we lost that particular day. I would relay that, via my brother Samuel Sandoval, to General Wheeler on the command ship. The Japanese would try to jam our radios all the time. They would shout, sing, or bang pots in order to disrupt our rhythm, but they never succeeded. Our messages went through because we knew each other's voices and the code so well that we could do it without any repeat or mistakes. On Iwo we were told that if we had a message, get it through the first time accurately, and then get off the radio. The familiarity with each other and the confidence we had in the code made it possible for us to do just that."[18]

By day four, the front lines were all tied in with one another, and communications posts were able to relay operational and artillery orders with relative ease. Combat efficiency, rated at about 68 percent, was the most serious problem facing Marine Corps commanders. Japanese defenders showed little signs of weakening, and the marines had little chance for rest and were eating mostly K and C rations. A cold drizzling rain did little to improve the morale, and progress would again be laborious. Generals Rockey and Cates decided to effect relief of some front-line units to provide impetus for the attack across the north tip of Motoyama 1.

Because of poor visibility in the heavy rain, plane support could not be launched, and by noon the advance had netted only 50-75 yards, with extremely high casualties. RCT 28 fared no better in its attempt to close the distance around the base of Suribachi. Demolition teams and flame throwers provided the only way to silence the enemy. Despite the weather and the enemy, RCT 28 managed to surround "HOTROCKS," a position just below the summit of Suribachi, by the end of February 23.

Cold, soaked to the skin and weary, marines dug in for the night and prepared to face another unrelenting mortar and artillery attack from the Japanese defenders. In places along the rocky aperture, marines could hear the sounds of Japanese talk and laughter filtering through the tunnels. This gave the marines the feeling that the enemy was just inches, not hundreds of feet, below their foxholes.

As the dark began to envelop Iwo, an order came down that would challenge the sanity of one white marine assigned to the 28th Regiment/H&S Company, 5th Division. "I remember one night, early in the campaign, a report that came in that some communication wires needed repairing. We were under orders not to move after dark, but the repairs were badly needed, and I was told to grab two other men to help me lay the wire," Henry Hisey Jr. recalled. "The Navajos were extremely dependable. They were the kind of guys you wanted in your foxhole, so I always tried to choose them when something had to be done. After the repair order came in, I got Teddy Draper and James Cohoe, both in my unit, to go with me.

"It was pitch black by the time we started out," Hisey continued. "I remember talking real loud as we walked, trying to use as many words with L's in them as possible. The Japs couldn't pronounce the L properly, and I figured that would alert the marines on either side of us that we were one of them. Well, things were going along just fine until Teddy and James started jabbering away in Navajo. I started hearing the click of safety latches come off weapons all around us. To Teddy and James, Navajo didn't sound anything like Japanese, but to anxious marines in their foxholes, it did! I yelled at them to keep quiet or we would all get shot for sure, but they just kept it up. Teddy said if he was going to die, he was going to die talking Navajo! Well, that was fine for Teddy and James, but I wasn't Navajo, and I wasn't ready to die! We made repairs and got back to our foxhole in one piece, but I'll never quite know how! Those two were my good friends, good marines, and their talking saved a lot of lives, so I guess I can forgive that one night."[19]

The objectives for day five were the securing of Suribachi and Motoyama 2. RCT 28 would follow the only path to the summit from the north face, while the 1st Battalion would take the attack south around the western side of the mountain. Motoyama 2 would be assaulted by the main body of the 4th Division, while the 5th Division lent fire support. The availability of aircraft support had been reduced the night before when Task Force 58 departed to continue strikes against Tokyo. The responsibility for providing close air support fell on the small carriers of Admiral Durgin's support force.

These vessels, already operating a full schedule, would cause delays in executing requests for air support, which impeded the progress of the 4th and 5th Divisions as they attempted to secure Motoyama 2. Nevertheless, the beaches were slowly being cleared of debris, and supplies containing badly needed 81mm shells and tanks were arriving from the cargo ships.

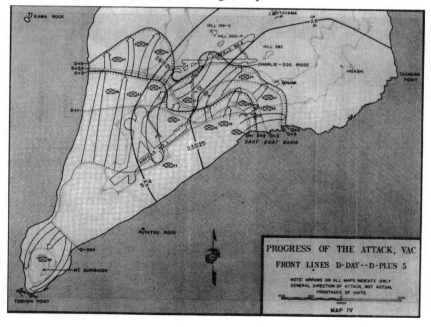

PROGRESS OF THE ATTACK, VAC

FRONT LINES D-DAY -- D-PLUS 5

NOTE ARROWS ON ALL MAPS INDICATE ONLY
GENERAL DIRECTION OF ATTACK, NOT ACTUAL
FRONTAGES OF UNITS

MAP IV

The flag is raised: *Schrier's E Company, left to right, Sgt. H.O. Hansen, Platoon Sgt. E.I. Thomas, 1st Lt. H.G. Schrier, Pfc. J.R. Michaels (holding the carbine), and Cpl. C.W. Lindberg. National Archives Photograph.*

Suribachi

The attack order for day five directed the 2nd Battalion/28th Regiment to secure and occupy the crest of Suribachi while Company E was directed by Lieutenant Colonel Chandler W. Johnson to "secure and occupy the summit."[5] First Lieutenant Harold G. Schrier, the executive officer of Company E, took his forty-man detachment and followed the forward three-man patrols heading up the north face of Suribachi. Since the number of Japanese defenders lurking inside the mountain was unknown, flankers were sent to guard against any ambush as Company E made its way upward.

As the platoon neared the summit, Schrier warned the troops to avoid any trail as it might be mined. They shortly found themselves on their hands and knees as the path became an almost vertical incline. As they inched toward the rim, they noted an eerie, disconcerting lack of enemy activity. When they spread out to encircle the rim, Schrier, uneasy with the intense silence, signaled the men to scoot over the edge, rise, and charge. A small defending force challenged the patrol, and a quick, hot fight developed but was quickly dispatched. A length of Japanese iron pipe was located, a small U.S. flag was lashed to one end, and at 10:20 A.M. the flag waved bravely from the summit.

Ashdla-ma-as-tso-si tse-nihl gah tkin nesh-chee dzeh Ashi-hi, Tkin Ts-a Ma-e A-Kha: Belasana Be Moasi. Bi-tsan-dehn ah-ja d-ah n-kih n-kih tseebii Dzeh Nakia, taa has-clish-nih Besh-legai-a-lah-ih Lin Klizzie dibeh moasi lin gah tkin ah-jah dah-nas-tsa klesh has-clish-nih gah wol-a-chee yeh-hes dibeh ah-nah be-No-da-ih Dibeh ma-e ah-jad tse-nihl klizzie do ye-zhe-al-tsisi-gi Klesh Ah-jah Bi-so-dih Bi-so-dih Tse-nihl neeznaa n-kih nos-bas.

To: 5th Marine Division, Info: ADC
From: LT 228 E Company, 3rd Platoon
1st Lieutenant H. G. Schrier's platoon raised U.S. flag and secured Mount Suribachi at 10:20.

"We were on the north slope of Motoyama 1, pinned down by Japanese machine gun fire, flat on our backs when we saw the flag go up on Suribachi," recalled Paul Blatchford. "All the white boys started yelling, 'Hey Chief, it's all over now!' I said, 'Not here!'"[20]

"I was close to 100 feet down on the north slope when Sergeant Ray told me to send a message that Suribachi had been secured and at what time and get it down to headquarters," Teddy Draper stated. "Then we received another message ordering us to regroup and resume the attack. I didn't see the flag go up, but I passed the message when it happened."[21]

Deep inside the tunnels at the bottom of Suribachi, Captain Samaji Inoye wept as he relayed a message to Kuribayashi that Suribachi had fallen. Suribachi, personally designed by Kuribayashi, fell in five days. What was left of Suribachi's defenders filtered through the interconnecting tunnels toward a spiny ridge located beyond Motoyama 2. Kuribayashi realized that with the fall of Suribachi, Iwo Jima would eventually become a U.S. possession. Resigning himself to this fate, he ordered his troops to make their last positions their graves and take as many Americans with them as possible.

Whereas the sight of the U.S. flag fluttering over the summit of Suribachi gave hope and heart to the weary marines, it enraged the Japanese. If the fighting had seemed fanatical up to that point, once the flag was raised, the combat became maniacal. Forbidden by Kuribayashi to execute banzai attacks, the Japanese defenders maximized the use of the interconnecting tunnels to pin down and slaughter marines.

Marine Corps command, on seeing the first flag raised on the summit, decided that a larger, more visible flag needed to be placed on top of Suribachi to keep hope and heart alive in the drive to secure the rest of the island. As Schrier's E Company returned down the same path it had ascended, RCT 28 made its way to the summit from the backside of Suribachi.

The second flag-raising, captured on film by photographer Joe Rosenthal, was witnessed by Teddy Draper. "I was about 100 feet away when I saw the men struggle with that long piece of pipe. I saw the lieutenant look around for an extra man to help,

CT28 celebrates the raising of the second, larger flag on Mt. Suribachi.
Code talker Teddy Draper Sr., shown as the 5th man from the left, sent the
message of this deed via the Navajo radio net to General Holland Smith's beach
command post. National Archives Photograph

then he yelled, 'Ira Hayes! Ira Hayes!' Then two more of the
guys jumped up to help them, and the big flag went up. It was a
sight to behold."[22]

The photograph of the second flag-raising was flashed around
the world with the proclamation that the marines were the finest
fighting force in the South Pacific. But none of the five men involved in that event considered themselves heroes. They were
simply good marines doing a job that had to be done. Marine
Corps Command asked Ira Hayes, a Pima Indian, to leave the
ongoing battle to tour the United States to promote the sale of
war bonds. The Marine Corps believed that Hayes exemplified
the courage, honor and tenacity of the marines currently fighting
on Iwo Jima. Hayes became an instant celebrity as a result of
Rosenthal's photograph, but he never felt comfortable when
people referred to him as a hero.

Wilsie Bitsie, who had become friends with Ira Hayes before
the war, recalled the many troubles Ira suffered due to that one

quirk of fate. "After we came back from the war," Bitsie remembered, "Ira and I used to talk about his troubles and his drinking. Ira told me, 'The maimed in the war just made me sick! Sometimes I wonder why it wasn't you in place of that third fellow that was right in front of me helping to raise the flag?' Me? Why? 'I just wish you had been there with me. Wilsie, if something happens to me, I told my mom you are going to get my flag.' Ira and I were great friends, and it hurts me when people call him a drunken Indian. They didn't understand what he experienced during and after the war. They still don't."[23]

Marine Corps commanders were very pleased with the securing of Mount Suribachi. For the first time in four bloody days of protracted fighting, the marines had finally gained an impressive advantage. During that afternoon, 2nd Battalion/28th Regiment continued mopping-up actions, sealing cave entrances and sniper positions.

This was a costly, brutal process which lasted until night came. "Every day we received replacements, and just about all of them ended up being either severely wounded or dead," Teddy Draper recalled. "There were a lot of new faces. I don't know where they all came from; all they do is get up and get killed. The lieutenant told me to try to look after the new guys while we were making our moves, and that is what I tried my best to do. Regroup, move out, and try to keep everybody alive, including myself.

"Once the mountain belonged to the marines," Draper continued, "it wasn't so dangerous for the men trapped on the beaches. The view from the top of Suribachi was spectacular. Once you looked over the island, it was easy to understand why the Japanese fought so hard not to lose it."[24]

Securing Suribachi gave the marine observer units an important place to establish flash-ranging equipment that would aid the fight to conquer the rest of the island. Murderous fire on the beachheads would cease, and marines and equipment would be able to move more freely. The securing of Suribachi proved to be a turning point in the battle to claim Iwo Jima. The cost to secure Suribachi consisted of 895 casualties, including four code talkers killed in action and one seriously wounded. Peter Johnson, Paul Kinlahcheeny, Sam Morgan and Willie Notah all died on day five; James Gleason, a code talker of the 2nd Battalion/27th Regiment/5th Division, lay wounded in his foxhole for two days before he was evacuated. Malissa Gleason, his widow, recalled what happened to him.

"Jimmie and Paul Kinlahcheeny were running messages when they got hit," Mrs. Gleason stated. "Machine gun fire caught both of them. Paul was hit right across the stomach, and Jimmie was shot in the left ankle. Paul's last words to Jimmie were, 'Tell my folks.' Jimmie crawled into a shell hole, and that was where he saw the flag being raised on the mountain. He was trapped in the middle of crossfire, and no one could get to him for two days.

"The *Gallup Independent* newspaper reported that Jimmie had been killed in action," Mrs. Gleason continued. "I saw the article and cut it out, but I never believed he was dead. Sure enough, about two weeks later I was notified that he was alive but seriously wounded. The bone in his left ankle had been shattered. About six months after the war was over they had to amputate his leg just below the knee.

"Jimmie liked being a marine," Mrs. Gleason stated. "Even after he had been wounded, he said that if they ever needed him again, he would go back. He liked using his language, and he liked his commanding officer, General Rockey. Jimmie was very proud to serve his country."[25]

Notes

1. Interview with Al Mertz, June 1991.
2. Lieutenant Colonel Whitman S. Bartley, USMC, Iwo Jima Amphibious Epic, The Battery Press, Inc., Nashville, Tennessee, 1954, p. 3.
3. Ibid. p. 12.
4. TF 56 Report of Planning, Operations, Iwo Jima Operation, 27Mar45 Encl A, 65A-445 Loc 09/30/05/7 A9-30, Marine Corps Historical Center.
5. Correspondence from J.P. Berkeley.
6. Interview with Samuel Billison, May 1993.
7. Interview with Al Mertz.
8. Interview with John Kinsel.
9. Interview with Thomas Begay, November 1992.
10. Interview with Samuel Billison.
11. Bartlett, Tom, *Leatherneck*, June 1980, p. 39.
12. Interview with Paul Blatchford.
13. Interview with John Kinsel.
14. Correspondence from Lieutenant General J.P. Berkeley USMC (Retired), March 1993.
15. Interview 1228, Doris Duke Collection.
16. Conversation with Teddy Draper Sr., March 1994.
17. Interview with Paul Blatchford.
18. Interview with Merril Sandoval, October 1991.
19. Conversation with Henry Hisey Jr., July 1993.
20. Interview with Paul Blatchford.
21. Interview 1163, Doris Duke Collection.
22. Ibid.
23. Interview with Wilsie Bitsie.
24. Interview 1163, Doris Duke Collection.
25. Interview with Malissa Gleason, August 1992.

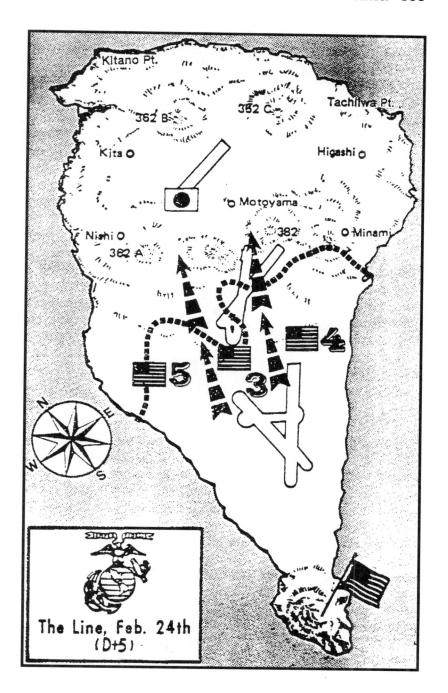

Kitano Pt.

362 B

362 C

Tachiiwa Pt.

Kita

Higashi

Motoyama

Nishi

362

Minami

362 A

5

4

3

N
E
W
S

The Line, Feb. 24th
(D+5)

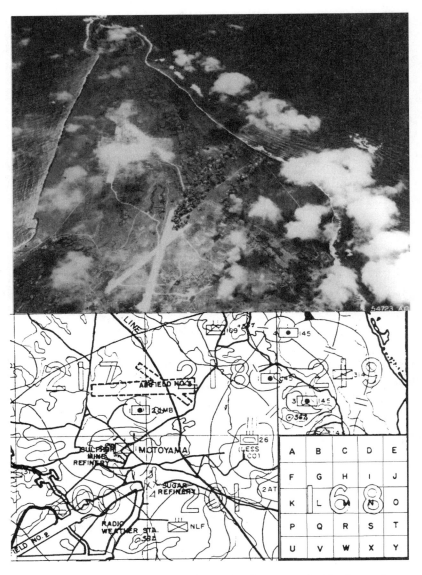

Motoyama 1 and Motoyama 2 airfields: *the white x's on the island were the primary reasons why the Americans needed Iwo Jima under their control. This island and its airfields would play a role in the final demise of the Empire of the Rising Sun. Photograph from the Air and Space Museum, Smithsonian Institution.* ***Motoyama area grid map*** *(below). Inset grid 168 shows letter designations.*

Fight for Motoyama Air Fields

Day Six Through Day Eleven

Motoyama 2 became the primary target for the 4th and 5th Divisions. On day six, the USS *Idaho* and *Pensacola* would hurl 14-inch battery salvos at grid map locations 200N and 200S, while howitzers and planes would carry rockets and bombs in preparation for the assault on Motoyama 2. The 5th Tank Battalion would proceed along the western taxiway to pave the way for ground troops. Company A, 5th Tank Battalion, leading the way along the western approach, encountered land mines and heavy anti-tank fire. Its advance was effectively blocked, and the western approach was abandoned. All tanks were directed to use the eastern approach, but it was also mined, and clearing a path took most of the morning.

"Charlie-Dog Ridge," named for the alphabet designations of the grid map in which it was located, ran along the southeast edge of Motoyama 2. On a lower level, to the southwest, was a semicircular rise of ground called the "Amphitheater," which contained some of the most formidable Japanese defenses on the island.

During the morning of day six, RCT 24/4th Division had made excellent progress toward the east end of the east-west runway on Motoyama 2 when heavy machine gun, rifle and antitank fire erupted from Charlie-Dog Ridge. The close proximity of RCT 24's front lines made air strikes too dangerous to consider, so the battalions turned to the 14th Marines for artillery support.

Bi-tsan-dehn: Tla-gin D-ah n-kih dii. Ah-woh a-kah: A-la-ih dii Be-al-doh-tso-lani Jo-Kayed-goh tseebii a-la-ih do hastaa nos-bas na-as-tso-si-a-ye-do-tish be-al-doh-cid-da-hi besh-ba-wa-chind ah-di n-kih nos-bas nos-bas Cha do-n-kih nos-bas nosbas A-chi.

To: CT 24
From: 14th Artillery
Request 81 and 60 millimeter mortar barrage at 200H and 200I.

Working under this type of cover fire, the marines were able to place four machine guns in position and advance nearly 300 yards by the end of the day. The enemy gunfire, coming from well-concealed emplacements and tunnels, allowed the marines only fleeting glimpses of the enemy. "We saw no dead Japanese," First Sergeant Herman J. Dupont reported. "As the Japanese fell, their fellow men would drag their bodies into the caves. It appeared that we were fighting ghosts."[1]

Significant progress had been made. Behind the front lines, command posts, artillery positions, medical aid stations and supply dumps were well established. This allowed General Schmidt to close his headquarters aboard the USS *Auburn* and assume command ashore. Operational orders stated, "When ordered to consolidate for the night, limited objective attacks may be made to improve position for the night. Ground once gained will not be voluntarily given up, except on 5th Division order."[2]

On day seven the 3rd Division assumed the task of clearing the central portion of Motoyama Plateau, while the 5th Division would carve a path toward Hill 362A. The 4th Division would assume the attack toward Hill 382, the Amphitheater, Turkey Knob and the destroyed village of Minami. This area would later be referred to as the "Meat Grinder."

The push forward by the 3rd Division would give three advantages to the marines: (1) they could drive laterally down to the coast; (2) they could use the routes in the interior for supply lines; and (3) this action would deny the enemy any position from which to fire on the beaches. It was emphasized that no division should advance too far ahead of the others. The additional task of providing troops for flank support would be hampered if this happened, and the division that advanced too far would also be under enemy fire from all directions.

Advances were measured in feet, not yards, for the next two days as the divisions inched their way toward the far end of Motoyama 2, the base of Hill 362A and Hill 382. The 26th Battalion/4th Division had captured the last two freshwater wells the Japanese had constructed, but many Japanese fought for weeks on Saipan with virtually no water. The loss of the freshwater wells was a minor setback for the Japanese; that they were inflicting major casualties on the marines gave them a moral boost to which a drink of water could not compare. By the end of day eleven, the Japanese still held three-fifths of Iwo Jima.

Harold Foster, a code talker of I Company/3rd Battalion/27th Regiment/5th Division, remembered how he used the code during the fight for control of Hill 362A. "Messages were coming in that enemy resistance on Hill 362A was intense. I was told to order one of the jeeps that had rocket launchers on it to move to a certain position, give the coordinates and the time they were to fire. Up on that hill was a big cave. I Company was up first, A Company was on our right flank, and B Company was the rear echelon. After they lifted the artillery, I was told to call in flamethrowers to help seal the entrances to that big cave. The next day we became the reserve for the 28th Regiment."

By the end of day eleven, the 5th Division held a 1,000-yard front along the crest of a ridge that ran east to west of Hill 362A. The 4th Division held Motoyama 2 and the commanding terrain to the north. The 3rd Division had carried its front lines 500 yards forward to within 600 yards of Motoyama 3.

Marine Corps commanders were debating which units out of the three divisions needed a break the most. The problem was that most of the marines were exhausted, hungry and desperately tired. A rotation system was set in place that allowed each company one day in reserve status every four days. The system did not always work, but there were periods of time when marines had a few hours to read a letter from home or write one, catch a little sleep, clean their weapons and spend a few precious moments not being shot at.

"One of the guys in my unit came over to my foxhole and

asked me if I had a cousin or uncle because he was on the radio asking for me," Bill Toledo remembered. "Frank Toledo was my uncle, I told him, and he said to get over to him and find out what he needed. Our position, the 3rd Division, was on the east side of the airfields, and Frank, with the 5th, was on the other side near the beaches. I made my way over to Frank's foxhole and he fixed me a cup of coffee. Actually, they were heat tablets, and we just started catching up on news from home, telling stories about what we had seen. He knew Ira Hayes, and he told me about what happened the day the flag was raised. We spent about thirty minutes visiting each other; then I went back to my unit. I don't know how he found out where I was, but it was a nice break and good to know that he was all right."[4]

"Milton Gishal and I were right next to the airfield when we smelled cooking," recalled Thomas Begay. "Fresh food, you could smell it anywhere! You could smell the death, too. Milton and I made up an excuse that our radio battery had run down and we needed to go back to headquarters for a new one. We took off, and just about 100 yards away a signal company had hot chow cooking. I grabbed my mess kit and joined the line. For days all we had were C rations, so we jumped at the chance for hot, fresh food."[5]

"We hadn't eaten anything but canned food for five days when suddenly I remembered my stash," John Kinsel said. "My stomach was growling so loud I thought it would give my position away to the Japanese! That's when I remembered I had a steak sandwich in my combat pack. I pulled it out, unwrapped it, and started munching away. All the guys around me could smell it and started yelling, 'Hey, give me some!' I said to heck with you guys; it was really good, and I wasn't going to share! It was the best steak sandwich I ever had! I can still remember how good it tasted!"[6]

The simple pleasures of a hot meal, a visit with a friend, and a five-day-old steak sandwich were just what these men needed. The first eleven days on Iwo had been filled with chaos, death, destruction, sleepless nights and endless hours spent on the radio. Some of the code talkers had experienced mortar attacks, machine gun fire and hand-to-hand combat situations that made them eternally grateful for the combat training they had received during boot camp. Because they were so closely allied to commanders, they also knew that the fight to completely secure Iwo had just begun. The campaign to take the rest of Iwo would require every marine to conduct himself above and beyond the call of duty.

Day Twelve Through Day Fifteen

The 3rd Division's primary target became Hill 362B, with the 5th Division serving as support along the boundary to the north and east of 362A. The 4th Division resumed its attack on Hill 382 and seized the high ground north of Turkey Knob. Turkey Knob contained a large blockhouse that served as a Japanese communications center, and it became imperative to neutralize this site so that marines could advance and lend support for the attack on Hill 382.

The approach to the plateau and Hill 362B was flat and offered little cover for the advancing troops. From the battalion commander's observation post, an area was spotted slightly forward of the front lines where tanks could be used to provide cover. As the infantry resumed its forward advance, it encountered intense small arms fire as it neared a piece of high ground in front of Hill 362B.

The 5th Division's first objective was an assault on the north side of Hill 362A: Nishi Ridge. The ridge ran west from the plateau directly across the front lines and almost to the water's edge. Caves honeycombed the north face of Hill 362A, which dictated that all infantry arms be used to the fullest extent. Bulldozers were called in to clear a path through the long antitank ditch that ran north from Hill 362A. This allowed tanks to travel 200 yards toward the base of the hill and shatter enemy gun emplacements.

The 4th Division began its forward advance toward the high ground overlooking the village of Minami. The marines held a north-south line that passed through the center of Hill 382 on the west side. Artillery and naval gunfire paved the way for the advances, but stiff opposition required the use of hand grenades,

60mm mortars, flame throwers, and bazookas to protect their precarious positions. The marines were being battered from all sides, and a smoke screen was called in to cover the withdrawal and evacuation of casualties. For all three divisions, it had been eight days of minimal advances laced with a crippling depletion of personnel.

By day thirteen, the 3rd Division had seized most of the high ground northeast of Motoyama 3 and was advancing toward the next target objective: Hill 357. While the 5th Division shored up the attack, the 3rd Battalion/9th Regiment remained in position as a division reserve between Motoyama 2 and Motoyama Village. They would spend the next three days reorganizing and resting in preparation for the next target: Hill 362C.

The 5th Division resumed its attack from the north position along the Nishi Ridge and relieved the 3rd Division units near Hill 362B. Casualties mounted fast as the troops drove through the rugged mazes where fierce hand-to-hand struggles raged, but by the end of the day the marines had managed to advance 200 yards northeast of Hill 362B. This had been dangerous ground for the marines, and it almost became fatal for one code talker.

"A corporal from A Company brought a message to lay wire to make a connection between two companies," Teddy Draper recalled. "The terrain was full of canyons that all looked alike, and if you weren't careful, you could get lost. I knew where we were: the Turkey Knob was to my left, the Meat Grinder was behind us, and the 4th Division was to our left. I took a little spool of wire on my hip and prepared to move out. One of the lieutenants, a new guy, decided that he wanted to come along, so we headed towards A Company.

"We got down and started to crawl," Draper continued, "and pretty soon I knew that we had gone too far to the left. I spotted a marine with a BAR [Browning Automatic Rifle], and that meant we were in no-man's-land, so we turned forward about 75 yards and almost ran smack into a Jap position. Then, just to the right, I noticed some amphibious tracks, and we followed them to A Company, connected the wires, and went back the same way we came. When we got back, a message came in saying, 'There is a Jap in marine clothes on the other side of the ridge.' Okay, who was just there? Me. I was the Jap in marine clothes! Boy that really killed me! The lieutenant explained what had happened, and I never saw him again after that. I don't know if he got killed or went to another company. Iwo was a bad place."[7]

Several code talkers were mistaken for Japanese, and one, Wilson Price, was almost shot by fellow marines. On Iwo, as on other islands, having any resemblance to the enemy was dangerous for the Navajos. As puzzling as it might have been for the Navajos to be compared to the Japanese, they never expressed a sense of outrage when they were mistaken for the enemy. Privately most of them simply chalked it up to white men's ignorance of Native Americans in general.

The bloody assault to the crest of Hill 362B continued with the aid of code talkers relaying vital information between units.

Than-zie a-kha: Hash-kay-gi-na-tah
Bi-tsan-dehn: Ah-jad D-ah taa n-kih tsotsid Tabaha.
Dibeh ah-jah a-chin be ah-deel-tahi deh-nah-as tso-si d-ah tlo-chin klesh dzeh tse-nihl ah-jad ta-atah tsa-ond naz-pas-tkin-tsah-jeha gah-ghil-keid-klesh do lin-daa-tsaa hastaa n-kih Shush.

To: Commanding Officer
From: LT 327 Regiment
Send demolition team to seal all caves and surrounding ridges and Hill 362B.

D-ah a-woh: Ashdla Be-al-doh-tso-lani.
Bi-tsan-dehn: Ah-jad D-ah taa n-kih tsotsid Tabaha.
Jo-kayed-goh be-al-doh-tso-lani besh-be-wa-chind n-kih a-la-ih tseebii Shush ah-di Jad-ho-loni us-dzoh taa ashdla D-ah a-kha shi-da gah d-ah tlo-chin ba-ah-hot-gli cha-gee al-tah-je-jay ne-ahs-jah tsah lin-daa-tsaa taa hastaa n-kih Shush.

To: 5th Artillery Battalion
From: LT 327 Regiment
Request artillery barrage 218B at K minus (-) 35 to K hour to support the attack on Hill 362B.[8]

The 5th Division's front lines by the end of the day were about 200 yards north of Nishi, with gains as much as 600 yards in some sectors and as little as 125 in others. The night was marked by sporadic mortar fire and minor attempts at infiltration. The patter of combat from day 13 to day 15 differed little: the enemy defended its position to the death while exacting heavy losses for every yard the marines gained.

Physically, emotionally, mentally and spiritually exhausted marines fought on despite the pressure of being engaged in attack after attack. The only cause for optimism was that the formidable main cross island defense belt of the Japanese had been penetrated and in some places broken. With the loss of the high ground, Japanese artillery operations were confined to small areas of firing.

Day Sixteen Through Day Twenty

All three divisions resumed their offensives on March 6 in an all-out effort to breach the final Japanese defensive lines around and on Hill 362C, advance north toward Kita, and then move east toward Higashi. These actions would push the remaining Japanese defenders toward the north end of the island near Kitano Point.

General Erskine, of the 3rd Division, felt that the old pattern of assault on 362C had thus far proved ineffective and decided that a surprise was in order. Marine tactics in the South Pacific campaigns had not included night attacks except for patrol purposes. The chance of a predawn assault being a complete surprise was good. It was so ordered. No messages concerning the night attack were transmitted over radio nets to preclude possible decoding by the enemy. Troops were cautioned to maintain absolute silence until they were detected by the enemy.

Surprise was complete! The marines quietly moved forward without detection and managed to kill many Japanese sleeping in their pillboxes and caves before the alarm was sounded. Hill 362C was taken around 2:00 A.M. along with Hill 357. The predawn attack had succeeded where days of daylight fighting had failed.

Although heavy casualties were inflicted, the marines had taken a 200-yard bite out of a stubborn core of Japanese resistance that had held them in check for six days.

The 3rd and 5th Divisions' progress was not quite matched by the 4th's because resistance along the southern edge of the Amphitheater/Turkey Knob area was considerable. The 4th spent most of the day reorganizing, strengthening defenses, re-equipping and resting. Sporadic enemy fire and infiltration lasted through the night, and frequent exchange of rifle fire and grenades occurred. It would continue this way for the duration of the 4th's push toward the East Boat Basin.

When the final phase of the campaign to secure Iwo began, the marines were in control of nearly four-fifths of the island. It was a precarious four-fifths because the Japanese remained underground, undetectable and capable of inflicting heavy casualties. When a hot spot was overrun, the marines found few of the dead and few, if any, weapons. Nevertheless, the marine advances created disruption, dispossession and disorganization among the Japanese defenders, which made the final phase easier to carry out.

Notes

1. First Lieutenant Herman J. Dupont, Camden Blue Team log, provided by Harold Foster.
2. CT-28 Journal, provided by Albert Hemingway.
3. Interview with Harold Foster.
4. Interview with Bill Toledo.
5. Interview with Thomas Begay.
6. Interview with John Kinsel.
7. Interview #1163, Doris Duke Collection.
8. CT-28 Journal.

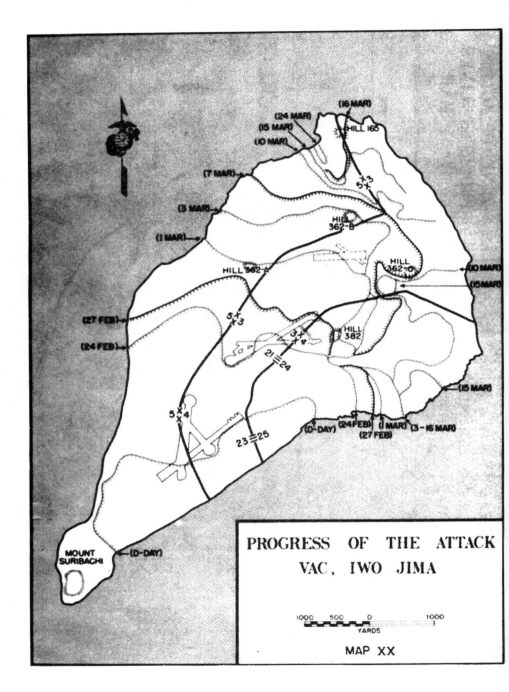

(16 MAR)

(24 MAR)
(15 MAR)
(10 MAR)
HILL 165

(7 MAR)

5×3

(3 MAR)

HILL
362-B

(1 MAR)

HILL
362-C
(10 MAR)
HILL 382-A

(15 MAR)

(27 FEB)

5×3

(24 FEB)

HILL
382

3×9

21≡24

(15 MAR)

5×4

(D-DAY)
(24 FEB) (1 MAR) (3 - 16 MAR)
(27 FEB)

23≡25

MOUNT
SURIBACHI
(D-DAY)

PROGRESS OF THE ATTACK

VAC, IWO JIMA

1000   500   0   1000
YARDS

MAP XX

Last Days

Day Twenty-one Through Day Twenty-six

Bah-has-tkih: Ye-nahl-nish Be-eh-ho-zini Ka-yah-bi-na-has-dzoh bi-tah-kiz Tabaha da-ahl-zhin-bi-tsa-na-dahl Gah Yil-doi tkin a-chin n-kih taa ashdla Klizzie-yazzie d-ah tlo-chin Ah-losz Tkele-cho-gi yeh-hes a-chin n-kih taa ashdla Ah-tad uhl-ne-ih d-ah ne-ahs-jah n-kih taa ashdla Shush Tsa uhl-ne-ih a-woh n-kih ashdla a-la-ih Ah-nah uhl-ne-ih a-woh a-kah n-kih ashdla a-la-ih Ah-jad uhl-ne-ih.

To: All units
From: Headquarters
Secret: Operational Orders
Boundary between regiments: RJ in 235K to RJ in 235G center to 235B N center to 251Q E center to 241L center.

While the 5th was beginning its forward push toward Kitano Point, the 3rd and 4th were slugging their way toward a section southwest of Hill 362C called "Cushman's Pocket," named after Lieutenant Robert E. Cushman. This territory consisted of deep crevices and sharp ridges that created a maze of cross-compartments; these provided excellent cover and concealment for the Japanese defenders.

Three battalions – 1st Battalion/9th Regiment, 2nd Battalion/9th Regiment and 3rd Battalion/21st Regiment – would attack simultaneously in an effort to sweep the enemy from this area, but it would take them nearly four days to accomplish this task. As in all actions against the Japanese, troops using flamethrowers, bazookas, grenades and demolition satchels made the defeat of these deeply entrenched and determined defenders possible. Frequent attempts to persuade the Japanese to surrender resulted in heavy return fire.

By the end of day 21, advances for all three divisions had been minimal, casualties had been heavy, and no shortages of weapons, troops or ammunition among the estimated 1,000 Japanese defenders had been found. The fighting along the division's front repeated the same pattern for the next three days until flame-throwing tanks could move forward to lend the support needed. It seems that flames were the only weapon that would drive the Japanese from their caves and rocky apertures, and it was used without hesitation.

"Towards the end of the battle, around the thirty-second day of the campaign, the army brought in tanks and barrels of gasoline and napalm," Paul Blatchford stated. "They would drag the barrels up those hills, punch a hole in it, and let it roll and bounce down, then set the trail on fire. Everything caught on fire, and the smell was something I can't describe! No matter how much fresh air you breathe after that you can never erase that smell from your memory."[1]

In a letter home Henry Hisey Jr. wrote of what he had witnessed on Iwo Jima. "Don't suppose anyone gets used to eating when they have corpses lying around in hot sunny weather and seeing big green flies on their C and K rations. There is not a lot I can tell you about how terrible it has been. I am one of the few that is able to write home, now. Bernice, it is about over now and I hope to be leaving here very soon. Could really handle a Pepsi Cola now. Am planning on putting a lot of time in the Virginia mountains and on the river when I get home."[2]

The gasoline/napalm tactics worked well, and they dislodged the last of the Japanese defenders from Kitano Point. The scorched, battered terrain was littered with broken weapons, dud bombs and Japanese who preferred death to surrender. Armored bulldozers tore paths through the rocky terrain that allowed flame-throwing tanks access as the marines inched their way forward. By the end of day twenty-six, the remaining Japanese defenders had been squeezed into the western tip of Kitano Point and a deep ravine to the southwest. For all intents and purposes, Iwo Jima had been conquered.

However, there were still some disturbing surprises left for the marines around Kitano Point. Harold Foster, a code talker for the 27th Regiment, recalled a particular cache discovered in a large cave. "When our unit reached Kitano Point and the area had been secured, demolition teams began cleaning and sealing caves. It was dangerous work because many of the caves were booby-trapped and the demolition men had to be very careful about what they touched. I was watching them when suddenly they began bringing out cases of canned goods. I didn't pay much attention to the cans at first, but then I heard the guys swearing out loud about those cans. I got curious and went over to where they had the cases stacked. I stopped dead in my tracks.

"I couldn't believe what I was seeing," Foster continued. "Box after box held canned whole tomatoes, fruit cocktail, pears, peaches, and evaporated milk, all with the American labels still on them! These cans could have only come from the food drive effort after the earthquake that Japan suffered through before the war. I stood there remembering how hard we had worked to raise money to donate towards buying canned goods for the people of Japan during that disaster. To see what we had sent to the people of Japan hidden away in caves on Iwo Jima was sickening. To think that the Japanese military took food from their own people's mouths shocked me; then it made me mad! I have never forgotten seeing those canned goods on Iwo Jima, and I never will."[3]

Secured

Than-zie tlo-chin: Ashdla Chal Din-neh-ih.
Bi-tsan-dehn: Hash-kay-gi-na-tah taa n-kih tsostsid Tabaha.
Ah-di a-la-ih tseebii nos-bas-nos-bas Shi-da Klesh ma-e ah-jad be-la-sana ah-tad gah tse-nill tkin dibeh ah-jah be a-kha tsah lin-daa tsaa a-la-ih hastaa ashdla. Tkin gloe-ih a-kha yil-doi a-chi be-tas-tni tse-nill ye-dshe-al-tsisi-gi. Ba-ha-this.

To: VAC (5th Amphibious Corps)
From: CO 327th Regiment
At 1800 U.S. flag raised on Hill 165. Iwo Jima secure. Over.[4]

March 16, 1945, 26 days and nine hours after the first marines had landed on the beaches of Iwo Jima, the island was declared secured. This was a technical security because there was a
500-man pocket of Japanese defenders located near the western
tip of Kitano Point that had to be dealt with. It would take another eight days to put an end to all Japanese resistance.

As soon as marine units could be relieved, they commenced
embarkation. The 4th Division departed for Maui on March 14;
the 5th began on March 18 and concluded on the 27th. The 3rd
Division assumed patrol and defense responsibilities until March
20 when the 147th Infantry arrived from New Caledonia to lend
support. On March 26, 1945 Iwo Jima was declared completely
secure. General Schmidt closed his command post, left Iwo by
air and joined the VAC Headquarters on the USS *President Mon-
roe*. The 3rd Division began embarking on March 27 after the
army's 147th assumed full responsibility for the defense of Iwo.

The importance of gaining control of Iwo Jima had been
impressed on marines long before any of them stepped foot on
the island. Operation Detachment was planned and executed in
accordance with the necessity of an air war against Japan. The
first emergency landing by a B-29 Superfortress, occurring on
day fourteen (March 4), proved that the strategic location of Iwo
Jima was worth the savage struggle. An excerpt from a wartime
publication of the Army Air Force described what Iwo Jima meant
to the pilots and crews making the long, dangerous bombing raids
on Japan:

> Located about midway between Guam and Japan, Iwo broke
> the long stretch, both going and coming. If you had engine
> trouble, you held out for Iwo. If you were shot up over Japan
> and had wounded aboard, you held out for Iwo. If the weather
> was too rough, you held out for Iwo. Formations assembled
> over Iwo, and gassed up at Iwo for extra-long missions. If
> you needed fighter escort, it usually came from Iwo. If you

had to ditch or bail out, you knew that air-sea rescue units were sent from Iwo. Even if you never used Iwo as an emergency base, it was a psychological benefit. It was there to fall back on.[5]

The 6,821 marines, sailors and soldiers who lost their lives did not do so in vain. The taking of Iwo Jima was crucial to bringing an end to the war with Japan. While the loss of life and wounded seemed a heavy price to pay for airfields, the Japanese losses were catastrophic. Out of the 22,000 Japanese soldiers and conscripted Korean laborers, only 1,083 surrendered or were captured. Kuribayashi's remains were never found, and his death, along with the loss of Iwo Jima, dealt a serious blow to the Japanese Ministry of Defense.

A battle is won or lost, not through one singular achievement of either men or machines, but through a concentrated effort of troops, equipment, coordination, communication and desire. Marine and navy personnel that participated in Operation Detachment reflected the highest levels of courage, determination, fortitude and honor. Admiral Chester W. Nimitz said it best when he remarked, "Among the Americans who served on Iwo Island uncommon valor was a common virtue."[6]

Post Observation Reports

Postaction reports on Operation Detachment unconditionally endorsed the continued use of Navajo code talkers and recommended that a minimum of 78 be assigned to each division.

Navajo Indian talkers were used extensively in the transmission of secret messages by voice radio. With the corps and division headquarters afloat for the first several days, this was the only available means for sending highly classified traffic over the air. Their complicated Navajo language was completely unintelligible to anyone not of the same tribe and security was assured.[7]

Signal Company, *Headquarters and Service Company, Radio Platoon, 5th Marine Dvision, Hawaii. Major Howard Conner (back row, 2nd from the right) commanded this platoon during some of the most intense fighting on Iwo Jima. His signal personnel included the following code talkers: Pfc Freeland Nez (3rd row, 5th from the left), Merril Sandoval (3rd row, 8th from the right), Thomas Begay (3rd row, 6th from the right), Sgt. Johnny R. Manuelito (3rd row, 5th from the right), Wilson Price (2nd row, 1st on the right). Photograph provided by Bert Clayton, first man on the right above the 2nd row.*

The "Iwo Jima Observer's Report on Communication Phases," prepared by Colonel H. G. Newhart, gave a detailed endorsement of the Navajo code talkers:

c. <u>Security</u>. A great deal of security has to be sacrificed in an amphibious operation. Practically no crypto-aids were employed for tactical messages other than the shackle code for numerals and use of voice call signs to denote organizations. Navajo Indians were employed for transmission of important classified traffic.

Ship shore traffic presented the most difficult problem in maintaining security. The only secure means of delivering classified traffic on these circuits within a reasonable time was via Navajo Talker. Navajos were of great value for ship-shore traffic and their assignment to Corps Headquarters should be continued.

d. <u>Navajo Indians</u>. Navajo Indians continued to be of great value in the operation. Organizations have commented most favorably upon the success of their employment as code talkers in previous operations. In this operation Navajos were utilized in Corps Headquarters for the first time for employment as code talkers between Corps Headquarters and Division Headquarters, as well as between echelons within Corps Headquarters.[8]

The success of the Navajo radio net assured Marine Corps commanders that the code could be used during a campaign.

Back at training areas on Hawaii, Navajo code talkers were assigned to retraining sessions to sharpen their skills, and practice transmitting the code for the impending campaign on Okinawa and the possible invasion of Japan.

Notes

1. Interview with Paul Blatchford.
2. Correspondence from Henry Hisey Jr., March 1994.
3. Interview with Harold Foster.
4. Ibid.
5. Iwo Jima Amphibious Epic, p. 210.
6. Ibid. p. III
7. 65A-4456 Loc 09/30-05-7 Box 17 A9-30.
8. Ibid.

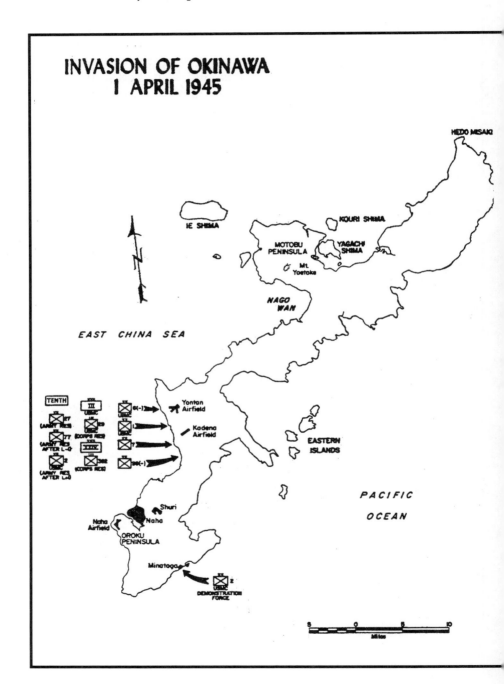

Okinawa

Return to Hawaii

The return to Hawaii from Iwo Jima was fairly uneventful. A majority of the marines slept for hours on end, making up for all the sleepless nights spent on Iwo. They had time to write letters home, but they kept talk to a minimum. The aftermath of what they had experienced on Iwo was too fresh in their minds; the loss of friends too painful to recall. For the duration of this voyage, there would be no regaling of deeds done or boasting of numbers of enemy dispatched to the great beyond. The subdued atmosphere was made even more somber when an announcement over the PA system declared that President Franklin D. Roosevelt had died.

"Along about April 12 we heard over the radio that Roosevelt had died," Samuel Billison remembered. "It was really sad. You could hear a pin drop."[1] "He was a fine man," Kee Etsicitty said. "We didn't even know who Truman was, and it made me a little uneasy that our president had died before the war was over. It was a sad trip back to Hawaii."[2]

Debarking in Hawaii and reporting to training areas, the men heard the next target was mainland Japan. "When we got back to the big island, we were told that on November 7th we would invade Japan," Samuel Billison recalled. "They gave us maps of Japan proper and the shoreline was all pillboxes, just like Iwo. It had been reconnoitered, and we were going back to the big island to regroup, retrain and then invade Japan. Realizing how small Iwo Jima was and how big Japan was, we looked forward to a bigger battle and a longer engagement with the enemy."[3] As

OKINAWA

ururururu   Edge of coral reef
●   Japanese strong point
Scale in yards
1000   0   1000

Zampa Misaki (Point Bolo)

Green 1
Green 2

6 Marines

Red 1
Red 2
Red 3
Blue 1
Blue 2

1 Marines

Yellow 1
Yellow 2
Yellow 3

Purple 1
Purple 2
Orange 1
Orange 2

7

White 1
White 2
white 3
Brown 1
Brown 2
Brown 3
Brown 4

96

Yontan Airfield

III Amphibious Corps
Bishi River
Corps Boundary

XXIV Army Corps

Kadena Airfield

the 3rd, 4th and 5th Divisions continued training for the possible invasion of Japan, the 1st, 2nd and 6th Divisions were enroute to their target campaign against Okinawa.

Operation Iceberg

Okinawa was not just another island in the push eastward; it was a primary objective within concurrent drives by Admiral Nimitz from the Central Pacific and General MacArthur from the Philippines. Okinawa, 325 nautical miles south of Japan, is one of the largest of the Ryukyu Islands. Seventy miles long and eighteen miles wide, Okinawa is heavily wooded with mountainous terrain in the north and rolling farmlands in the south. Japan has always considered Okinawa a part of Japan proper, and the island, whose name means "Shrine," is used as a spiritual/vacation retreat.

The Japanese Imperial General Staff intended to protect Okinawa with all the available forces, including the kamikaze or "divine wind." Okinawa, commanded by General Mitsuri Ushijima, was garrisoned by the 32nd Army, which held more than 100,000 troops. Ushijima's Chief of Staff, Major General Isamu Cho, assisted in the defense preparations around the capital city of Naha. Lieutenant General Takeo Fujioka's 9th and 62nd Divisions covered the beachheads near Hagushi, while Lieutenant General Tatsumi Ammiya's 24th Division patrolled the Yontan airfield.

Between these two units were batteries of the 1st and 23rd Medium Artillery Regiments, the 7th Heavy Artillery Regiment, and the 110th Heavy Artillery Battalion. Their gun sizes ranged from 75mm to 150mm. There were also three machine gun companies, four oversized anti-aircraft battalions, and four antitank battalions buried up to their turrets and commanded by Major General Wada.

The third defense line was north on the Motobu Peninsula. Japanese lines of defense now stretched north of Naha, through Shuri Castle in the center, past the airfield, and on toward the peninsula. This in-depth defense, such as that designed on Peleliu and Iwo Jima, had three primary features: no counter attacks in force, no attacks without reinforcements and large-scale infiltration at night.

While the Japanese were preparing for the ultimate defense of their empire, the largest invasion force ever assembled – some 180,0000 troops, including 81,165 marines, sailed from the Ulithi Atoll on March 18. D-day was April 1, and the 1st and 6th Marine Divisions were figured into the pre-invasion planning. The 2nd Marine Division would be used to draw attention away from the actual designated landing beaches. The 1st and 6th, along with the Army, would land abreast on the Hagushi beaches on the eastern shores and head for the airfields located at Yontan and Kadena. General Geiger's III Amphibious Corps would proceed north to clean out the upper defenses, while the army wheeled south toward the Shuri Castle/Naha area.

D-Day

On April 1, 1945, Easter Sunday, the 2nd Marine Division executed the perfect diversionary landing at Minatoga, Okinawa. The Japanese rushed toward the defense of this harbor city, only to find that it was not threatened at all. This tactic allowed the landing forces a peaceful entry onto Okinawa. Marines and soldiers advanced 4,000 yards inland without encountering any Japanese defenders. The eerie silence of a clean landing did not sit well with marines who were accustomed to hitting the deck the moment they set foot on any Japanese-held island. In fact, this type of landing made them more cautious and nervous as they waited for the enemy to disgorge its venom on them. As men and equipment poured from LSTs, command and communication posts were quickly put into action.

"During our beach assault and island operations," Sergeant Dolph Reeves of Radio Intelligence recalled, "Navajo talkers were worth their weight in gold and were thoroughly professional. On Easter Sunday and April Fool's Day 1945, I was aboard the AGC-13 USS *Panamint* for the landing on Okinawa. I was a radio supervisor in Joint Operations. I had at least two code talkers with me at all times. When a message was given to me for delivery, and there was plenty going on in Joint Ops, I immediately checked the classification. If classified, I would instruct the operator on the appropriate circuit to request a talker for the other end. Then with a few grunts and unusual sounds from our talker, and an acknowledgment from the other end, the message was delivered.

"Time saved by omitting the crypto center, and by delivering a plain language message that no one other than another Navajo talker could decipher, was enormous. Their contributions to marine operations in the South Pacific were probably unmeasurable."[4]

The absence of enemy troops puzzled everyone, and when civilians were questioned it became clear that the Japanese had retreated to the rugged northern section of Okinawa. Both airfields and the hills surrounding them were secured with little effort by the 10th Army before D-Day was over. By the end of day four, the 7th Infantry Division and the 1st Marine Division had reached the east coast and the Katchin Peninsula. The marines then proceeded toward the northern half of Okinawa and met serious Japanese resistance near the Motobu Peninsula. The 96th Army Division found similar resistance near the Shuri Castle, east of the capital city of Naha. The positions of both the army and the marines would remain stagnant for the next eight days.

Day Ten Through Day Sixteen

Coupled with fierce enemy resistance, the marines were faced with daily drenching rains that hampered their movements. During this time, the code talkers discovered a way to help relieve stress and tension, and it came in the form of an unattended BAR. The majority of the code talkers were issued M1 rifles and .45 pistols for protection; it was rare for them to have access to a BAR. When they did, they behaved like little children with a new Christmas toy. "I remember one night," recalled Alex Williams, a code talker from the 1st Division, "when one of the white boys found a BAR. He said, 'Hey, we've got a powerful rifle now, we ought to use it. It's raining hard so nobody would hear if any code talker wants to use it.' During the next three nights we used it. The third morning somebody checked the magazine clip; it was empty. I used it one of the nights so I guess I contributed to the guilt of those empty magazines."[5] While emptying a BAR of all its ammunition just for fun was not the smartest thing to do in a combat zone, it was good therapy nonetheless.

By April 12 the rains had ceased. The 4th and 29th Regiments of Shepherd's 6th Division were then able to move toward the eastern portion of the Motobu Peninsula. Their target was the 1,200-foot Mount Yaetake. The 1st Division was ordered south to the Shuri Castle/Naha area to lend support in routing the 24th and 62nd Japanese units. The defenders were entrenched in the caves and gullies surrounding Shuri and Naha.

Navajo-directed naval gunfire along with 27 battalions of artillery poured 19,000 rounds for forty minutes into the Shuri/ Naha area. This was topped off with a 650-plane sortie that rained bombs, rockets, napalm and machine gun fire in the hope that this attack would either destroy the Japanese or leave them so stunned that they would be immobilized.

As was the case on Peleliu and Iwo, the Japanese were neither destroyed nor immobilized. When the marine and army assault platoons began to advance through the debris and smoke, they were stopped cold. The well-concealed defenders stepped out from their deep protected caves and gullies and staffed their undamaged defense positions. As usual, all hell broke loose.

Jo-kayed-goh chay-da-gahi ba-ah-hot-gli ashdla nos-bas a-del-tal nish-cla-jih-goh toh-ni-tkal-lo Dzeh Nakia shil-loh.

Request tank support 50 yards left of E Company immediately!

Jo-kayed-goh be-al-do-cid-da-hi coh n-kih ashdla a-del-tahl be-kah-dehn Wol-la-chee Nakia.

Request mortar fire 25 yards behind A Company.

Jo-kayed-goh A-zay da-ne-lei woh-neh d-ah a-kha be-kadehn who-dzah Shush Nakia.

Request medical personnel report to rear echelon of B Company.

The Navajo radio net began sending and receiving countless messages from the front lines to the rear echelons. For the next five days, bitter fighting continued, and forward progress was measured in small bloody yards. The Japanese fought tenaciously, exacting a heavy toll for each yard the army and marine units gained. Naval gunfire and air support were applied when possible, but for the most part this battle was going to be a repeat of the infantry actions that had occurred on Peleliu and Iwo. By the evening of April 23, General Ushijima's outer perimeter had been penetrated at several points, and he withdrew his forces from Naha to set a ring of defense around Shuri Castle. His retreat was effected under cover of dense fog and artillery barrages. When soldiers moved out the next morning, they encountered only stragglers.

This pattern of attack, penetration and forced abandonment lasted until Okinawa was declared secure. By May 8 General Shepherd's 6th Division had captured Machinato airfield and was proceeding across the Asa Kawa River to the next target: a place called "Sugar Loaf." Sugar Loaf was the last outer Japanese bastion that denied access to the rear entrance to Shuri Castle, the Asato River, and the city of Naha. Two hundred yards south of Sugar Loaf were two hills: the Horseshoe and the Half Moon. General Cho had carefully tunneled this area with plenty of artillery and machine gun nests. The 22nd Regiment was dispatched to secure the Horseshoe, while the 29th was ordered to secure the Half Moon. Ten days of repeated assaults against these two targets were mounted before the Japanese defenders were neutralized. The worst aspects of these maneuvers were the constant night attacks and infiltrations by the Japanese.

From May 16 to May 30, rains once again pounded the island and bogged down tanks, artillery pieces and soldiers. After two months of bitter, protracted fighting, the 10th Army finally managed to occupy Naha on May 27. Two days later, the Japanese 32nd Army began withdrawing from the ruins of Shuri Castle. On May 29 A Company/1st Battalion/5th Regiment captured the remains of Shuri Castle. The 10th Army chased and squeezed the remnants of the Japanese defenders toward the extreme southern tip of Okinawa.

During the first week in June, the 2nd Marine Division returned to Okinawa from the Mariana Islands, attached to the 1st Division, and aided the army's effort to push the Japanese into surrender. On June 19 Lieutenant General Ushijima sent farewell messages to Japan, ordered what was left of his army to fight to the death and committed hara-kiri. On June 21 the 10th Army drove through the Ara Saki area and announced the organized resistance had ceased. Okinawa was declared secure on June 22, 1945. Mopping up continued until September 7, when a Japanese commander formally surrendered to General Joseph A. Stilwell.

The battle for Okinawa was the most costly and prolonged campaign in the South Pacific after Guadalcanal. The logistics of this battle, however, were greatly enhanced through the use of the Navajo radio nets.

The size of the island and the troop strength of the Japanese exacted an enormous toll of navy, marine and army personnel and equipment. The sacrifice, however, was worth the price as the capture of Okinawa forced the Japanese Ministry of Defense to face the inevitable. Japan's surrender in August 1945 saved many thousands of soldiers, sailors and marines from suffering and death in an assault on the Japanese homeland.

Notes

1. Interview with Samuel Billison.
2. Interview with Kee Etsicitty.
3. Interview with Samuel Billison.
4. Correspondence from Dolph Reeves.
5. Oral History Transcript VE 25.A1 M37, Marine Corps University.

Japan surrenders: *General Umezu (left) and Mr. Shigemitsu (right) represent the government of Japan during surrender ceremonies aboard the USS Missouri in Tokyo Bay. Photograph from the private collection of F.D. McClain, USN, Retired. (Note that during the photographic printing process of this picture it is flopped relative to the picture on page 216. The military braid on the shoulder of general Umezu is on his left shoulder in this picture and on his right in the picture on page 216. Also Mr. Shigumitsu's cane moves from his right hand to his left.)*

War's End

The victories on Okinawa and the Philippines raised the hope that the war would soon be over. The possibility of invading Japan sent shudders down the spines of the South Pacific forces. By now there was hardly a soldier, sailor or marine who wanted to face the prospect of trying to conquer the Japanese homeland. Experience had shown them that the Japanese were relentless and unyielding. Propagandist "Tokyo Rose" made clear in her radio broadcasts that if U.S. soldiers dared to set one foot on Japanese soil, they would pay more dearly than they had in any battle to date.

The very idea that U.S. soldiers would be forced to fight women, children and elderly people was beyond distasteful; it was abhorrent. The U.S. hoped that with the defeat of Germany, the Japanese government would compromise and end the war before any invasion could take place. The tool used came in the most awesome, frightening and deadly form of warfare: the atomic bomb.

The Light From Hell

On August 6, 1945, the bomber plane *Enola Gay* left Saipan bound for its target destination: Hiroshima, Japan. On board was the first atomic bomb, and its use changed the world forever. Navajos working at CinComSoPac knew that something big was in the wind. They had heard about "Fat Man" and "Little Big Boy," nicknames for the plutonium and uranium bombs, and realized that the war would soon be over one way or another.

When the results of the atomic blast on Hiroshima did not

effect Japan's surrender, a second bomber plane, *Bock's Car*, departed Saipan on August 9 and headed for its target destination: Nagasaki. These two attacks panicked the people of Japan but had little effect on the ruling military leaders. These men were prepared to fight down to the last child if necessary.

Allied command, desperate to bring this war to an end, ordered a 1,600-plane strike attack on Tokyo on August 13. The enormous resulting fire storm nearly leveled the entire city, and thousands of civilians were injured or killed. This action finally forced Emperor Hirohito to override the voices of the military and accept the proclamation of surrender on August 14, 1945. The war was finally over.

On August 30, 1945, U.S. forces began the postwar occupation of Japan. "I served occupation duty in Japan inspecting all the houses," Paul Blatchford recalled. "All the women and children headed for the mountains; they were afraid of what the soldiers might do to them. Our assignment was to confiscate any weapons and ammunition. I did this for about three days; then I was sent to Nagasaki to help guard displaced Japanese soldiers.

One day one of the men in the company asked, 'Hey, Chief, why don't you find out where the head is? We need to go to the head.' I started thinking, but I forgot what the Japanese called it, so I thought, I'll wait until the next train comes and ask the first Japanese that speaks English. So I waited, and here came a fellow and he said, 'Good morning,' and I replied, 'Good morning. Say, where is your head?' He looked at me and asked 'Oh, you sick in the head?' I said, 'In the Marine Corps we call it a head. I mean toilet. Where is the toilet?' He just shook his head and went on his way.

"The fellows kept saying, 'Hurry up, Chief, we need to go to the head!' Just then another man got off the train, and I said, 'Hello,' and then it just hit me! The Japanese word for toilet was 'benjo,' so I asked the man, and he pointed the place out to me. In Japan the men and women use the same facility. It's just a large round house with holes in the floor. So I took the guys over there, and we went in, and when they saw the mixed company, they said, 'Chief, you brought us to the wrong place!' I told them they better use it because there wasn't going to be anything better."[1]

"I was on Hawaii when word got out that if you had 140 points, you could go home," Harold Foster remembered. "I wanted to serve in the post-occupation force and see the country that had become our powerful enemy. We were given booklets showing us how to speak simple words in Japanese to communicate and rules of conduct. We were told that we were representing the United States of America and the Marine Corps and to behave like ambassadors at all times."[2]

The bulk of the occupation forces divided their time among confiscating weapons, guarding streets and neighborhoods, and distributing food and clothing. The Japanese were in pathetic shape. Hunger was rampant, and U.S. bombing raids had destroyed massive sections of houses and buildings. The Japanese were bowed and silent in their role as a conquered people.

U.S. forces also occupied cities in China: Tientsen (Tianjin), Tsingtao (Qingdao), and Peking (Bejing). The official surrender of Japan occurred aboard the USS *Missouri* in Tokyo Harbor on September 2, 1945. Another surrender took place in Tsingtao (Qingdao) and involved the 6th Marine Division. Major General

Lemuel Shepherd Jr. accepted Japan's surrender and addressed the 6th Division with the following speech:

> Officers and men of the Sixth Marine Division: You are about to participate in the formal surrender of the Japanese Military forces in the Tsingtao area. It is an historic event which each of you should long remember. It is the goal for which we have fought during these past four years, and I am sure the personal satisfaction each of you obtains from witnessing the local Japanese Army Commander lay down his sword in complete defeat will, in a small measure, compensate for the dangers and hardships to which you have been exposed during your service in this war.
>
> We of the Sixth Marine Division have every reason to be proud of our accomplishments in the Pacific War and of our part in bringing victory to our cause. Melanesia, Micronesia, and the Orient truly describe the scope of our contribution during the progress of the war. And in the same fashion the Crusader's sword emblazoned on our shield typifies the striking power characteristic of the Sixth Marine Division. From the initial landing of Marines in the summer of 1942 on Makin Island, through the bitter battles from Guadalcanal and Guam to the final decisive campaign on Okinawa in which our Division played such a glorious part, units of the Sixth Division have repeatedly distinguished themselves.
>
> To have commanded this splendid body of men is the greatest honor that I shall ever receive. It is with a deep sense of humility and pride that I stand before you this day and, as your representative, receive the surrender of the enemy, for whose defeat we have fought and bled through the years.[3]

The war with the Empire of the Rising Sun was indeed finally over. Back in the United States, people poured into the streets in wild, joyous celebrations and began planning welcome home festivities for their soldiers. In Japan the people moved quietly and painfully through the streets littered with garbage, remnants of houses and buildings, and corpses. There would be no joyous welcome for their soldiers; the majority of them were dead, and those who had managed to survive were treated as disgraces to their families and country. The suffering of the Japanese was intense, and for the survivors of Hiroshima and Nagasaki, the suffering had just begun.

Although the war with Japan had reached its end, many code talkers continued to use the code. This time, however, they were using it for the scientific community. "One morning the captain came up to me and said, 'You and Rex Malone report to intelligence at Nagasaki,'" Paul Blatchford recalled. "We were told that the army and navy intelligence wanted reports of the atomic bomb effects sent back to San Francisco in code. Information like, How many buildings were destroyed? Was there any vegetation left? How many people died on impact? How many had died since? I had never seen anything like what I saw at Nagasaki. Not even the destruction on Iwo Jima came close to what had happened here. The Japanese survivors had no medical supplies whatsoever, the wounded were using newspapers for bandages, and the infection rate was really high.

"We sent all of that back to the States in code," Blatchford continued. "We used the alphabet to do this, and we transmitted from midnight to 6:00 A.M. because the intelligence people didn't want anyone to know what was being sent. I never knew the names of the Navajos that received the information Rex and I sent; we just transmitted the documents the army and navy wrote down. During the day, we didn't have much to do, and sightseeing was something we weren't allowed to do. It was depressing work. After two weeks of this duty, I was told that I was eligible for discharge, and they sent me back to Sasebo. I don't know who took my place, but Rex stayed there for about six months. I came home aboard the transport *Franklin* and was discharged from San Diego."[4]

The occupation of Japan lasted until December 31, 1946, when World War II was officially declared over, although the final peace treaty was not signed until April 28, 1952. According to statistics released by the Japanese Ministry of Health and Welfare in 1956, fatalities, both military and civilian, from July

1937 to August 1945 amounted to 2.3 million. This figure does not include the thousands of MIAs and post-atomic deaths. Japan suffered grievous losses for the treachery of Pearl Harbor, the Philippines and the many island groups in the South Pacific. The "Greater East Asia Co-Prosperity Sphere" blueprint was knocked from its foundation by determined, tenacious and honorable members of the Army, Navy and Marine Corps. The South Pacific war had cost the Marine Corps 19,733 dead and 67,207 wounded. Eighty Medals of Honor were awarded. The South Pacific Fleet Marine Force was finally, and deservedly, at peace.

Postwar Observations

The Navajo code talkers served with dedication and precision during every campaign in the South Pacific from Guadalcanal to Okinawa. Some code talkers were borrowed from division to division, and from one organization to another within Marine Corps operations. They served in Raider Battalions, Signal Companies, JASCO (Joint Signal Assault Company), Headquarters & Service, Infantry, Artillery, Engineer and Tank Battalions, Shore Party Teams, Reconnaissance, Paramarines, Marine Air Wing groups and on every class of Navy vessels.

One postwar observation critic complained that because of the special status of their service the code talkers were considered part of regular communication personnel, but should have been classed under another group.

> One is that they are not susceptible to a high standard of training for use as wire men, or radio men, and therefore, are valuable only as code talkers; but they are nevertheless counted as part of the authorized allowances of communication personnel. Thus each Indian assigned to a division results in one less radio operator or wire man available to the division. That is considered undesirable and unsatisfactory from a communication standpoint.[5]

This critic was right in stating that the code talkers were not "ordinary" communication personnel. They were used primarily for "coded" communications but were not considered on the same level as Radio Intelligence. This made them, in a sense, orphans. They belonged to anyone who needed and used them, but no single organization held sway over them. The following men describe the true worth of the Navajo code talkers during the war.

"The Navajo code talkers assigned to our Regiment was my first contact with these outstanding Marines," George Strum, Chaplin/25th Regiment states. "I was in awe of how important they were to our operations and their great contributions to the success of our division and regiments.

"Most of them were very young men. They were clean cut, very military and just simply outstanding Marines. I never had any problems that I had to deal with, as a Chaplain, with these fine Marines.

"Of course, their task was dangerous with high casualties during landings," George continued. "They were most courageous in all their duties. The sacrifice for freedom given by these very brave men was incredible. I feel that all the Marines respected them very highly, including the Officers. Their contribution to the victories in the South Pacific was most important."[6]

"I was attached to a Marine Special Forces group on July 1, 1943 aboard a light cruiser the USS *Manchester*," Davey Baker states. "On the 5th of July we pulled alongside the USS *Harlan R. Dickson*, a light destroyer in the 3, 000 ton class, and at the time we were not told our mission or location. It turned out, a few days later, that we were close to New Guinea. When we met the USS *Dickson* we took aboard three Navajo Marines. Ships orders were, 'Ask no questions, and give them a wide berth.'

"In late July we were given our task mission. The Navajos were code talkers and our mission was to get them on land. That turned out to be the Gilbert Islands. The task mission was stated to us under 'for your ears only' and everything was very hush, hush. Our orders and the Navajos were under Admiral Chester W. Nimitz who wanted the Japanese cleared from the central and northern Solomans ASAP. He needed these islands for sea and air force bases to conquer the islands close to Japan.

"On October 6th, 0200 hours, we loaded our code talkers

and two fire teams on a mosquito or PT motor torpedo boat and ran about two hours following coded signal and night lamp signals to contact a local coast watcher," Davey continued. "We left our 'coders' in the hands of the watcher and returned to the ship. I never did learn the name of the island we shored that night but I'm sure I was there again on November 20-23, 1943. The names were Tarawa, Makin, and Apamama Atolls in the Gilbert Islands. Makin and Apamama fell easily but we lost nearly 1, 000 Marines for the victory on Tarawa. Two months later came the Marshall Islands, then onto the Marianas where we lost 25,000 troops.

"We saw 'coders' later on in the summer of 1944 on the Palau Islands, Manila and New Guinea. They were all combat set and looked as if they were off to another island. Most Marines and Army personnel never had a clue what the 'coders' were and what major part they played in our war. If God alone may know, they saved thousands of American lives yet their tale has been hidden by the very role they played: Talk silent, speak swift, stay alive."[7]

And so the war was over and so was the need for the code talkers. They had served wherever they were sent without question or complaint and now it was time to return home. They would depart the same way they had enlisted: quietly and shrouded in secrecy. The secrecy would last for twenty-four years.

Notes

1. Interview with Paul Blatchford.
2. Interview with Harold Foster.
3. Smith, S.E. *The United States Marine Corps in World War II*, p. 930.
4. Interview with Paul Blatchford.
5. 65A-4556, Location 09/30-05-7 Box 17 A9-30.
6. Correspondence from George Strum, June 1993.
7. Correspondence from Davey Baker, April 1994.

Spider Rock. *Photo by Beth McClain*

Epilogue
Home to the Diné Bikéyah

The marines began their discharge process from all over the South Pacific: New Caledonia, Australia, New Zealand, Guadalcanal, China, Japan and Hawaii. Massive convoys set sail in colorful flotillas toward San Francisco and San Diego. Towns and cities across the country celebrated the safe return of their sons, brothers, husbands and fathers. It was a glorious time to celebrate being alive, respected and loved. Not everyone who had served in the armed forces received a welcome home celebration, and the Navajos were some of those who did not.

"I was discharged from the Marine Corps in April 1946 from San Diego," Harold Foster recounted. "I met William Yazzie [Dean Wilson] there, and we were held in quarantine for two weeks. Dean had a pass to get chow at the R center so he took me with him. After the quarantine period was over, I was given my discharge papers. They gave me my base pay plus mileage, and we had to pay for our transportation home out of that money. I went up to Los Angeles and spent a few days with my second cousin Sam Begay; then I headed for home.

"I went back the same way I went in; a train from Los Angeles to Santa Fe and then a bus to the reservation. My brother was already home, and I just showed up. He had his healing ceremony just before I arrived, and I had mine shortly after. There was no fuss made over my brother or me for serving in the war. We did our duty, and we were both expected to look for work and get on with our lives. I became an interpreter for the BIA Health Services and held that position for 39 years.

"I joined the Marine Corps because I liked the uniform on the recruiting poster," Foster continued. "Once I was accepted into the Corps, I was treated like a real human being. The marines gave me a sense of self-respect that I knew I could use the rest of my life. When you are given a rifle and a radio, it becomes your responsibility to take care of them. The marines gave me confidence that I could do what was asked of me and succeed."[1]

Quiet, no-fuss homecomings occurred all over the reservation. There were no organized celebrations, no public recognition for any returning veteran. This attitude stemmed from the traditional belief that only the Holy People (Spider Woman, the Hero Twins, etc.) should be celebrated. This response was not lack of respect for what these young men had accomplished during the war, nor was it meant to diminish what they had experienced. The Navajos are a quiet, unassuming, modest people who consider celebrating deeds of expected behavior akin to bragging. The Navajos who joined the battle to protect the people and the land were doing what was expected of them. To throw a parade or make a fuss would simply not be the Navajo way. The veterans understood and respected this tradition.

All of the code talkers were told not to talk about what they had done until "Uncle Sam says it is okay to do so." The rules that had applied while they were learning the code were enforced after the war as well: don't tell wives, children, girlfriends, mothers, fathers, brothers, sisters, or anyone else.

"After the battle on Iwo Jima," Foster remembered, "my commanding officer told me that the 642 would not be typed on my discharge papers. He said that we might be at war with Russia in the next few years, and the code talkers might be needed again."[2] True to his word, many of the code talkers of the 5th Division did not have the 642 typed on their discharge papers. The *United States Marine Corps Manual of Military Occupational Specialties* defined 642 "Code Talker" as follows: "Transmits and receives messages in a restricted language by radio and wire. Sends and receives messages by means of semaphores and other visual signal devices. May perform field lineman, switchboard operator, or other communication duties."[3]

The secrecy surrounding what they had done during the war created problems for code talker veterans. Veterans say that returning home from any conflict is stressful, that the period of adjustment back to civilian life can be confusing, depressing and filled with nightmares. Support groups enabled veterans to release feelings connected to war and help them find ways to cope. Talking about the war was something the code talkers could not do. Since this avenue of release was not open to them, they resorted to the one thing white veterans did not have: traditional ceremonies.

Purification ceremonies and other rituals were performed for those men and families that requested them.

"I used to get nightmares after I came back home," Paul Blatchford said. "I couldn't afford a private Squaw Dance, so I went to the big ones whenever they held them and just paid for the medicine. Sure enough, after the dance I was cured of my nightmares. I used to see all of the horror of the war, but it faded after the Squaw Dance ceremony."[4]

"I didn't have a ceremony when I came home," Carl Gorman said. "I didn't quite believe in it anymore. A medicine man that was an old friend suggested that I have one, but I didn't have the money to pay him to perform it. He agreed to do a one night sing over me for free. I participated in the sing and felt a great weight leave my mind and body. I felt very rested afterwards. I realized then that I needed to make peace with what I had experienced during the war."[5]

"I was sick at night," Dan Akee remembered. "I was having nightmares all the time. Every time I shut my eyes I would see or hear the enemy coming at me, and I'd find myself screaming. This continued for over a year until I went completely deaf. The doctors couldn't find a cause for my deafness and couldn't help me. Finally, my father put up a Gourd Dance for me. It was just unbelievable what happened to me.

"The first night I heard a drum and my ear popped and I could hear again! ....After the Gourd Dance, I gained back my weight, and the nightmares slowly faded."[6]

Many veterans participated in ceremonies, while others found different ways to make peace with what they had experienced in the war. Teddy Draper Sr. wrote a poem that later turned into a song that helped him heal.

Iwo-Iwo, Iwo-Iwo, at the place called Iwo Jima.
Our soldiers, it happened, were almost killed,
heye, yana,
Iwo-Iwo, Iwo-Iwo, at the place called Iwo Jima.
Our soldiers, it happened, were almost killed,
heye yana,
Suribachi, Suribachi, Suribachi, on top of it
Up there flying, it happened, up there was the
flag,
hiyi, yana
Suribachi, Suribachi, Suribachi
On the third day, our soldiers, it happened
up there,
Flying, it happened, up there, the flag,
hiyi, yana
Red, white and blue stripped, up there flying,
hiyi, yana
Suribachi, Suribachi, Suribachi, on top of it,
Up there flying, it happened, up there flying,
hiyi, yana
Red white and blue stripped, up there flying,
heye yana,
Iwo-Iwo, Iwo-Iwo, at the place called Iwo Jima,
Ours, on top, flying, it happened on top, flying,
heye yana,
Iwo-Iwo, Iwo-Iwo, at the place called Iwo Jima,
Ours, on top, flying, it happened on top, flying,
heye, yana, yana.[7]

Whatever methods the Navajo veterans incorporated in the transition from military back to civilian life, certain facts were clear: (1) they had seen worlds beyond their imaginations, and (2) they had recognized the value of an education. The code talkers had served with officers that had college degrees and admired their knowledge and how well they understood and spoke the English language.

The Navajo veterans had also experienced equality for the first time. The Marine Corps had shown them that whether they were just ordinary foot soldiers or officers, they were treated with respect. How they conducted themselves counted more than the color of their skin. Kee Etsicitty put the Marine Corps experience in perspective when he said, "The Marine Corps is like a wheel with many different spokes. The code talkers were one spoke in the Marine Corps wheel, an important one, but contained within the whole."[8]

The Marine Corps experience was so positive for some of the Navajos that they stayed in and became "twenty-year" men: Dean Wilson, William Kien and Wilson Price. Other Navajos joined different branches of the service and fought in Korea. A number of the men took advantage of the GI bill and finished their educations. They applied to colleges, universities, vocational schools and trade schools all across the country. They became engineers, ranchers, teachers, carpenters, mechanics, electricians, artists and small business owners. They participated in tribal government and helped shape policies the Navajo Nation enforces to this day. They had seen and experienced things that prepared and propelled them to strengthen the Navajo people.

The path these veterans walked was filled with obstacles not only from the outside world but also from some of their own people. Many members of the tribe had trouble accepting the changes the veterans were suggesting: education reform, job training, loans for small businesses and promotion of tourism. Job opportunities within the reservation were scarce and drought had been a severe problem during the war. Crop and animal production were at an all-time low, and many families were suffering hardships from the sudden loss of military pay.

The border towns surrounding the reservation continued to treat the Navajos with the same disdain after the war as they had before and during. Navajo artists were still treated unfairly on payments for their work, and bars made Navajos easy targets for assaults by allowing them to drink themselves into total stupors. The saying that "the more things change, the more they stay the same" held true for the Navajos for years to come.

The one provision of the GI bill that the Navajo veterans were not allowed to enjoy was the housing program. If a veteran wanted to build a house on a piece of reservation land and tried to secure the loan through a bank, it was denied. The problem was that the BIA would not sign a waiver for the title to the land (the U.S. government holds title in-trust to Navajo reservation land), and there was no way to secure a GI or Veterans Administration loan without it.

The inability to build a home on land that veterans could prove their ancestors had lived on for generations infuriated them! They had suffered through the war like every other veteran, yet the option to build a house of their own design and liking was denied them. If they wanted to live on the reservation, they would have to accept the government-built houses or save their own money until they could afford to build. Some of the veterans took over houses that belonged to their parents after they passed away, but if there was an older brother or sister involved, they lost out. Other veterans had to find available housing in the border towns and face landlords not crazy about renting or selling to Navajos. The housing inequity created feelings of anger and despair in veterans that are present to this day.

First Honors

As the postwar years marched along and memories of the war faded, the Navajo code talkers settled into normal patterns of life on and off the reservation. These quiet, uneventful years later gave way to the first public recognition of their contribution during the war. The 22nd reunion of the 4th Marine Division Association was scheduled to be held in 1969 in Chicago, Illinois, and Lee Cannon, a member of the Honors Committee, was asked to help organize the event. The purpose of these annual reunions was to raise scholarship funds for the children of marines who had been killed or disabled during the South Pacific war.

As a major function of the reunions, someone was selected for special honors. Typically the recognition was given to Medal of Honor recipients, generals and regimental commanders. Lee Cannon, a World War II veteran knowledgeable about the role the Navajos had performed during the war, suggested that the reunion honor a group of veterans who had never been given public recognition: the Navajo code talkers. The reunion committee welcomed Cannon's suggestion and set about making plans for the appropriate symbol for the tribute.

Cannon did not approach the project casually. He knew from personal experience that the symbol of honor should be consistent with Navajo values and sensitivities. He made several exploratory trips to the Navajo reservation and discussed the issue with many people. It was decided that the tribute would follow the tradition in which great Native Americans had been honored by Anglos in the past: the code talkers would be awarded specially engraved medallions hanging from leather thongs adorned with red, white and blue Indian beads.

Cannon spent the better part of 1968 traveling at his own expense between Washington, D.C. and the reservation to bring all the necessary elements together for the pending celebration. First, the code talkers had to be located and assembled; second, permission from the Marine Corps to honor the men had to be granted. For this reason, Cannon sought the advice and help of Commandant General Leonard F. Chapman, Jr. At this point, Cannon was not aware of the secrecy surrounding the code talker program and probably unknowingly set the wheels in motion for the declassification of the Navajo dictionary (see Appendix for dictionary).

The most serious problem that needed to be addressed was how to obtain the money necessary to produce the medallions. Cannon asked for and received an interview with W. Clement Stone, founder of the Positive Mental Attitude Philosophy, who granted the money for the medallions. Brigadier General Jay W. Hubbard, the director of the Division of Information at Marine Corps Headquarters, assured Cannon and the committee that a special transport would pick up the Navajos in Albuquerque and fly them to Chicago on June 25, 1969.

The design of the medallion was inspired by a painting of Ira Hayes by Joe Ruiz Grandee. The painting depicted Hayes dressed in the hunting regalia of the Pima tribe and sitting astride an Indian pony. In the mist of the background is the famous image of the second flag raising on Iwo Jima. Cannon received permis-

First honors: *Code talkers pose beneath a statue of a World War II soldier during their trip to Chicago in 1969. Kneeling from left to right: Dean Wilson, 1st Division; Thomas Begay, 5th Division; Albert Smith, 2nd Division. Standing from left to right: Johnny Tabaha, 4th Division; Peter Sandoval, 4th Division; Sammy Silversmith, 4th Division; William Kien, 5th Division; Frank Chee Willeto, 4th Divison. Photograph courtesy of Camp Pendleton Photographic Section, negative No. 014-247-88. Shown in the upper left is a reproduction of the medallion presented to the code talkers by the 4th Marine Division Association.*

sion from Grandee to use his painting on the medallions.

Fifteen Navajo code talkers of the 4th Division along with one code talker representing the 1st, 2nd, 3rd, 5th and 6th Divisions arrived in Chicago on June 25. They were greeted by Harry Larrison, Chicago Chairman of the Honor Committee; Gunnery Sergeant G. R. Smith, a corps photographer; and the Drum and Bugle Corps of the 4th Marine Air Wing. During the next two days, the Navajos were treated to sightseeing tours of the city and were entertained at a pow wow sponsored by the Indians of Chicago at the American Indian Center.

June 28, the day of the honors, began with a parade through downtown Chicago that finished with a memorial service at Pioneer Court. The night of the banquet was charged with unspoken emotion when Cannon asked the Navajos to step front and center as their names were called to receive the medallions for Meritorious Service in Communications. After the last Navajo had been decorated, Cannon stated, "These men are quiet; they kept their trust; they are Fourth Division heroes – every one of them! To them, our heartiest congratulations!"[9]

For the first time since the war ended, the Navajo code talkers found a measure of the importance of what they had done during the war. They were stunned by the outpouring of respect and affection from the 4th Division members and had difficulty finding words that expressed what they were feeling. Outwardly they appeared to be the same stoic, unperturbed Navajos, but inside they were deeply moved. As the war changed them in ways they could not have imagined, so did this first taste of recognition. They began to realize the enormous gift they had given this country in its time of need, and it was one of the proudest moments in their lives.

The Birth of the Association

The first honoring of the Navajo code talkers encouraged them to form an organization. One objective was to educate the Navajo people and the general public about the role the code talkers had played in the war. Sixty-nine code talkers gathered for a reunion July 9-10, 1971. During this reunion the Navajo Code Talkers Association was formed. They elected John Benally as Chairman, James Nahkai as Vice Chairman and William McCabe as Secretary-Treasurer. A member from each of the six marine divisions was elected to the board.

During the reunion, a team of interviewers from the Doris Duke Oral History project at the University of Utah recorded approximately 60 hours of taped sessions with the code talkers. It was the first time since the war that they were free to answer questions about what they had done. Some of the code talkers just briefly answered the questions asked, while others literally gushed their experiences without seeming to take a breath! There was trouble in the wind when Philip Johnston showed up and was given credit for things he did not do. He told the interviewers and code talkers that he had created the first code, which did not sit well with William McCabe, Carl Gorman, Dean Wilson, John Benally, or Eugene Crawford! These normally quiet, polite Navajos jumped all over him and let him know that what he was saying simply was not true! Johnston was cornered and had to be rescued by Jimmy King, who helped straighten out the ruffled feelings. King's diplomatic way of handling this issue quelled tempers and restored order to the meeting. But the issue of Philip Johnston's role concerning the code talker program is a sore point to this day.

By 1973 the Navajo Code Talkers Association had designed a logo, flag and uniform consisting of a turquoise cap (later changed to red), gold velveteen shirt and khaki trousers. Members began appearing as a unit in Veteran's Day parades all over the Southwest. They traveled to schools both on and off the reservation, giving lectures about what they had done during World War II.

Lee Cannon arranged for the Navajo code talkers to march in the 1975 Tournament of Roses parade, and they served as the color guard for the 350-member All-Arizona Marching Band in the bicentennial parades in Washington, D.C. and Philadelphia. This recognition led to an invitation to march in President Jimmy Carter's inauguration parade on January 20, 1977.

Although the parades and travel were gratifying for the code talkers, two other events helped them realize that they had be-

39th Anniversary of the "First 29." *Navajo code talkers gathered at Red Rock State Park, NM during a ceremony given by the United States Marine Corps. The Marines recruited an all-Navajo platoon in honor of the first Navajos who joined the Marine Corps in 1942. Photo courtesy of Kenji Kawano.*

come more than just a curiosity. The first unfolded when the Marine Corps announced that it was going to come to the reservation and recruit another all-Navajo platoon in honor of the 39th anniversary of the First 29. Many of the young men selected were grandsons, great-nephews and cousins of many of the World War II Navajo code talkers. This also marked the first and only time that the Marine Corps publicly acknowledged the Navajo code talkers for their contribution in the South Pacific. This was a pleasing moment for the code talkers.

The second event that brought them great satisfaction was the passing of a resolution by Congress that designated August 14, 1982 as National Navajo Code Talkers Day. President Ronald Reagan's official proclamation stated:

By House Joint Resolution 444, the Congress has requested

me to designate August 14, 1982, as National Navajo Code Talkers Day.

NOW, THEREFORE, I, RONALD REAGAN, President of the United States of America, do hereby designate August 14, 1982 as National Navajo Code Talkers Day, a day dedicated to all members of the Navajo Nation and to all Native Americans who gave of their special talents and their lives so that others might live. I ask the American people to join me in this tribute, and I call upon Federal, State and local officials to commemorate this day with appropriate activities.[10]

News of this national day of recognition reached the shores of Japan and was reported in a Tokyo newspaper, the *Fuji Evening*. Its headline stated, "JAPANESE MILITARY FORCES DEFEATED BY INDIANS." The article tried to explain how the

Defenders of Liberty: *members of the Navajo Code Talkers Association pose beneath the statue of Abraham Lincoln during a visit to Washington, D.C. during the summer of 1983. Photo courtesy of Kenji Kawano.*

Navajo code talkers had affected the Japanese forces in the South Pacific war. "If the Japanese Imperial Intelligence Team could have decoded the Navajo messages, the outcome of the battles on Saipan and Iwo Jima might have been different. Without the activities of the Navajo tribe, the history of the Pacific War might have turned out completely different."[11]

This is the most potent explanation to date of why the Marine Corps initiated the Navajo code talker program. That the Japanese realized the importance of the Navajo code validated the reasons so many Navajos had joined the Marine Corps.

From 1982 to the present, Navajo code talkers have continued to be recognized. The code talkers were honored with an exhibit in the Pentagon Museum in September 1993, and on March 10, 1994, they received an honor from the most unusual place: the Northern Mariana Islands. Juan N. Babauta, Representative from the United States Commonwealth of Northern

Proud veterans: *Navajo code talkers prepare to march in the Navajo Nation Fair, September 1989. Members of the Navajo Code Talkers Association participate in many events throughout the Navajo Nation. Photo courtesy of Kenji Kawano.*

Mariana Islands, hosted a banquet at the Navajo Nation Inn, Window Rock, Arizona, to personally thank the Navajo code talkers for their role in helping end Japanese rule during the war.

"World War II, and every war, extracts an immeasurable price on the soul of mankind," said Juan Babauta. "Sometimes too easily overshadowed by the sadness of those days of war are the memories of friendships made and personal acts of human kindness. I humbly stand here to say that you and your deeds have not been forgotten by the peoples of Saipan, Tinian, and the rest of the Northern Mariana Islands."[12]

Reaction to this heartfelt tribute ranged from surprise to tears. Carl Gorman expressed what most of the men felt when he said, "We went to war to protect a way of life, our land and our people. We went to war to liberate people who were being enslaved. Most of the time what we ended up fighting for and liberating was a deep water harbor or airfields. It was beautiful to meet someone whose life had been changed through actions you carried out long before they were even born."[13]

As a special treat and challenge for readers, the Navajo code talkers have sent a message. Every word was constructed from the alphabet of the final revised Navajo dictionary. Use it to decode this message:

"Na-as-tso-si tse-nihl tsah-as-zih d-ah lin ah-jah A-chin wol-la-chee a-keh-di-glini be-la-sana yil-doi ne-ahs-jah Tsan tse-nill a-woh tkin tlo-chin a-chin dzeh tsah be shi-da gah ah-nah chuo A-kha ah-losz bela-sana ah-jad ah-jad d-ah a-chi be-tas-tni dzeh than-zie tlo-chin tla-gin a-kha tsin-tliti ah-jah."[14]

Notes

1. Interview with Harold Foster.
2. Ibid.
3. Navajo Code Talker file, Marine Corps Historical Center.
4. Interview with Paul Blatchford.
5. Conversation with Carl Gorman, March 1994.
6. Interview 1159, Doris Duke Collection.
7. Correspondence from Teddy Draper Sr., March 1994.
8. Interview with Kee Etsicitty.
9. Correspondence from Lee Cannon, April 1994.
10. Navajo Code Talker Association Banquet Program, 1986.
11. *Fuji Evening*, 1983, translated by Hiroshi Akima, 1991.
12. Chris Murphy, "Islanders Thank Code Talkers," *Gallup Independent*, March 10, 1994.
13. Conversation with Carl Gorman.
14. Oral History Transcript, Jimmy King Sr., Marine Corps University.

Perfect recruiting poster candidate: *Carl Gorman, respected Elder, teacher, philosopher, artist and oldest member of the "First 29." This picture says it all.*

Appendix 1

Proposed Plan
for
Recruiting
Indian Signal Corps Personnel
[JOHNSTON'S PROPOSAL]

1. <u>General</u>. The American Indian comprises a distinct racial subdivision, presumed by anthropologists to have migrated from Asia by way of "the landbridge" at Bering Strait. Dates of these migrations have not been fixed, but recent excavations have disclosed human remains in association with those of the now extinct giant sloth–an indication that earlier migrations occurred more than 20,000 years ago.

Present Indian population of the United States is 361,816, comprising 180 tribes. These are divided into distinct linguistic stocks, each of whose languages have apparently evolved from a common source. The total number of tribes in the United States, Canada, and British Columbia is 230, which represent 56 linguistic stocks. The language of a tribe belonging to one linguistic stock is completely alien to that of another stock; and in most cases variations of the tongues within a linguistic stock may be so great as to be mutually unintelligible.

All Indian languages are classed as "unwritten" because no alphabets or other symbols of purely native origin are in existence. In a few cases, these aboriginal tongues have been reduced to writing by American scholars, who have developed alphabets adapted to the expression of the difficult consonants involved. A notable instance in point is the Navajo Dictionary compiled by the Franciscan Fathers of Saint Michaels, Arizona, who have also translated portions of the Bible, and written other texts in the Navajo tongue for the use of their students. Recently, the United States Bureau of Indian Affairs has inaugurated a program of writing Navajo texts for study in reservation schools. However, a fluency in reading Navajo can be acquired only by individuals who are first highly educated in English, and who, in turn, have made a profound study of Navajo, both in its spoken and written form. An illiterate Navajo is, of course, entirely unable to read his own language.

Because of the fact that a complete understanding of words and terms comprising the various Indian languages could be had only by those whose ears had been highly trained in them, these dialects would be ideally suited to communication in various branches of our armed forces. Messages sent and received between two individuals of the same tribe could not, under any circumstances, be interpreted by the enemy; conversations by telephone or short-wave radio could be carried on without possibility of disclosure to hostile forces.

2. Tribes Available for Recruitment. A logical approach to the problem of selection of suitable personnel for an Indian Signal Corps would be to consider the largest tribes in the United States. Reference to accompanying map will show locations of each of the following:

Tribe	Population
Navajo	49,338
Sioux (in South Dakota)	20,670
Chippewa	17,443
Pima-Papago	11,915

The Pima and Papago tribes are so closely allied in language as to be mutually intelligible.

Percentage of literacy among the foregoing tribes would be in direct proportion to the length of time each has been in contact with educational facilities. The Chippewa would have the highest percentage, with the Sioux second, the Pima-Papago third, and the Navajo fourth. It should be noted, however, that a prerequisite to effective service in transmitting code messages is an excellent command of both the native tongue and of the English. In some cases, individuals of a tribe which has had long contact with white residents may have largely forgotten his native tongue.

Since only a minute percentage of the foregoing tribes are college graduates, it is unlikely that 250 members of each, between the ages 21-30, would be available for recruitment. However, a fair number have attended government and public schools, and completed twelve grades, equivalent to high school. Without doubt a large majority of these would have sufficient command of both their native tongues and of English to qualify for service in the signal corps. It is also probable some individuals with even less schooling, by reason of constant use of the English language, might be qualified for Signal Corps service. This matter could readily be ascertained by giving each applicant an examination to show his fluency in both tongues.

3. <u>Recruitment of Navajo Indians</u>. This tribe is selected as an example of a possible plan for recruitment because of the writer's intimate knowledge of its reservation, the people, and their language. Most of the factors discussed would apply top the other three tribes in varying degrees.

With an area of 25,000 square miles, and an approximate population of 50,000, the Navajo reservation is one of the most sparsely populated sections of the United States. It is traversed by unimproved roads and trails; and many of its outlying portions are accessible only on horseback. Culturally and linguistically, the Navajo has been autonomous, and apart from surrounding white population. But in recent years, an increasing number of Navajo children have attended schools established by the government on this reservation, where they have received grammar school instruction; and a large percentage of these students have graduated from other schools of higher grades located at points remote from the reservation, where the curricula include native arts and crafts, as well as various trades and occupations taught in accredited schools throughout the United States.

Because the manner of life on the Navajo reservation provides small opportunity for educated Indians to set up a standard of living compatible with their training, a large portion of them have sought employment in government agencies and institutions, and in towns near the reservation. Therefore, an effective program to contact suitable personnel for recruitment would require publicity designed to reach every Navajo whose age and education qualifies him for service. The most important feature of such a program would be a bulletin prepared to set forth the following:

(a) That the Navajos are in a unique position to render service in the defense of the United States – a service which will be of inestimable value.

(b) That such a service would involve the transmission of messages in their own tongue, which is not understood by any other people in the world.

(c) That meritorious service in such a capacity may result in advancement in the service.

(d) That applications for enlistment are received at designated localities.

The best location for a central recruiting station would be at the Central Navajo Agency, Window Rock, Arizona, or Gallup, New Mexico (see enclosed map). Secondary stations for contact of local applicants should be located at several points throughout the reservation, preferably at Tuba City, Arizona, Chin Lee, Arizona, and Shiprock, New Mexico. Special efforts should also be made to contact Navajos through government school superintendents at Leupp, Fort Defiance, Kayenta, and Keams Canyon, Arizona, and Crownpoint, New Mexico.

A considerable number of eligible applicants will also be

found among the following categories:

(a) Navajos attending non-reservation government schools, such as those located at Phoenix, Arizona, and Albuquerque, New Mexico.

(b) Educated Navajos employed at the foregoing schools, and in various capacities by the government.

(c) Educated Navajos who are employed off the reservation, principally in the cities of Flagstaff, Winslow, Gallup, and Albuquerque.

(d) Navajos who have already enlisted, or have been inducted into the armed forces, who might be transferred to the Marine Corps for special training in signal work.

4.   <u>Indian Affairs Officials</u>.   Direct contact with the Navajo Reservation should be made through Mr. E. R. Fryer, Superintendent, Central Navajo Agency, Window Rock, Arizona. Contact with proper authorities among the other three tribes listed can be made through the Honorable John Collier, Commissioner of Indian Affairs, Washington, D.C.

Appendix 2

**Original Text of Letter
From: Lt. Col. Wethered
Woodworth
To: Director, Division of Recruiting
Subject: Enlistment of Navajo
Indians**
[MEETING WITH BIA OFFICIALS, MARCH 25, 1942]

HEADQUARTERS U. S. MARINE CORPS
WASHINGTON

26 March 1942

From: Lieutenant Colonel Wethered Woodworth.
To: The Director, Division of Recruiting.

Subject: Enlistment of Navaho Indians.

Reference: (a) Ltr, Director, Division of Plans and Policies,
                         dated 20 March 1942.

    1.   The undersigned met with the following officials
of the Bureau of Indian Affairs in the office of the Commissioner
of that bureau on 25 March 1942:

           Mr. Fred H. Daiker, Acting Chief of Welfare
           Mrs. Lucy W. Adam, Chief of Community, Service Bureau
              and Education
           Dr. L. W. White, Assistant Director of Health
           Mr. J. C. McCaskill, Chief of the Planning Division

    2.   The ideas set forth in Section 2 of reference
letter above was explained and information was requested as to
whether or not the Bureau of Indian Affairs felt that the enlistment
and employment of Navaho Indians was practicable and feasible.

    3.   After some discussion the following factors
developed:

        (1) There are approximately 50,000 Navahos on the
reservation of which some 8,000 are males, 75% of whom are
of military age.

        (2) About 3,000 males are between the ages of 21
and 25 of which some five or six hundred have had high
school education.

        (3) Of the above group a large proportion are con-
versant to some extent to communication methods as they have
not only used the telephone but in many instances been employed
by the general superintendent of the reservation for radio

-1-

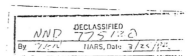

broadcasting which is used to some extent for the dissemination of information on the reservation.

(4) Some 4,677 males registered for the draft, eighty-five (85) individuals up to date voluntarily enlisted in some branch of the service and approximately two-hundred twenty-five (225) have been inducted under the Selective Service Act.

(5) The Selective Service Board in covering the area of the reservation has to a large degree deferred the induction of many of the tribe on the grounds of insufficient education. This has created a bad feeling in the tribe as on the whole they are most anxious to serve and be treated as other Americans.

(6) Mrs. Adam, who has taught school for years on the reservation states that should we undertake an enlistment program it will be partly supported by the Tribal Council and we will have more applicants than we can use.

4.   Some discussion was held as to whether or not the Navaho language would be a fit medium of communication and as to whether or not it would be intelligible to other people. All of the bureau personnel present agreed that for ordinary involved military communications the Navaho language would be an ideal medium of communication and that messages so delivered would be intelligible to anyone other than the Navahos themselves. They all agreed that transmitting messages by this method would be exceptionally fast as the individuals could translate as they received and it would do away with any coding or transcoding of any sort.

5.   The Opinion was requested as to the manner in which a recruiting campaign should be carried out and as to the manner in which the recruit should be handled and trained.

6.   As a result of the above discussion it is believed that the program if undertaken should be carried out as follows:

(1) Before any effort to enlist Indians is undertaken personal contact should be made with Mr. E. R. Fryer, General Superintendent, Navaho Reservation, Window Rock, Arizona (between Wingate and Gallop).

(2) With the cooperation of Mr. Fryer contact should be made with the Tribal Council and the program under consideration should be laid before that body and their cooperation asked for.

(3) It should be pointed out to the Tribal Council that the services required are particularly valuable to the military effort and that the men employed will be in the status of specialist of an unusual order. It is the

-2-

opinion of the undersigned that if enlistments are made the
Indians should be placed in Class V, Marine Corps Reserve
and should be trained as a group as specialists rather
than be put through the ordinary recruit training. This
opinion is based on the ideas put forth by the members of
the Indian Bureau which in the main emphasized the fact that
"face" means a great deal to the Indian and that better
cooperation and effort might be obtained if the individuals
recruited felt themselves to be singled out in an unusual
manner for an unusual job.

  (4) Mrs. Adam stated that, of course, there were
no military terms in the Indian vocabulary and it might be
well to employ during the training period two or three of the
older Indians (40 to 50 years old) who are expert interpreters
and who would be invaluable in helping the recruits develop
the proper vocabulary. It will be necessary for them to
invent new terms. Mrs. Adams and Mr. Daiker both felt that
the Bureau of Indian Affairs would be willing to detail their
interpreters for this duty if the Marine Corps could house
and subsist the same should the training be given at some
place other than the reservation.

  (5) Mr. Daiker stated that he was sure we could give
the initial training on the reservation if it was so desired
and that it might be well to do so as interpreters would
always be available and we would have the benefit of the
cooperation and advice of the superintendent in setting up
the scheme.

5.   As a result of the above conference it was felt
that the suggestion as to enlisting initially thirty (30)
Navahos for training and experimental duty is both practicable
and feasible and that the same should be initiated. Before
any moves are made, however, it is recommended that someone
be detailed to call on Mr. Fryer, the General Superintendent of
the reservation and perfect the general principles under which
the program is to be carried out.

6.   The undersigned gave Mr. Daiker to understand
that no move would be made by this headquarters until the same
had been cleared with his office. This, not so much for their
approval, as they stated this was not necessary, but to assure
cooperation from that office to the greatest extent possible.

7.   It is believed that there are certain factors
that should be given consideration in the building up of an
Indian force and that these should be discussed at length with

-3-

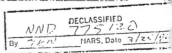

the General Superintendent and other members of the Bureau of
Indian Affairs as the whole effort might be ~~evaluated~~ if, in
the initial steps a false approach is made.

WETHERED WOODWORTH,
Lieutenant Colonel, U. S. Marine Corps.

- -

Appendix 3

Original Code

The following is a list of 263 terms created by the first 32 Navajos enrolled in the Marine Corps Communications School located at Camp Elliott.

Alphabet	Navajo	Meaning
A	Wol-la-chee	Ant
B	Shush	Bear
C	Moasi	Cat
D	Be	Deer
E	Dzeh	Elk
F	Ma-e	Fox
G	Klizzie	Goat
H	Lin	Horse
I	Tkin	Ice
J	Tkele-cho-gi	Jackass
K	Klizzie-yazzie	Kid
L	Dibeh-yazzie	Lamb
M	Na-as-tso-si	Mouse
N	Nesh-chee	Nut
O	Ne-ahs-jah	Owl
P	Bi-sodih	Pig
Q	Ca-yeilth	Quiver
R	Gah	Rabbit
S	Dibeh	Sheep
T	Than-zie	Turkey
U	No-da-ih	Ute

V	A-keh-di-glini	Victor
W	Gloe-ih	Weasel
X	Al-an-as-dzoh	Cross
Y	Tsah-as-zih	Yucca
Z	Besh-do-gliz	Zinc

Military Designations

Corps	Din-neh-ih	Clan
Division	Ashi-hi	Salt
Regiment	Tabaha	Edge-water
Battalion	Tacheene	Red Soil
Company	Nakia	Mexican
Platoon	Has-clish-nih	Mud
Section	Yo-ih	Beads
Squad	Dibeh-li-zini	Black Sheep

Communications

Telephone	Besh-hal-ne-ih	Telephone
Switchboard	Ya-ih-e-tih-ih	Central
Wire	Besh-le-chee-ih	Copper
Telegraph	Besh-le-chee-ih Be-hane-ih	
		Communication By Copper Wire
Semaphore	Dah-ha-a-tah-ih Be-hane-ih	
		Flag Signals
Blinker	Coh-nil-kol-lih	Fire Blinder
Radio	Nil-chi-hal-ne-ih	Radio
Panels	Az-kad-be-ha-ne-ih	Carpet Signals

Officers

Brigadier General	So-a-la-ih	One Star
Major General	So-na-kih	Two Stars
Colonel	Astah-besh-le-gai	Silver Eagle
Lt. Colonel	Che-chil-be-tah-besh-le-gai	
		Silver Oak Leaf
Major	Che-chil-be-tah-ola	Gold Oak Leaf
Captain	Besh-le-gai-nah-kih	Two Silver Bars
1st Lieutenant	Besh-le-gai-a-lah-ih	One Silver Bar

2nd Lieutenant	Ola-alah-ih-ni-ahi	One Gold Bar

Airplanes:	**Wo-tah-de-ne-ih**	**(Air Corps)**
Dive Bomber	Gini	Chicken Hawk
Torpedo Plane	Tas-chizzie	Swallow
Observation Plane	Ne-as-jah	Owl
Fighter Plane	Da-he-tih-hi	Hummingbird
Bomber	Jay-sho	Buzzard
Patrol Plane	Ga-gih	Crow
Transport Plane	Astah	Eagle

Ships:	**Toh-dineh-ih**	**(Water Clan Fleet)**
Battleship	Lo-tso	Whale
Aircraft Carrier	Tsidi-ney-ye-hi	Bird Carrier
Submarine	Besh-lo	Iron Fish
Mine Sweeper	Cha	Beaver
Destroyer	Ca-lo	Shark
Transport	Dineh-nay-ye-hi	Man Carrier
Cruiser	Lo-tso-yazzie	Small Whale
Mosquito Boat	Tse-e	Mosquito

Months		
January	Yas-nil-tes	Crusted Snow
February	Astah-be-yaz	Small Eagle
March	Woz-cheind	Squeaky Voice
April	Tsha-chill	Small Plant
May	Tah-tso	Big Plant
June	Be-ne-eh-eh-jah-tso	Big Planting
July	Be-ne-ta-tsosie	Small Harvest
August	Be-neen-ta-tso	Big Harvest
September	Ghan-jih	Half
October	Nil-chi-tsosie	Small Wind
November	Nil-chi-tso	Big Wind
December	Kesh-mesh	Christmas

Countries		
Africa	Zhin-ni	Blackies
Alaska	Beh-hga	With Winter

America	Ne-he-mah	Our Mother
Australia	Cha-yes-desi	Rolled Hat
Britian	Toh-ta	Bounded By Water
China	Ceh-yehs-besi	Braided Hair
France	Da-gha-hi	Beard
Germany	Besh-be-cha-he	Iron Hat
Iceland	Tkin-ke-yah	Ice Land
India	Ah-le-gai	White Clothes
Italy	Doh-ha-chi-yali-tchi	Stutter
Japan	Beh-na-ali-tsoisi	Slant Eyed
Philippines	Keyah-da-na-ilhe	Floating Land
Russia	Sila-goche-ih	Red Army
South America	Sha-de-ah-ne-mah	South Our Mother
Spain	Debeh-de-nih	<u>Sheep</u>/Pain

General Vocabulary

Action	Ah-ha-tinh	Action
Advance	Nas-say	Ahead
Airdrome	Nilchi-began	Air House
Alert	Ha-ih-des-ee	Watchful
Allies	Nih-hi-cho	Our Friends
Along	Wol-la-chee-snez	Long Ant
Also	Eh-do	Also
Alternate	Na-kee-go-ne-nan-dey-he	
		Second Position
Amphibious	Chal	Frog
And	Do	And
Annex	Ih-nay-tani	Addition
Approach	Bi-chi-ol-dah	Moving To
Are	Gah-tso	Large Rabbit
Area	Haz-a-gih	Area
Armored	Besh-ye-ha-da-di-teh	Iron Protected
Arrive	Il-day	Came
Army	Lei-cha-ih-yil-knee-hi	Dog Faces
Artillery	Be-al-doh-tso-lani	Many Big Guns
As	Ache	Ace
Assault	Altseh-e-jah-he	First Strike
Attached	A-hid-day-tih	Attached

Available	Ta-shoz-teh-ih	Available
Battery	Bih-be-al-doh-tka-ih	Three Guns
Base	Bih-tsee-dih	Foundation
Be	Tses-nah	Bee
Been	Tse-nah-nesh-chee	Bee/<u>N</u>ut
Before	Bih-tse-dih	Prior
Begin	Ha-hol-ziz	Start
Belong	Tse-nah-snez	Long Bee
Block	Da-dey-than	Block
Bombs	A-ye-shi	Eggs
By	Be-gah	By
Camp	To-alsteh-hogan	Temporary House
Camouflage	Di-nes-ih	Hide
Can	Yah-di-zini	Can
Cannoneer	Be-al-doh-tso-dey-dil-don-igi	
		Big Gun Operator
Capacity	Be-nel-ah	Capacity
Capitol	Tkah-chae	Sweat House
Captured	Yis-nah	Captured
Casualty	Bih-din-ne-day	Out Of Action
Class	Alth-a-a-teh	Class
Coast Guard	Ta-bas-dsissi	Shore Runner
Code	Yil-tas	Peck
Column	Alth-kay-ni-zih	Column
Combat	Da-ah-jih-gahn	Fighting
Combination	Al-tkas-ei	Mixed
Commander	Bih-keh-he	Senior
Commanding Officer	Hash-kay-gi-na-tah	War Chief
Concentrate	Ta-la-hi-jih	One Place
Confidential	Na-nil-in	Keep Secret
Conquered	A-keh-des-dlin	Won
Convoy	Tkal-kah-o-nei	Move On Water
Counter-attack	Woltah-al-ki-gi-jeh	Counter-act
Creek	Toh-nil-tsanh	Little Water
Debouchment	Dzilth-gahn-ih	Apache

Defense	Ah-kin-gil-toh	Defend
Department	Hogan	Central House
Dispositions	A-ho-tay	Disposition
Displace	Hih-do-nal	Move
Do	Tse-le	Small Pup
Echelon	Who-dzoh	Line
Engineer	Day-dil-jah-hi	Fire Builder
Enlist	Bih-zih-a-da-yi-lah	Signature
Escape	A-zeh-ha-ge-yah	Escape
Establish	Has-tay-dzah	Set Up
Estimate	Bih-ke-tse-shod-des-kez	Guess
Execute	A-do-nil	Will Happen
Fail	Cha-al-cind	Fail
Field	Clo-dih	Outside
Fire	Coh	Fire
Flank	Dah-di-kad	Side
Flare	Wo-chi	Light Streak
Grenades	Ni-ma-si	Potatoes
Guard	Ni-dih-da-hi	Guard
Have	Jo	Have
Headquarters	Na-ha-tah-ba-hogan	Main House
Hospital	A-zey-al-hi	Place Of Medicine
Install	Ehd-thah	Put In
Invade	A-tah-gi-nah	Move Into
Is	Seis	Seven
Island	Seis-keyah	Seven Land
Left	Nish-cla-jih	Left
Location	A-kew-eh	Spot
Machine Gun	A-knah-as-dinih	Rapid Fire Gun
Magnetic	Na-e-lahi	Pick Up Iron
Maneuver	Na-na-o-nalth	Move Around

Manufacture	Besh-be-eh-el-ih-dih	Metal Factory
Mechanic	Chiti-a-nayl-inih	Car Repairman
Message	Hane-al-neh	Message
Military	Sila-go-keh-goh	Soldiers
Mine	Ha-gade	Mine
Mortar	Be-al-doh-cid-da-hi	Sitting Gun
Navy	Tal-kah-sila-go	Sea Soldiers
Not	Ni-dah-than-zie	No/Turkey
Objective	Bi-ne-yei	Goal
Observed	Hal-zid	Seen
Occurred	Yeel-tsod	Taken
Of	Toh-ni-tkal-lo	Ocean Fish
Or	Eh-dodah-goh	Either
Order	Be-eh-ho-zini	Direct
Ordinance	Lei-az-iah	Underground
Overlay	Be-ka-has-tsoz	Over Lap
Parenthesis	Astanh	Rib
Penalize	Tah-ni-des-tanh	Set Back
Primary	Altseh-nan-day-hi-gih	1st Position
Proceed	Nay-nih-jih	Go
Protect	Ah-chanh	Self Defense
Railhead	A-do-geh-hi	Shipping & Receiving Point
Rally	A-lah-na-o-glalth	Gathering
Range	An-zeh	Distance
Reached	Baz-ni-tsood	Reached
Reconnaissance	Ha-a-cidi	Inspector
Reinforce	Nal-dzil	Reinforce
Relieved	Nah-jih-co-nal-ya	Remove
Replacement	Ni-na-do-nil	Replacement
Report	Who-neh	Got Words
Representative	Tka-naz-nili	Triple Men
Request	Jo-kayed-goh	Ask For
Retreat	Ji-din-ned-chanh	Move Back

River	Toh-yil-kal	Much Water
Route	Gah-bih-tkeen	Rabbit Trail
Runner	Nih-dzid-teih	Runner
Sabotage	A-tkel-yah	Hinder
Saboteur	A-tkel-el-ini	Troublemaker
Sailors	Cha-le-gai	White Caps
Seamen	Tkal-kah-dineh-ih	Seamen
Secret	Bah-has-tkin	Secret
Side	Bosh-keesh	Side
Signal	Na-eh-eh-gish	By Sign
Shell	Be-al-doh-be-ca	Shell
Short	Be-oh	Short
Space	Be-tkah	Between
Stream	Toh-ni-lin	Running Water
Submerged	Tkal-cla-yi-yah	Under Water
Submit	A-nih-leh	Send
Such	Yis-cleh	Socks
Supplementary	Tka-go-ne-nan-dey-he	3rd Position
Supply	Nal-yeh-hi	Supply
Territory	Ke-yah	Land
That	Than-zie-cha	Turkey Hat
The	Cha-gee	Blue Jay
There	Bih	There
They	Ni-ghai	They
Together	Ta-bil	With
Torpedo	Lobe-ca	Fish Shell
Tracer	Beh-na-al-kah-hi	Track
Traffic Diagram	Hane-ba-na-as-dzoh	Story Line
Troops	Nal-deh-hi	Troops
Unit	Da-az-jah	Bunch
Vicinity	Na-hos-ah-gih	There About
Was	Ne-teh	Was

Weapons	Beh-dah-a-hi-jah-geni	Weapons
Zone	Bah-na-has-dzoh	Area

Punctuation

Colon :	Naki-alh-deh-da-al	Two Spots
Comma ,	Tsa-na-dahl	Tail
Dash -	Us-dzoh	Dash
Parenthesis ( )	Astsanh	Rib
Period .	Da-ahl-zin	Black Spot
Question ?	Ah-jah	Ear
Semi Colon ;	Da-ahl-zhin Bi-tsa Na-dahl	
		Spot Tail

Appendix 4

Letter from Carl I. Wheat of Wheat and May Attorneys at Law

WHEAT AND MAY
ATTORNEYS AT LAW

Washington 5, D. C.
March 10, 1944

William F. Friedman
3932 Military Road, N. W.
Washington, D. C.

Dear Colonel Friedman:

A letter going into greater detail on the matter of which I spoke to you last night has just arrived, and rather than write to Johnston today I thought I might pass on the pertinent passages of his letter to you. If, after you have reflected on the matter, you should wish me to write him, I shall be glad to do so, or you might wish to write him direct, or to have someone see him and look his program over on the ground.

He is TSgt. Philip Johnston, address Field Signal Battalion, Training Center, Camp Pendleton, Oceanside, California. As I told you, I have known him for many years. He is an engineer and grew up in the Navajo country. Years ago he and I talked at length of just what he is now doing, – training Navajos for war communications purposes. The import portions of his letter follow:

"Since our brief visit the other day, a highly significant development has taken place. The Commandant of the Marine Corps has reached a final decision regarding the use of Navajo communication in this branch of the service. A definite number of Indians will be attached to each division, and when these quotas are filled, the procurement program will be terminated. While the total number of personnel thus provided will be somewhat less than that recommended by officers who have made use of our system, it will, nevertheless, be adequate to provide all divisions in the field with enough trained Navajos for essential purposes. The men I now have here in school, together with those already graduated and transferred to various units, will practically fill all quotas; which means that my job in the Marine Corps (or at least this phase of it) is nearly finished.

"Right on the heels of the foregoing news comes a dispatch from the Italian front proving beyond all doubt that the Navajo system would be of inestimable value to the army. It has been revealed that a critical situation on the Anzio Beachhead was further complicated by the fact that the commander of our forces was unable to transmit information regarding his plight without, at the same time, revealing his weakness to the enemy. Mountain passes were closed by blizzards, barring the passage of couriers, and any attempt to make use of radio communication would have apprised the enemy of his predicament. Here, then, is a classical illustration of how a method of radio communication which is <u>absolutely</u> <u>secure</u> against enemy interception would be of <u>priceless</u> value. Moreover, it is reasonable to believe that the Secretary of War might now be in a highly receptive frame of mind to give the most serious consideration to a proposal that the Army start a program to train Navajo personnel in the system of communication which the Marine Corps is already using."

Mr. Johnston then suggests that I might know the people in the Army who handle these matters, and wonders whether it would be possible for an Army Signal Officer to be assigned to visit Camp Pendleton "for a demonstration of Navajo communication." Such officer could then determine the lay of the land, and Johnston states that, if authorized Navajo communicators could be made available for service at the front "in a surprisingly short time." He adds, in support of this conclusion:

"1. When all Marine Corps divisions are supplied with their quotas of Navajos, it is probable that I will be discharged for 'mission completed,' after which I would be available for service in the Army. If the Chief of Staff should decide to start the program before that time, he could no doubt secure my release from this branch of the service if he desired me to take charge of it. In such an event, the school here could be carried on efficiently in my absence, since I have built up a competent staff of instructors who would be able to continue their work with a little general supervision.

"2. At present I have eleven Navajos in my school who are either acting as instructors, or who are competent to do so. Two or three of these would be ample to finish the training program authorized for the Marine Corps. The balance, say eight men, might be loaned to the Army for a limited period (about eight weeks) if such a request were made by the proper authority. Each of these men could instruct a class of twenty. Assume that eighty percent of this group of 160 men qualified, as trainees have done here, and we would have about 128 men ready for communication duty. A few of these could be retained as instructors, and the balance sent to the locale where they are most needed.

"3. There is an abundance of Navajos already serving in the Army who could be qualified for communication in their native language. In a recent radio broadcast, the Vice Chairman of the Navajo Tribal Council stated that some 2000 of this tribesmen were in the armed forces. The most intelligent of such men now in the Army could be selected for training, which would require about eight weeks."

I offer this to you for what it may be worth. My own view is that the experience of Johnston in this particular activity should not be lost sight of, now allowed to be wasted. He knows the Navajos, and has actually been training them in this work, so this is not in any sense a mere theory. I sincerely trust that, at the very least, this matter may be seriously investigated in some appropriate manner. I am, of course, assuming that you are in the current of such matters. If I can be of any further assistance, please call on me.

Sincerely,

[signed] Carl I. Wheat

Appendix 5

Marine Corps Response to Wheat and May Letter
SRH 120 Document

THE USE OF NAVAJO INDIANS FOR RADIO TRANSMISSION SECURITY PURPOSES

The following information was obtained in a conference between Lt. Col. Smith of the Marines (Arlington Annex-Room 2126) and Lt.—————— of A. H. S. on 15 April, 1944, 1300-1430 inclusive.

The training of Navajo Indians for security purposes in radio voice transmission has been a Marine project for some time. Up to the present writing approximately 250 of these Indians have been trained in this respect. This training has been under the guidance of T/Sgt Johnston at Camp Pendleton, California.

The course itself runs a minimum of twenty weeks, with the first eight weeks being an infantry indoctrination course, and the remainder being a training period in the native tongue, English, signal and radio procedure, and field signal training.

The source of these Navajo Indians has been tapped to the very limit of Marine resources, and the procurement curve is approaching the zero mark. The Army, however, has quite a few of these Indians scattered through its ranks and a numerical count should be instituted before any training is contemplated or undertaken.

The use of Indians is not a theory, it is an actuality. These Indians have been used on the combat front at Guadalcanal, Bougainville and Tarawa. The 1st, 2d, 3d, 4th and 5th Marine Divisions have these Indians in their Division Signal Companies and Lt. Col. Snedaker (Arlington annex) Lt. Col. McGill (Arlington Annex) and Lt. Col. Nelson (Quantico) can give accounts of their use on the combat front.

The normal Marine set-up is 38 such Indians per Marine Division. This is the highest headquarters to which they are assigned. The breakdown of the 38 is 2 per Bn., 2 per Reg't., and 8 per Div. Sig. Co.

All of these Indians are so trained to be just as versatile as possible. A few are trained as radio operators, many as runners, and all as basic infantrymen. Their work as runners is outstanding, and on their own in jungle or wooded area, they are much more hardy and self supporting than the normal white man.

In general, the Navajo vocabulary does not suffice for military purposes. but the Marines augment or supplement the regular parent tongue with original phonetic words coined expressly in the Navajo tongue for military purposes.

To date, none of these Indians have been captured or killed. They seem to have a knack for agile escape and adequate self-protection. From this, Col. Smith seems to feel fairly certain no compromise have been effected.

The ability of these Indians to receive and transmit under battle conditions and noises is as good, if not better, than their English-speaking fellow soldiers.

Stereotyped forms of messages are used, and although this is a definite deficiency from a cryptanalytic view-point, Marine officers state that the gibberish of the Indians is so unintelligible that this does not hasten its compromise in the least.

Both officers concerned agree that the more Navajos employed in this type of signal communication the less secure the system will be, which is a natural; deduction, but not necessarily a true one.

Code books used in this type of communication are never taken far enough forward to place in danger of capture and the men are definitely trained to develop their memories. Retentiveness of learned material is outstanding in the Navajo.

Use of Navajo Indians for Communication.

1. Director of Communications

1. In reply to your informal request of 7 June
1944 regarding the attitudes expressed by the Army Research Ground Forces and Army Air Forces on the use of Navajo Indians for use in radio telephone transmissions, the following information has been obtained:

Army Ground Forces: Lieutenant Colonel James M. Kimbrough, Jr. of the Signal Section of Army Ground Forces informed the writer that Colonel G. B. Rogers and Colonel O. K. Sadtler took this matter up with G-2 and obtained their feelings and opinions on it. Apparently, G-2 was dead set against the adoption of the plan to use Indians, since it was felt that the security features inherent in the Navajo tongue were not sufficient enough to warrant development for general radio telephone transmissions. It was further objected to that the enemy could obtain translators and after the re-cordations of sufficient plain test had been obtained, the entire language be subject to successful analysis and compromise.

Therefore, the Army Ground Forces did not feel justified in screening the entire army in search of Navajo linguists.

<u>Army Air Forces:</u> As yet no answer has been received to our request of 13 June 1944 directed to the Army Air Forces on the same subject and we are therefore unable to express to you their feelings on this matter. Upon receipt of this infor-mation, it will be immediately forwarded to your attention

Chas. E. Henshall
1st Lt., SPSIS-4
17 June 1944
Ext. 307

SIS
<u>Date 6/17/44   Sig JB</u>

Appendix 6

Navajo Dictionary
Revised as of 15 June, 1945
Final Revised Edition

Alphabet

A. (Wol-la-chee)	Ant	G. (Jeha)	Gum
A. (Be-la-sana)	Apple	H. (Tse-gah)	Hair
A. (Tse-nill)	Axe	H. (Cha)	Hat
B. (Na-hash-chid)	Badger	H. (Lin)	Horse
B. (Shush)	Bear	I. (Tkin)	Ice
B. (Toish-jeh)	Barrel	I. (Yeh-hes)	Itch
C. (Moasi)	Cat	I. (A-chi)	Intestine
C. (Tla-gin)	Coal	J. (Tkele-cho-gi)	Jackass
C. (Ba-goshi)	Cow	J. (Ah-ya-tsinne)	Jaw
D. (Be)	Deer	J. (Yil-Doi)	Jerk
D. (Chindi)	Devil	K. (Jad-ho-loni)	Kettle
D. (Lha-cha-eh)	Dog	K. (Ba-ah-ne-di-tinin)	Key
E. (Ah-jah)	Ear	K. (Klizzie-yazzie)	Kid
E. (Dzeh)	Elk	L. (Dibeh-yazzie)	Lamb
E. (Ah-nah)	Eye	L. (Ah-jad)	Leg
F. (Chuo)	Fir	L. (Nash-doie-tso)	Lion
F. (Tsa-e-donin-ee)	Fly	M. (Tsin-tliti)	Match
F. (Ma-e)	Fox	M. (Be-tas-tni)	Mirror
G. (Ah-tad)	Girl	M. (Na-as-tso-si)	Mouse
G. (Klizzie)	Goat	N. (Tsah)	Needle

N. (A-chin)	Nose	S. (Dibeh)	Sheep
O. (A-kha)	Oil	S. (Klesh)	Snake
O. (Tlo-chin)	Onion	T. (D-ah)	Tea
O. (Ne-ahs-jah)	Owl	T. (A-woh)	Tooth
P. (Cla-gi-aih)	Pant	T. (Than-zie)	Turkey
P. (Bi-so-dih)	Pig	U. (Shi-da)	Uncle
P. (Ne-zhoni)	Pretty	U. (No-da-ih)	Ute
Q. (Ca-yeilth)	Quiver	V. (A-keh-di-glini)	Victor
R. (Gah)	Rabbit	W. (Gloe-ih)	Weasel
R. (Dah-nes-tsa)	Ram	X. (Al-na-as-dzoh)	Cross
R. (Ah-losz)	Rice	Y. (Tsah-as-zih)	Yucca
		Z. (Besh-do-tliz)	Zinc

A.	Able	J.	Jig	S.	Sugar
B.	Baker	K.	King	T.	Tare
C.	Charlie	L.	Love	U.	Uncle
D.	Dog	M.	Mike	V.	Victor
E.	Easy	N.	Nan	W.	William
F.	Fox	O.	Oboe	X.	X-ray
G.	George	P.	Peter	Y.	Yoke
H.	How	Q.	Queen	Z.	Zebra
I.	Item	R.	Roger		

Names of Various Organizations

Corps	Din-neh-ih	Clan
Division	Ashih-hi	Salt
Regiment	Tabaha	Edge Water
Battalion	Tacheene	Red Soil
Company	Nakia	Mexican
Platoon	Has-clish-nih	Mud
Section	Yo-ih	Beads
Squad	Debeh-li-zini	Black Sheep

Officers

Commanding General	Bih-keh-he (G)	War Chief
Major General	So-na-kih	Two Star
Brigadier General	So-a-la-ih	One Star
Colonel	Atsah-besh-le-gai	Silver Eagle

Lieutenant Colonel	Che-chil-be-tah-besh-legai	
		Silver Oak Leaf
Major	Che-chil-be-tah-ola	Gold Oak Leaf
Captain	Besh-legai-na-kih	Two Silver Bars
Lieutenant	Besh-legai-a-lah-ih	One Silver Bar
Commanding Officer	Hash-kay-gi-na-tah	War Chief
Executive Officer	Bih-da-hol-nehi	Those In Charge

Names of Countries

Africa	Zhin-ni	Blackies
Alaska	Beh-hga	With-winter
America	Ne-he-mah	Our Mother
Australia	Cha-yes-desi	Rolled Hat
Britain	Toh-ta	Between Waters
China	Ceh-yehs-besi	Braided Hair
France	Da-gha-hi	Beard
Germany	Besh-be-cha-he	Iron Hat
Iceland	Tkin-ke-yah	Ice Land
India	Ah-le-gai	White Clothes
Italy	Doh-ha-chi-yali-tchi	Stutter
Japan	Beh-na-ali-tsosie	Slant Eye
Philippine	Ke-yah-da-na-lhe	Floating Island
Russia	Sila-gol-che-ih	Red Army
South America	Sha-de-ah-ne-hi-mah	South Our Mother
Spain	Deba-de-nih	Sheep Pain

Names of Airplanes

Planes	Wo-tah-de-ne-ih	Air Force
Dive Bomber	Gini	Chicken Hawk
Torpedo Plane	Tas-chizzie	Swallow
Observation Plane	Ne-as-jah	Owl
Fighter Plane	Da-he-tih-hi	Humming Bird
Bomber Plane	Jay-sho	Buzzard
Patrol Plane	Ga-gih	Crow
Transport	Atsah	Eagle

Names of Ships

Ships	Toh-dineh-ih	Sea Force

Battle Ship	Lo-tso	Whale
Aircraft	Tsidi-ney-ye-hi	Bird Carrier
Submarine	Besh-lo	Iron Fish
Mine Sweeper	Cha	Beaver
Destroyer	Ca-lo	Shark
Transport	Dineh-nay-ye-hi	Man Carrier
Cruiser	Lo-tso-yazzie	Small Whale
Mosquito Boat	Tse-e	Mosquito

Names of Months

January	Atsah-be-yaz	Small Eagle
February	Woz-cheind	Squeeky Voice
March	Tah-chill	Small Plant
April	Tah-tso	Big Plant
May	Tah-tsosie	Small Plant
June	Be-ne-eh-eh-jah-tso	Big Planting
July	Be-ne-ta-tsosie	Small Harvest
August	Be-neen-ta-tso	Big Harvest
September	Ghaw-jih	Half
October	Nil-chi-tsosie	Small Wind
November	Nil-chi-tso	Big Wind
December	Yas-nil-tes	Crusted Snow

Vocabulary

Word	*Navajo*	*Literal Translation*
Abandon	Ye-tsan	Run Away From
About	Wola-chi-a-he-gahn	Ant Fight
Abreast	Wol-la-chee-be-yied	Ant Breast
Accomplish	Ul-so	All Done
According	Be-ka-ho	According To
Acknowledge	Hanot-dzied	Acknowledge
Action	Ah-ha-tinh	Place Of Action
Activity	Ah-ha-tinh- (Y)	Action Ending In Y
Adequate	Beh-gha	Enough or Sufficient
Addition	Ih-he-de-ndel	Addition
Address	Yi-chin-ha-tse	Address
Adjacent	Be-gahi	Near or Close By
Adjust	Has-tai-nel-kad	Adjust

Advance	Nas-sey	Ahead
Advise	Na-netin	Advise
Aerial	Be-zonz	Stinger
Affirmative	Lanh	Affirmative
After	Bi-kha-di (A)	After
Against	Be-na-gnish	Against
Aid	Eda-ele-tsood	Aid
Air	Nilchi	Air
Airdrome	Nilchi-beghan	Airdrome
Alert	Ha-ih-des-ee	Alert
All	Ta-a-tah (A)	All
Allies	Nih-hi-cho	Allies
Along	Wolachee-snez	Long Ant
Also	Eh-do	Also
Alternate	Na-kee-go-ne-nan-dey-he	
		2nd Position
Ambush	Khac-da	Ambush
Ammunition	Beh-eli-doh-be-cah-ali-tas-ai	
		All Sort Of Ammunition
Amphibious	Chal	Frog
And	Do	And
Angle	Dee-cahn	Slanting
Annex	Ih-nay-tani	Addition
Announce	Beh-ha-o-dze	Announce
Anti	Wol-la-chee-tsin	Ant Ice
Anticipate	Ni-jol-lih	Anticipate
Any	Tah-ha-dah	Any
Appear	Ye-ka-ha-ya	Appear
Approach	Bi-chi-ol-dah	Approach
Approximate	To-kus-dan	Approximate
Are	Gah-tso	Big Rabbit
Area	Haz-a-gih	Area
Armor	Besh-ye-ha-da-di-teh	Iron Protector
Army	Lei-cha-ih-yil-knee-ih	Army
Arrive	Il-day	Arrive
Artillery	Be-al-doh-tso-lani	Many Big Guns
As	Ahce	As
Assault	Altseh-e-jah-he	First Striker

Assemble	De-ji-kash	Bunch Together
Assign	Bah-deh-tahn	Assign
At	Ah-di	At
Attack	Al-tah-je-jay	Attack
Attempt	Bo-o-ne-tah (A)	Try
Attention	Giha	Attention
Authenticator	Hani-ba-ah-ho-zini	Know About
Authorize	Be-bo-ho-snee	Authorize
Available	Ta-shoz-teh-ih	Available
Baggage	Klailh (B)	Baggage
Banzai	Ne-tah	Fool Them
Barge	Besh-na-elt	Barge
Barrage	Besh-ba-wa-chind	Barrage
Barrier	Bih-chan-ni-ah	In The Way
Base	Bih-tsee-dih	Base
Battery	Bih-be-al-doh-tka-ih	Three Guns
Battle	Da-ah-hi-dzi-tsio	Battle
Bay	Toh-ah-hi-ghinh	Bay
Bazooka	Ah-zhol	Bazooka
Be	Tses-nah	Bee
Beach	Tah-bahn (B)	Beach
Been	Tses-nah-nes-chee	Bee Nut
Before	Bih-tse-dih	Before
Begin	Ha-hol-ziz	Commence From
Belong	Tses-nah-snez	Long Bee
Between	Bi-tah-kiz	Between
Beyond	Bilh-la Di	Down Below
Bivouac	Ehl-nas-teh	Brush Shelter
Bomb	A-ye-shi	Eggs
Booby Trap	Dineh-ba-whoa-blehi	Man Trap
Borne	Ye-chie-tsah	Born Elk
Boundary	Ka-yah-bi-na-has-dzoh	
		(B) Boundary
Bull Dozer	Dola-alth-whosh	Bull Sleep
Bunker	Tsas-ka	Sandy Hollow (Bedlike)
But	Neh-dih	But
By	Be-gha	By

Cable	Besh-lkoh	Wire Rope
Caliber	Nahl-kihd (C)	Move Around
Camp	To-altseh-hogan	Temporary Place
Camouflage	Di-nes-ih	Hid
Can	Yah-di-zini	Can
Cannoneer	Be-al-doh-tso-dey-dil-don-igi	
		Big Gun Operator
Capacity	Be-nel-ah	Capacity
Capture	Yis-nah	Capture
Carry	Yo-lailh	Carry
Case	Bit-sah	Case
Casualty	Bih-din-ne-dey	Put Out Of Action
Cause	Bi-nih-nani	Cause
Cave	Tsa-ond	Rock Cave
Ceiling	Da-tel-jay	Seal
Cemetary	Jish-cha	Among Devils
Center	Ulh-ne-ih	Center
Change	Thla-go-a-nat-zah	Change
Channel	Ha-talhi-yazzie	Small Singer
Charge	Ah-tah-gi-jah	Charge
Chemical	Ta-nee	Alkali
Circle	Nas-pas	Circle
Circuit	Ah-heh-ha-dailh	Circuit
Class	Alth-ah-a-teh	Class
Clear	Yo-ah-hol-zhod	Clear
Cliff	Tse-ye-chee	Cliff
Close	Ul-chi-uh-nal-yah	Close
Coast Guard	Ta-bas-dsissi	Shore Runner
Code	Yil-tas	Peck
Colon	Naki-alh-deh-da-al-zhin	
		Two Spots
Column	Alth-kay-ne-zih	Column
Combat	Da-ah-hi-jih-ganh	Fighting
Combination	Al-tkas-ei	Mixed
Come	Huc-quo	Come
Comma	Tsa-na-dahl	Tail Drop
Commercial	Nai-el-ne-hi	Commercial
Commit	Huc-quo-la-jish	Come Glove

Communication	Ha-neh-al-enji	Making Talk
Conceal	Be-ki-asz-jole	Conceal
Concentration	Ta-la-hi-jih	One Place
Concussion	Whe-hus-dil	Concussion
Condition	Ah-ho-tai	How It Is
Conference	Be-ke-ya-ti	Talk Over
Confidential	Na-nil-in	Kept Secret
Confirm	Ta-a-neh	Make Sure
Conquer	A-keh-des-dlin	Won
Consider	Ne-tsa-cas	Think It Over
Consist	Bilh (C)	Consist
Consolidate	Ah-hih-hi-nil	Put Together
Construct	Ahl-neh	To Make
Contact	Ah-hi-di-dail	Come Together
Continue	Ta-yi-teh	Continue
Control	Nai-ghiz	Control
Convoy	Tkal-kah-o-nel	Moving On Water
Coordinate	Beh-eh-ho-zin-na-as-dzoh	Known Lines
Counter Attack	Woltah-al-ki-gi-jeh	Counter Act
Course	Coh-ji-goh	Course
Craft	Ah-toh	Nest
Creek	Toh-nil-tsanh	Very Little Water
Cross	Al-n-as-dzoh	Cross
Cub	Shush-yahz	Bear Cub
Dash	Us-dzoh	Dash
Dawn	Ha-yeli-kahn	Dawn
Defense	Ah-kin-cil-toh	Defense
Degree	Nahl-kihd	Degree
Delay	Be-sitihn	Deer Lay
Deliver	Be-bih-zihde	Deer Liver
Demolition	Ah-deel-tahi	Blow Up
Dense	Ho-dilh-cla (D)	Wet
Depart	Da-de-yah	Depart
Department	Hogan	Department
Designate	Ye-khi-del-nei	Point Out
Desperate	Ah-da-ah-ho-dzah	Down To Last

Detach	Al-cha-nil	Detached
Detail	Be-beh-sha	Deer Tail
Detonator	Ah-deel-tahi (OR)	Blown Up
Difficult	Na-ne-klah	Difficult
Dig In	Le-eh-gade	Dig In
Direct	Ah-ji-go	Direct
Disembark	Eh-ha-jay	Get Out
Dispatch	La-chai-en-seis-be-jay	Dog Is Patch
Displace	Hih-do-nal	Move
Display	Be-seis-na-neh	Deer Is Play
Disposition	A-ho-tay	Disposition
Distribute	Nah-neh	Distribute
District	Be-thin-ya-ni-che	Deer Ice Strict
Do	Tse-le	Small Pup
Document	Beh-eh-ho-zinz	(D) Document
Drive	Ah-nol-kahl	Drive
Dud	Di-giss-yahzie	Small Dummy
Dummy	Di-giss-tso	Big Dummy
Each	Ta-lahi-ne-zini-go	Each
Echelon	Who-dzah	Line
Edge	Be-ba-hi	Edge
Effective	Be-delh-need	Effective
Effort	Yea-go	With All Your Might
Element	Ah-na-nai	Troop Representing Other
Elevate	Ali-khi-ho-ne-oha	Elevate
Eliminate	Ha-beh-to-dzil	Eliminate
Embark	Eh-ho-jay	Get On
Emergency	Ho-nez-cla	Emergency
Emplacement	La-az-nil	Emplacement
Encircle	Ye-nas-teh (E)	Encircle
Encounter	Bi-khanh	Go Against
Engage	A-ha-ne-ho-ta	Agreed
Engine	Chidi-bi-tsi-tsine (E)	Engine
Engineer	Day-dil-jah-he	Engineer
Enlarge	Nih-tsa-goh-al-neh	Make Big
Enlist	Bih-zih-a-da-yi-lah	Enlist
Entire	Ta-a-tah (E)	Entire

Entrench	E-gad-ah-ne-lih	Make Ditch
Envelop	A-zah-gi-ya	Envelop
Equipment	Ya-ha-de-tahi	Equipment
Erect	Yeh-zihn	Stand Up
Escape	A-zeh-ha-ge-yah	Escape
Establish	Has-tay-dzah	Establish
Estimate	Bih-ke-tse-hod-des-kez	
		Estimate
Evacuate	Ha-na	Evacuate
Except	Neh-dih (E)	Except
Except*	Na-wol-ne	Expect
Exchange	Alh-nahl-yah	Exchange
Execute	A-do-nil	Execute
Explosive	Ah-del-tahi (E)	Explosive
Expedite	Shil-loh (E)	Speed Up
Extend	Ne-tdale	Make Wide
Extreme	Al-tsan-ah-bahm	Each End

This is a typo. It should read "Expect."

Fire	Coh	Fire
Fail	Cha-al-eind	Fail
Failure	Yees-ghin	Failure
Farm	Mai-be-he-ahgan	Fox Arm
Feed	Dzeh-chi-yon	Feed
Field	Clo-dih (F)	Field
Fierce	Toh-bah-ha-zsid (F)	Afraid
File	Ba-eh-chez	File
Final	Tah-ah-kwo-dih	That Is All
Flame Thrower	Coh-ah-ghil-tlid	Flame Thrower
Flank	Dah-di-kad	Flank

Fortification	Ah-na-sozi	Cliff Dwelling
Fortify	Ah-na-sozi-yazzie	Small Fortification
Forward	Tehi	Let's Go
Fragmentation	Besh-yazzie	Small Metal
Frequency	Ha-talhi-tso	Big Singer
Friendly	Neh-hecho-da-ne	Friendly
From	Bi-tsan-dehn	From

Furnish	Yeas-nil (F)	Furnish
Further	Wo-nas-di	Further
Garrison	Yah-a-da-hal-yon-ih	Take Care Of
Gasoline	Chidi-bi-toh	Gasoline
Grenade	Ni-ma-si	Potatoes
Guard	Ni-dih-da-hi	Guard
Guide	Nah-e-thlai	Guide
Hall	Lhi-ta-a-ta	Horse All
Half Track	Alh-nih-jah-a-quhe	Race Track
Halt	Ta-akwai-i	Halt
Handle	Bet-seen	Handle
Have	Jo	Have
Headquarter	Na-ha-tah-ba-hogan	Headquarter
Held	Wo-tah-ta-eh-dahn-oh	Held (past tense)
High	Wo-tah	High
High Explosive	Be-al-doh-be-ca-bih-dzil-igi	Powerful Shell
Highway	Wo-tah-ho-ne-teh	High Way
Hold	Wo-tkanh	Hold
Hospital	A-zey-al-ih	Place Of Medicine
Hostile	A-nah-ne-dzin	Not Friendly
Howitzer	Be-el-don-tso-quodi	Short Big Gun
Illuminate	Wo-chi (I)	Light up
Immediately	Shil-loh (I)	Immediately
Impact	A-he-dis-goh	Impact
Important	Be-has-teh	Important
Improve	Ho-dol-zhond	Improve
Include	El-tsod	Include
Increase	Ho-nalh	Increase
Indicate	Ba-hal-neh	Tell About
Infantry	Ta-neh-nal-dahi	Infantry
Infiltrate	Ye-gha-ne-jeh	Went Through
Initial	Beh-ed-de-dlid	Brand
Install	Ehd-tnah	Install
Installation	Nas-nil	In Place

Instruct	Na-ne-tgin	Teach
Intelligence	Ho-yah (I)	Smart
Intense	Dzeel	Strength
Intercept	Yel-na-me-jah	Intercept
Interfere	Ah-nilh-khlai	Interfere
Interpret	Ah-tah-ha-ne	Interpret
Investigate	Na-ali-ka	Track
Involve	A-tah	Involve
Is	Seis	Seven
Island	Seis-keyah	Seven Island
Isolate	Bih-tsa-nel-kad	Separate
Jungle	Woh-di-chil	Jungle
Kill	Naz-tsaid	Kill
Kilocycle	Nas-tsaid-a-kha-ah-yeh-ha-dilh	
		Kill Oil Go Around
Labor	Na-nish (L)	Labor
Land	Kay-yah	Land
Launch	Tka-ghil-zhod	Launch
Leader	Ah-na-ghai	Leader
Least	De-be-yazie-ha-a-ah	Lamb East
Leave	Dah-de-yah	He Left
Left	Nish-cla-jih-goh	Left
Less	Bi-oh (L)	Less
Level	Dil-konh	Level
Liaison	Da-a-he-gi-eneh	Know Other's Action
Limit	Ba-has-ah	Limit
Litter	Ni-das-ton (L)	Scatter
Locate	A-kwe-eh	Spot
Loss	Ut-din	Loss
Machine Gun	A-knah-as-donih	Rapid Fire Gun
Magnetic	Na-e-lahi	Pick Up
Manage	Hastni-beh-na-hai	Man Age
Maneuver	Na-na-o-nalth	Moving Around
Map	Kah-ya-nesh-chai	Map

Maximum	Bel-dil-khon	Fill To Top
Mechanic	Chiti-a-nayl-inih	Auto Repairman
Mechanized	Chidi-da-ah-he-goni	Fighting Cars
Medical	A-zay	Medicine
Megacycle	Mil-ah-heh-ah-dilh	Million Go Around
Merchant Ship	Na-el-nehi-tsin-na-ailh	
		Merchant Ship
Message	Hane-al-neh	Message
Military	Silago-keh-goh	Military
Millimeter	Na-as-tso-si-a-ye-do-tish	
		Double Mouse
Mine	Ha-gade	Mine
Minimum	Be-oh (M)	Minimum
Minute	Ah-khay-el-kit-yazzie	Little Hour
Mission	Al-neshodi	Mission
Mistake	O-zhi	Miss
Mopping	Ha-tao-di	Mopping
More	Thla-na-nah	More
Mortar	Be-al-doh-cid-da-hi	Sitting Gun
Motion	Na-hot-nah	Motion
Motor	Chide-be-tse-tsen	Car Head
Native	Ka-ha-teni	Native
Navy	Tal-kah-silago	Sea Soldier
Necessary	Ye-na-zehn	Want
Negative	Do-ya-sho-da	No Good
Net	Na-nes-dizi	Net
Neutral	Do-neh-lini	Neutral
Normal	Doh-a-ta-h-dah	Normal
Not	Ni-dah-than-zie	No Turkey
Notice	Ne-da-tazi-thin	No Turkey Ice
Now	Kut (N)	Now
Number	Beh-bih-ke-as-chinigih	What's Written
Objective	Bi-ne-yei	Goal
Observe	Hal-zid	Observe
Obstacle	Da-ho-desh-zha	Obstacle
Occupy	Yeel-tsod	Taken

Of	Toh-ni-tkal-lo	Ocean Fish
Offensive	Bin-kie-jinh-jih-dez-jay	
		Offensive
Once	Ta-lai-di	Once
Only	Ta-ei-tay-a-yah	Only
Operate	Ye-nahl-nish	Work At
Opportunity	Ash-ga-alin	Opportunity
Opposition	Ne-he-tsah-jih-shin	Opposition
Or	Eh-dodah-goh	Either
Orange	Tchil-lhe-soi	Orange
Order	Be-eh-ho-zini	Order
Ordnance*	Lei-az-jah	Under Ground
Originate	Das-teh-do (O)	Begin
Other	La-e-cih	Other
Out	Clo-dih (O)	Out Side
Overlay	Be-ka-has-tsoz	Overlay

This is a typo. It should read "Ordinance."

Parenthesis	Atsanh	Rib
Particular	A-yo-ad-do-neh	Particular
Party	Da-sha-jah- (P)	Party
Pay	Na-eli-ya	Pay
Penalize	Tah-ni-des-tanh	Set Back
Percent	Yal	Money (all sorts)
Period	Da-ahl-zhin	Period
Periodic	Da-al-zhin-thin-moasi	Period Ice Cat
Permit	Gos-shi-e (P)	Permit
Personnel	Da-ne-lei	Member
Photograph	Beh-ghi-ma-had-nil	Photograph
Pill Box	Bi-so-dih-dot-sahi-bi-tsah	
		Sick Pig Box
Pinned Down	Bil-dah-has-tanh-ya	Pinned Down
Plane	Tsidi	Bird
Plasma	Dil-di-ghili	Plasma
Point	Be-so-de-dez-ahe	Pig Point
Pontoon	Tkosh-jah-da-na-elt	Floating Barrel
Position	Bilh-has-ahn	Position
Possible	Ta-ha-ah-tay	Possible

Post	Sah-dei	Post
Prepare	Hash-tay-ho-dit-ne	Prepare
Present	Kut (P)	Present
Previous	Bih-tse-dih (P)	Previous
Primary	Altseh-nan-day-hi-gih	1st Position
Priority	Hane-pesodi	Priority
Probable	Da-tsi	Probable
Problem	Na-nish-tsoh	Big Job
Proceed	Nay-nih-jih	Go
Progress	Nah-sai (P)	Progress
Protect	Ah-chanh	Self Defense
Provide	Yis-nil (P)	Provide
Purple	Dinl-chi	Purple
Pyrotechnic	Coh-na-chanh	Fancy Fire
Question	Ah-jah	Ear
Quick	Shil-loh	Quick
Radar	Esat-tsanh (R)	Listen
Raid	Dezjay	Raid
Railhead	A-de-geh-hi	Shipping Point
Railroad	Konh-na-al-bansi-bi-thin	Railroad
Rallying	A-lah-na-o-glalth	Gathering
Range	An-zah	Distance
Rate	Gah-eh-yahn	Rabbit Ate
Ration	Na-a-jah	Ration
Ravine	Chush-ka (R)	Ravine
Reach	Il-day (R)	Reach
Ready	Kut (R)	Ready
Rear	Be-ka-denh (R)	Rear
Receipt	Shoz-teh	Receipt
Recommend	Che-ho-tai-tahn	Recommend
Reconnaissance	Ha-a-cidi	Inspector
Reconnoiter	Ta-ah-ne-al-ya	Make Sure
Record	Gah-ah-nah-kloli	R-E-Rope
Red	Li-chi	Red
Reef	Tsa-zhin	Black Rock

Reembark	Eh-na-jay	Go In
Refire	Na-na-coh	Refire
Regulate	Na-yel-na	Regulate
Reinforce	Nal-dzil	Reinforce
Relief	Aganh-tol-jay	Relief
Relieve	Nah-jih-co-nal-ya	Remove
Reorganize	Ha-dit-zah	Reorganize
Replacement	Ni-na-do-nil	Replacement
Report	Who-neh	Got Word
Representative	Tka-naz-nili	Triple Men
Request	Jo-kayed-goh	Ask For
Reserve	Hesh-j-e	Reserve
Restrict	Ba-ho-chinh	Restrict
Retire	Ah-hos-teend	Retire
Retreat	Ji-din-nes-chanh	Retreat
Return	Na-dzah	Came Back
Reveal	Who-neh (L)	Reveal
Revert	Na-si-yiz	Turn About
Revetment	Ba-nas-cla (R)	Corner
Ridge	Gah-ghil-keid	Rabbit Ridge
Riflemen	Be-al-do-hosteen	Riflemen
River	Toh-yil-kal	Much Water
Robot Bomb	A-ye-shi-na-tah-ih	Egg Fly
Rocket	Lesz-yil-beshi	Sand Boil
Roll	Yeh-mas	Roll
Round	Naz-pas (R)	Round
Route	Gah-bih-tkeen	Rabbit Trail
Runner	Nih-dzid-teih	Runner
Sabotoge	A-tkel-yah	Hindered
Saboteur	A-tkel-el-ini	Trouble Maker
Sailor	Cha-le-gai	White Caps
Salvage	Na-has-glah	Pick Them Up
Sat	Bih-la-sana-cid-da-hi	Apple Sitting
Scarlet & Red	Lhe-chi (S & R)	Red
Schedule	Beh-eh-ho-zini	Schedule
Scout	Ha-a-sid-al-sizi-gih	Short Recon.
Screen	Besh-na-nes-dizi	Screen

Seaman	Tkal-kah-dineh-ih	Seaman
Secret	Bah-has-tkih	Secret
Sector	Yoehi (S)	Sector
Secure	Ye-dzhe-al-tsisi-gi	Small Security
Seize	Yeel-stod (S)	Seize
Select	Be-tah-has-gla	Took Out
Semi Colon	Da-ahl-zhin-bi-tsa-na-dahl	
		Dot Drop
Set	Dzeh-cid-da-hi	Elk Sitting
Shackle	Di-bah-nesh-gohz	S-shackle
Shell	Be-al-doh-be-ca	Shell
Shore	Tah-bahn (S)	Shore
Short	Bosh-keesh*	Short
Side	Bosh-keesh	Side
Sight	Ye-el-tsanh	Seen
Signal	Na-eh-eh-gish	By Signs
Simplex	Alah-ih-ne-tih	Inner Wire
Sit	Tkin-cid-da-hi	Ice Sitting
Situate	A-ho-tay	(S) Situate
Smoke	Lit	Smoke
Sniper	Oh-behi	Pick 'Em Off
Space	Be-tkah	Between
Special	E-yih-sih	Main Thing
Speed	Yo-zons	Swift Motion
Sporadic	Ah-na-ho-neil	Now And Then
Spotter	Eel-tsay-i	Spotter
Spray	Klesh-so-dilzin	Snake Pray
Squadron	Nah-ghizi	Squash
Storm	Ne-ol	Storm
Straff	Na-wo-ghi-goid	Hoe
Straggler	Chy-ne-de-dahe	Straggler
Strategy	Na-ha-tah (S)	Strategy
Stream	Toh-ni-lih	Running Water
Strength	Dzhel	Strength
Stretch	Desz-tsood	Stretch
Strike	Nay-dal-ghal	Strike
Strip	Ha-tih-jah	Strip
Stubborn	Nil-ta	Stubborn

Subject	Na-nish-yazzie	Small Job
Submerge	Tkal-cla-yi-yah	Went Under Water
Submit	A-nih-leh	Send
Subordinate	Al-khi-nal-dzl	Helping Each Other
Succeed	Yah-taygo-e-elah	Make Good
Success	Ut-zah	It Is Done
Successful	Ut-zah-ha-dez-bin	It Is Done Well
Successive	Ut-zah-sid	Success Scar
Such	Yis-cleh	Sox
Suffer	To-ho-ne	Suffer
Summary	Shinh-go-bah	Summer Mary
Supplementary	Tka-go-ne-nan-dey-he	3rd Position
Supply	Nal-yeh-hi	Supply
Supply Ship	Nalga-hi-tsin-nah-ailh	Supply Ship
Support	Ba-ah-hot-gli	Depend
Surrender	Ne-na-cha	Surrender
Surround	Naz-pas (S)	Surround
Survive	Yis-da-ya	Survive
System	Di-ba-tsa-as-zhi-bi-tsin	System

This is a typo. It should read "Be-oh."

Tactical	E-chihn	Tactical
Take	Gah-tahn	Take
Tank	Chay-da-gahi	Tortoise
Tank Destroyer	Chay-da-gahi-nail-tsaidi	Tortoise Killer
Target	Wol-doni	Target
Task	Tazi-na-eh-dil-kid	Turkey Ask
Team	Deh-na-as-tso-si	Tea Mouse
Terrace	Ali-khi-ho-ne-oha (T)	Terrace
Terrain	Tashi-na-hal-thin	Turkey Rain
Territory	Ka-yah (T)	Territory
That	Tazi-cha	Turkey Hat
The	Cha-gee	Blue-jay
Their	Bih	Their

Thereafter	Ta-zi-kwa-i-be-ka-di	Turkey Here After
These	Cha-gi-o-eh	The See
They	Cha-gee (Y)	The Y
This	Di	This
Together	Ta-bilh	Together
Torpedo	Lo-be-ca	Fish Shell
Total	Ta-al-so (T)	Total
Tracer	Beh-na-al-kah-hi	Tracer
Traffic Diagram	Hane-ba-na-as-dzoh	Diagram Stroy* Line
Train	Coh-nai-ali-bahn-si	Train
Transportation	A-hah-da-a-gha	Transportation
Trench	E-gade	Trench
Triple	Tka-ih	Triple
Troop	Nal-deh-hi	Troop
Truck	Chido-tso	Big Auto
Type	Alth-ah-a-teh (T)	Type

*This is a typo. It should read "Story."

Under	Bi-yah	Under
Unidentified	Do-bay-hosen-e	Unidentified
Unit	Da-az-jah (U)	Unit
Unshackle	No-da-eh-nesh-gohz	U-shackle
Until	Uh-quo-ho	Until

Vicinity	Na-hos-ah-gih	There About
Villiage	Chah-ho-oh-lhan-ih	Many Shelter
Visibility	Nay-es-tee	Visibility
Vital	Ta-eh-ye-sy	Vital

Warning	Bilh-he-neh (W)	Warning
Was	Ne-teh	Was
Water	Tkoh	Water
Wave	Yilh-kolh	Wave
Weapon	Beh-dah-a-hi-jih-gani	Fighting Weapon
Well	To-ha-ha-dlay	Well
When	Gloe-eh-na-ah-wo-hai	Weasel Hen
Where	Gloe-ih-qui-ah	Weasel Here
Which	Gloe-ih-a-hsi-tlon	Weasel Tied Together

Will	Gloe-ih-dot-sahi	Sick Weasel
Wire	Besh-tsosie	Small Wire
With	Bilh (W)	With
Within	Bilh-bigih	With In
Without	Ta-gaid	Without
Wood	Chiz	Fire Wood
Wound	Cah-da-khi	Wound
Yard	A-del-tahl	Yard
Zone	Bih-na-has-dzoh	Zone

Terms Used in the Field

Colors

Red	Lichii
Green	Tatlid-go-dootizh
Yellow	Ltso
Blue	Dootizh
White	Lighi

Numbers

1	A-la-ih	One
2	N-kih	Two
3	Taa	Three
4	Dii	Four
5	Ashdla	Five
6	Hastaa	Six
7	Tsostsid	Seven
8	Tseebii	Eight
9	Hahast-ei	Nine
10	Neeznaa	Ten
Pass	Bi-sodih-be Jilchii	Pig/Ass

Appendix 7

Known Navajo Code Talkers

The following list of Navajo code talkers was compiled through documents found in the "Navajo Code Talker" file, Marine Corps Historical Center, Philip Johnston Collection and the Navajo Code Talkers' Association. Because the Navajo Communication School records have not been made available, the following list is considered incomplete and in some cases unverified.

Akee, Dan
Alfred, Johnny
Allen, Perry
Anderson, Edward B.
Anthony, Franklin A.
Apache, Jimmie
Arviso, Bennie
Ashley, Regis
Augustine, John
Ayze, Lewis Franklin
Babiya, Don
Bahe, Henry
Bahe, Woody
Baldwin, Benjamin C.
Beard, Harold
Becenti, Ned D.
Becenti, Roy Lewis
Bedoni, Sidney
Begay, Carlos

Begay, Charley Y.
Begay, Charlie H.
Begay, Charlie Tsosie
Begay, George K.
Begay, Henry
Begay, Jerry Claschee
Begay, Jimmie M.
Begay, Joe N.
Begay, Lee H.
Begay, Leo B.
Begay, Leonard
Begay, Notah
Begay, Paul   KIA Okinawa
Begay, Roy
Begay, Samuel Hosteen Nez
Begay, Thomas H.
Begay, Walter
Begay, Walter Kescoli
Begay, Wilson

Begaye, Fleming D.
Begody, David Maize
Begody, Roger
Belinda, Wilmer
Belone, Harry
Benallalie, Jimmie D.
Benally, Harrison Lee
Benally, Harry
Benally, Jimmie L.
Benally, John Ashi
Benally, Samuel
Bentone, Willie
Bernard, John
Betone, Lloyd
Bia, Andrew
Billey, Wilfred E.
Billie, Ben
Billiman, Howard
Billison, Samuel
Billy, Sam Jones
Bitse, Peter John
Bitsie, Wilsie H.
Bitsoi, Delford Baldwin
Bizard, Jesse
Blacj, Jesse
Blatchford, Paul H.
Bluehorse, David
Bowman, John Henry
Bowman, Robert
Brown, Arthur C.
Brown, Clarence Paul
Brown, Cosey Stanley
Brown, John
Brown, N.A.
Brown, Tsosie Herman
Brown, William Tully
Buck, Wilford
Burke, Bobby

Burnie, Jose
Burnside, Francis A.
Burr, Sandy
Cadman, William
Calledito, Andrew
Carroll, Oscar Tsosie
Cattle Chaser, Dennis
Cayedito, Del
Cayedito, Ralph
Charley, Carson Bahe
Charlie, Sam
Chase, Frederick
Chavez, George
Chee, Guy Claus
Chee, John
Clah, Stewart
Clark, Jimmie
Claw, Thomas
Cleveland, Benjamin H.
Cleveland, Billie
Cleveland, Ned
Cody, Leslie
Cohoe, James Charles
Craig, Bob Etsitty
Crawford, Eugene Roanhorse
Crawford, Karl Lee
Cronemeyer, Walter
Crosby, Billy
Curley, David
Curley, Rueben
Dale, Ray
Damon, Anson Chandler
Damon, Lowell Smith
Davis, Tully
Deel, Martin Dale
Dehiya, Dan
Dennison, George H.
Dennison, Leo

Dixon, James
Dodge, Jerome Cody
Dooley, Richard
Doolie, John
Draper, Nelson
Draper, Teddy, Sr.
Etsicitty, Kee
Etsitty, Deswood
Evas, Harold
Foghorn, Ray
Foster, Harold
Fowler, King
Francisco, Jimmy
Freeman, Edwin
Gatewood, Joe Patrick
George, William M.
Gishall, Milton Miller
Gleason, James
Goodluck, John V.
Goodman, Billie
Gooldtooth, Emmett
Gorman, Carl Nelson
Gorman, Tom
Gray, Harvey
Grayson, Bill Lewis
Greymountain, Yazzie
Guerito, Billy Lewis
Gustine, Tully
Guy, Charles
Harding, Ben William
Harding, Jack W.
Hardy, Tom
Harrison, Tom
Haskie, Ross
Hawthorne, Roy Orville
Haycock, Bud
Hemstreet, Leslie
Henry, Albert

Henry, Edmund Juan
Henry, Kent Carl
Hickman, Dan Junian
Holiday, Calvin
Holliday, Samuel T.
Housewood, Johnson *(KIA Guam)*
Housteen, Dennie
Howard, Ambrose
Hubbard, Arthur Jose
Hudson, Lewey
Hunter, Tom
Ilthma, Oscar B.
James, Benjamin
James, Billy
James, George
Jenson, Nevy
Johle, Elliott
John, Charlie Tsihi
John, Edmund
John, Leroy
Johnny, Earl
Johnson, Deswood Remy
Johnson, Francis Taylor
Johnson, Johnny
Johnson, Peter *(KIA Iwo Jima)*
Johnson, Ralph
Jones, Jack
Jones, Tom
Jordan, David
Jose, Teddy
June, Allen Dale
June, Floyd
Keams, Percy
Keedah, Wilson
Kellwood, Joseph H.
Kescoli, Alonzo
Ketchum, Bahe
Kien, William

King, Jimmy Kelly
Kinlahcheeny, Paul *(KIA Iwo Jima)*
Kinsel, John
Kirk, George Harlan
Kirk, Leo
Kiyaani, Mike
Kontz, Rex T.
Lapahie, Harrison
Largo, James
Leonard, Alfred
Leroy, John
Leuppe, Edward
Little, Keith Morrison
Lopez, Tommy K.
MacDonald, Peter
Malone, Max
Malone, Rex T.
Malone, Robert
Maloney, James
Maloney, Paul Edward
Manuelito, Ben Charles
Manuelito, Ira
Manuelito, James C.
Manuelito, Johnny R.
Manuelito, Peter R.
Marianito, Frank
Mark, Robert
Martin, Matthew
Martinez, Jose
McCabe, William
McCraith, Archibald
Mike, King Paul
Miles, General
Moffitt, Tom Clah
Morgan, Herbert
Morgan, Jack C.
Morgan, Ralph *(KIA Cape Gloucester)*
Morgan, Sam *(KIA Iwo Jima)*

Morris, Joe
Moss, George Alfred
Multine, Oscar Phillip
Murphy, Calvin H.
Nagurski, Adolph N.
Nahkai, James Thomas
Nakaidinae, Peter
Napa, Martin
Naswood, Johnson
Negale, Harding
Newman, Alfred K.
Nez, Arthur
Nez, Chester
Nez, Freeland
Nez, Howard Hosteen
Nez, Israel Hosteen
Nez, Jack
Nez, Sidney
Notah, Roy
Notah, Willie A. *(KIA Iwo Jima)*
O'Dell, Billy
Oliver, Lloyd
Oliver, Willard V.
Ottero, Tom
Paddock, Layton
Pahe, Robert D.
Parrish, Paul A.
Patrick, Amos Roy
Patterson, David E.
Peaches, Alfred James
Peshlakai, Sam
Pete, Frank Denny
Peterson, Jose
Pinto, Gual
Pinto, John
Platero, Richard
Preston, Jimmie
Price, Joe Frederick

Price, Wilson Henry
Reed, Sam
Roanhorse, Harry C.
Sage, Andy
Sage, Denny
Salabiye, Jerry Edgar
Sandoval, Merril Leo
Sandoval, Peter Paul
Sandoval, Samuel
Sandoval, Thomas
Scott, John
Sells, John Captain
Shields, Freddie
Shorty, Robert Tom
Silversmith, Joe A.
Silversmith, Sammy
Singer, Oscar Jones
Singer, Richard B.
Singer, Tom *(KIA Peleliu)*
Skeet, Wilson Chee
Slinky, Richard T.
Slivers, Albert James
Slowtalker, Balmer
Smiley, Arcenio
Smith, Albert
Smith, Enock
Smith, George
Smith, Raymond R.
Smith, Samuel Jessie
Soce, George Bill
Sorrell, Benjamin G.
Spencer, Harry
Tabaha, Johnnie
Tah, Alfred
Tah, Edward
Talley, John
Tallsalt, Bert
Thomas, Edward

Thomas, Richard
Thompson, Claire M.
Thompson, Everitt M.
Thompson, Francis Tso
Thompson, Frank T.
Thompson, Nelson S.
Todacheene, Carl Leo
Todacheenie, Frank Carl
Tohe, Benson
Toledo, Bill Henry
Toledo, Curtis
Toledo, Frank
Toledo, Preston
Toledo, Willie
Towne, Joseph H.
Towne, Zane
Tracy, Peter
Tso, Chester Housteen
Tso, Howard Benedict
Tso, Paul Edward
Tso, Samuel N.
Tsoie, Harry *(KIA Bougainville)*
Tsosie, Alfred *(KIA Cape Gloucester)*
Tsosie, Cecil Gorman
Tsosie, Collins D.
Tsosie, David W.
Tsosie, Howard
Tsosie, Kenneth
Tsosie, Samuel
Tsosie, Woody
Upshaw, John
Upshaw, William R.
Vandever, Joe
Visalia, Buster
Wagner, Oliver
Walley, Roberts
Werito, John
Whitman, Lyman Jimmie

Willeto, Frank Chee
Williams, Alex
Williams, Kenneth
Willie, George Boyd
Willie, John W.
Wilson, Dean
Woodty, Clarence Bahe
Yazhe, Harrison A.
Yazza, Peter
Yazza, Vincent
Yazzie, Charlie
Yazzie, Clifton
Yazzie, Daniel
Yazzie, Eddie Melvin
Yazzie, Edison Kee
Yazzie, Felix
Yazzie, Francis
Yazzie, Frank Harold
Yazzie, Harding
Yazzie, Joe Shorty
Yazzie, John
Yazzie, Justine D.
Yazzie, Lemuel Bahe
Yazzie, Ned
Yazzie, Pahe D.
Yazzie, Peter
Yazzie, Raphael D.
Yazzie, Robert
Yazzie, Sam
Yellowhair, Leon
Yellowhair, Stanley
Yellowman, Howard Thomas
Yoe, George Edward
Zah, Henry

Bibliography

Books

Arthur, Anthony. *Bushmasters.* New York: Saint Martin's Press, 1987.

Bartley, Lieutenant Colonel Whitman S. USMC. *Iwo Jima Amphibious Epic.* Nashville: The Battery Press, Inc., 1954.

Costello, John. *The Pacific War.* New York: Rawson, Wade Publishers, Inc., 1981.

Dunn, William J. *Pacific Microphone.* College Station: Texas A & M University Press, 1988.

Foster, John. *Guadalcanal General.* New York: William Morrow and Company, 1966.

Gow, Ian. *Okinawa 1945 Gateway to Japan.* Garden City: Doubleday & Company, 1985.

Hemingway, Abert. *Ira Hayes, Pima Marine.* Lanham, Mass.: University Press of America, 1988.

Hoyt, Edwin P. *Japan's War: The Great Pacific Conflict.* New York: McGraw-Hill Book Company, 1986.

Hoyt, Edwin P. *To the Mariana's War in the Central Pacific: 1944.* New York: Van Nostrand Reinhold Company, 1980.

Kahn, David. *Codebreakers: The Story of Secret Writing.* New York: MacMillan, 1967.

Kahn, David. *Kahn on Codes: Secrets of the New Cryptography.* New York: MacMillan, 1983.

Kawano, Kenji. *Warriors, Navajo Code Talkers.* Flagstaff: Northland Publishing Company, 1990.

Mason, John T. Jr. *The Pacific War Remembered.* Annapolis: Naval Institute Press, 1986.

Morison, Samuel Eliot. *Aleutians, Gilberts and Marshalls, June 1942-April 1944.* Boston: Little Brown and Company, 1962.

Morison, Samuel Eliot. *The Struggle for Guadalcanal August 1942-February 1943.* Boston: Little Brown and Company, 1962.

Morison, Samuel Eliot. *Victory in the Pacific 1945.* Boston: Little Brown and Company, 1962.

Newcomb, Richard F. *Iwo Jima.* New York: Holt, Reinhart and Winston, 1965.

Ross, Bill D. *Iwo Jima: Legacy of Valor.* New York: Vanguard

Press, 1985.

Smith, S.E. *The United States Marine Corps in World War II.* New York: Random House, 1969.

Steinberg, Raphael. *Island Fighting.* Alexandria, VA: Time-Life Books, 1978.

Toland, John. *Infamy.* Garden City: Doubleday and Company, Inc., 1982.

Tregakis, Richard. *Guadalcanal Diary.* New York: Random House, 1943.

Wheeler, Richard. *A Special Valor.* New York: Harper and Row Publishers, 1983.

Wheeler, Richard. *Iwo.* New York: Lippincott and Crowell, 1980.

Zich, Arthur. *The Rising Sun.* Alexandria, VA: Time-Life Books, 1977.

Documents

National Archives Military Reference Branch, Washington, D.C.
NND913070 127, 46A, Box 1 Folder 5 1020-1365/1365-10.
NND913070 127, 46A, Box 21 Folder 3 155-1610.
NND913070 127, 46A, Box 23 Folder 3 1975-1990.
NND913070 127, 46A, Box 24 Folder 8.
NND913070 127, 46A, Box 32 Folder 10 1020-1365-30.
NND913070 127, 46A, Box 36 Folder 2.
SRH-120 Report.

National Archives Suitland Reference Branch, Suitland, Maryland.

RG-127 1365-15 to 1365-150 (5/42-8/43) Box 600 Folder 6.
RG-127 1365-150-50 to 1365-150-20-40, Box 356 Vol: 2P.
RG-127 1365-150-20-20 Box 353.
RG-127 1365-150-50 to 1365-150-20, Box 356, Folder 1.
RG-127 1365-150-50 to 1365-150-20, Box 356, Folder 4.
RG-127 1535-75 (1/42-1/49) Box 600, Folder 4.
RG-127 1535-75, Box 600, Folder 13.
RG-127 1535-75, Box 600, Folder 14.
RG-127 1535-140 to 1535-130, Box 613, Folder 4.
RG-127 1535-75, (10/42-1/43) Box 599.
RG-127 1535-75, Box 598, Folder 17.
RG-127 1535-75, Box 598, Folder 18.
RG-127 1535-75, Box 600, Folder 12.
RG-127 1535-75, box 597, Folder 19.
RG-127 1535-75, Box 597, Folder 20.
RG-127 1535-75, Box 600, Folder 13.
RG-127 1520-30-160 (1/41-5/43) Box 526, Folder 8.
RG-127 2185-20, Box 1427, Folder 4.

Marine Corps Historical Center listings, Washington Navy Yard, Washington D.C.
62A-2086 Loc 02/35-38-3, Box 14 Folder "Navajo Code Talkers."
65A-2086 Loc 09/30/05/7, Box 17, A9-30 Iwo Jima.
127-76-30 Loc 0/13-49-6-3 F5,

Box 1.
127-76-30 Loc 9/13/49-6-3
GU-30 Box 5.
"Navajo Code Talkers" file.

Private Collections

Philip Johnston Collection, Museum of Northern Arizona, Flagstaff.
Doris Duke Collection, Mariott Library, University of Utah, Salt Lake City.
Albert Hemingway: CT28 Journal.

Newspapers

Chevron. May 16, 1942 issue.
Chevron. July 3, 1942 issue.
Chevron. January 28, 1943 issue.
Fuji Evening. Tokyo, Japan, August 16, 1982.
Gallup Independent. March 10, 1994.
Leatherneck. June 1980 issue.
Oklahoma Tribune. Oklahoma City, Oklahoma 1987.
San Diego Union. San Diego, California, January 1943.
VFW Magazine. November 1991.
The Voice. Edition 1, Volume VIII, Chicago, Illinois, November

Correspondence

George C. Strum, May 4, 1992.
Lieutenant General J. P. Berkeley, USMC (Retired), April 3, 1993.
Sergeant Major Dolph Reeves, USMC (Retired), January 14, 1994.
Henry Hisey, Jr., March 3, 1994.
Thomas Randant, March 4, 1994
Davey Baker, April 18, 1994.
Carl & Mary Gorman, June 7, 1994.

Interviews

Thomas Begay, Auguast 1992.
Samuel Billison, May 31, 1993.

Wilsie Bitsie, June 2, 1993.
Paul Blatchford, October 1991.
Richard Bonham, July 20, 1993.
Kee Etsicitty, April 16, 1992.
Harold Foster, October 1991, April 13, 1992.
Malissa Gleason, August 1992.
John Goodluck, July 20, 1991.
John Kinsel, July 20, 1991.
Al Mertz, April 11, 1992.
Merril Sandoval, October 1991.
Bill Toledo, August 19, 1993.

Maps and Illustrations

Maps and illustrations were provided by the Marine Corps Historical Center, Washington Navy Yard, Washington, D.C.

Miscellaneous

Navajo Code Talker Association, Banquet Program, Gallup, New Mexico, February 22, 1986

Index